THE PARLOUR AND THE STREETS

T0385673

THE INDIA LIST

Solvyns: A Kan singer

Sumanta Banerjee

THE PARLOUR
AND THE STREETS

ELITE AND POPULAR CULTURE IN
NINETEENTH-CENTURY CALCUTTA

LONDON NEW YORK CALCUTTA

Seagull Books, 2019

Text © Sumanta Banerjee, 1989, 2019
ISBN 978 0 8574 2 617 8

First published by Seagull Books in 1989

British Library Cataloguing-in-Publication Data
A catalogue record for this book is available from the British Library

Typeset by Seagull Books, Calcutta, India
Printed and bound by Hyam Enterprises, Calcutta, India

CONTENTS

ACKNOWLEDGEMENTS

I express my gratitude to Professor Arun Das Gupta of the Depart-
ment of History, Calcutta University; Dr Pradip Sinha of the
Department of History, Rabindra Bharati University, Calcutta;
Dr Asok Sen of the Centre for Studies in Social Sciences, Calcutta;
Mr Paromesh Acharya of the Indian Institute of Management,
Calcutta; and Ms Ratnabali Chatterjee of the Department of Islamic
History, Calcutta University, for helping me to clarify my thoughts
on several points during my research programme. The opinions
expressed here are, however, my own.

I wish to acknowledge the help and cooperation that I received
from the librarians and staff of the following organizations:
National Library, Calcutta; Bangiya Sahitya Parishad Library, Calcutta; Victoria Memorial Hall, Calcutta; Visva-Bharati Library,
Santiniketan; and Asiatic Society, Calcutta.

I am grateful to the Indian Council of Social Science Research,
New Delhi, for providing funds for my research project on which
the present book is based. I am also grateful to the Indian Institute
of Management, Calcutta, for kindly agreeing to house the project
during my research work in Calcutta.

Thanks are due for permission to reproduce the Kalighat *pats*
from the B. K. Birla Collection and Nandan Museum, Kala Bhavan,
Santiniketan. The pictures by Alex Hunter and F. B. Solvyns appear
here courtesy The National Library and Victoria Memorial Hall
respectively.

New Delhi, 1989

The present book was first published by Seagull Books in 1989, around 30 years ago. Since then fresh researches have been undertaken by a new generation of young scholars in the history of Calcutta's popular culture of the nineteenth century—and the subject of this book. They have come up with findings that lend wider dimensions to the subject, and throw light on some of the corners of that history that I may have been unaware of at the time when I wrote it.

I should therefore, on this occasion of the republication of my book, pay tribute to these scholars who have not only enriched my knowledge, but have also expanded the frontiers of academic research in the field of urban popular culture by retrieving rare literary, oral and visual evidences from archives and other sources. I welcome in particular, the publication of two important volumes in Bengali—the first entitled *Battalar Boi: Unish Shatoker Dush-prapyo Kuriti Boi* (Gangchil, 2011), within the folds of which two young scholars, Adrish Biswas (now sadly deceased) and Mou Bhattacharya, brought together rare prints of popular farces and satirical verses which they painstakingly gathered from the India Office collection of the British Museum library in London. The other important publication is in English, entitled *Power In Print: Popular Publishing and the Politics of Language and Culture in a Colonial Society* (Oxford University Press, 2006) by Anindita Ghosh, who offers a deeply analytical study of these cheap prints from the nineteenth-century presses in Battala in north Calcutta that represented a collaboration among printer-publishers, authors and readers—all of whom came mostly from the city's plebeian background. She reopens the debate on some of the questions that I raised in my book—on the social structure of literacy among the lower-class milieu and its relationship with the Bengali bhadralok society. Both the above-mentioned scholars have added fresh inputs to my understanding of Battala literature, which is a major topic in my book.

I also welcome another young scholar, Devajit Bandyo-padhyay, who has come out with a *Bengali book: Beshyasangeet aiji-sangeet* (Subarnarekha, 2001), a collection of songs by high-class courtesans (baijis) as well as lower-class prostitutes (beshyas) in nineteenth-century Calcutta—their voices blending in common articulation of their living experiences, sometimes sad, sometimes comic. By meticulously documenting these songs from old gramo-phone records, Devajit has enriched the oral history of Bengali pop-ular culture of that period. Personally, I thank him for unwinding the long-forgotten songs of these women, which helps me to replenish my collection of their cultural output that I had earlier quoted in my book *Dangerous Outcast: The Prostitute in Nineteenth-Century Bengal* (Seagull Books, 1998[2019]).

I thank Naveen Kishore of Seagull Books for bringing out a new edition of this book, and hope that it will generate interest among readers, as well as reinvigorate the spirit among academic circles for further research in the variegated and colourful contours of urban popular culture not only in nineteenth-century Calcutta, but also in other cities of India, both in the past and the present.

Hyderabad, 2019

INTRODUCTION

This work seeks to compare the cultural productions of two socio-economic groups of Bengalis in nineteenth-century Calcutta that emerged in the course of the growth and development of a metropolitan city under a colonial administration.

It is a study of the major types of representation in Bengali, in the print (published literature) and audiovisual (songs, dramatic performances, paintings, etc.) media—as they reflect the patterns of behaviour and attitudes acquired from the past by the respective socioeconomic groups, and as they were modified by the contemporary environment; as well as their responses to the social trends of the period.

Of the two socioeconomic groups, one is the Bengali elite composed predominantly of banians and dewans (intermediaries helping the East India Company to conduct business and administration in relation to the indigenous people) at the beginning; absentee landlords (rentiers appointed by Lord Cornwallis as government agents to collect rents from landed estates under the Permanent Settlement) at a later stage; and as we reach the end of the nineteenth century, a middle class consisting of professionals who were products of an English colonial education system (conforming in many ways to the standard set by Thomas Babington Macaulay in his famous Minute of 1835, 'a class of persons, Indian in blood and colour, but English in taste, in opinions, in morals and in intellect'), who evolved a concept of nationalism acceptable within the set-up of the colonial administration. Through all these various stages of development, the elite demonstrated a certain sense of continuity in shaping a distinct literature of its own, an indigenous school of music and a taste in fine arts. The other group consists of the Bengali lower orders—migrants who came to Calcutta from the neighbouring villages in search of jobs. A large number of them were traditional artisans and craftsmen who practised and patronized the rural cultural forms which became considerably modified in the new metropolitan environment and thus evolved into a new urban folk culture, to become marginalized by the end of the nineteenth century.

A few explanatory notes about the use of certain terms may be necessary in this connection. We have used the terms 'folk culture' and 'popular culture'—often interchangeably—to describe the culture of the city's lower orders. Some critics make a distinction between the two terms. 'Popular art . . . has in common with folk art the genuine contact between audience and performer; but it differs from folk art in that it is individualized art, the art of the known performer.'[1] In the culture of the lower orders of nineteenth-century Calcutta, as we shall see in the course of our survey, in some art forms the artistes emerged from anonymity and became 'known performers'. In some other art forms, the performance as well as the composition continued to retain the collective anonymity of traditional folk culture. In the latter part of our study, we use the term 'mass culture' or 'mass entertainment' to describe the art forms served through the modern commercial media industry.

> Where popular art . . . exists only through the medium of a personal style, mass art has no personal quality but, instead, a high degree of personalization. . . Mass art uses the stereotypes and formulae to simplify the experience, to mobilize stock feelings and to get them going . . .[2]

The conditions under which both the elite and the lower orders lived and produced their respective art and literature were generated by the process of urban development introduced in a pre-industrial society and governed by the commercial and administrative needs of the British colonial power. As a centre of commerce dominated by foreign traders and colonialists, right from the beginning of the eighteenth century, Calcutta drew a heterogeneous indigenous population made up of both the rich and the poor. The prevailing relationships of people, based not on any traditional moral order, but on business or administrative convenience, produced new states of mind in Calcutta, which could be described as a 'heterogenetic' centre as opposed to the 'orthogenetic' type of old cities (like Beijing or Kyoto) which carried forward, developed and elaborated a long-established local culture or civilization. Calcutta, on the other hand (like London, New York or Osaka), created new modes of thought, both among the rich and the poor, that were in conflict with the old culture. These new modes either superseded or modified thoughts associated with the old cultures.[3]

Theoretical Approach

The theoretical approach of this work involves two disciplines—sociology and cultural criticism. Until comparatively recent times, there had been a marked tendency to see the two disciplines as to some degree antithetical. But this breach is now showing real signs of being closed.

The old assumptions that culture can be explained solely in terms of commercial or economic structures on the one hand, or explicated only by the rules of aesthetic analysis on the other, have given way to a pluralistic approach such as to be found in the studies carried out by the Centre for Contemporary Studies at Birmingham (founded in 1964 by Richard Hoggart as a research grouping within the English Department of the University), or in the numerous products of interdisciplinary research like E. P. Thompson's *Making of the English Working Class* (1963); John Berger's *Ways of Seeing* (1972); and Raymond Williams' articles.[4]

The theories regarding development of culture in a colonial society, in the context of nineteenth-century Calcutta, can be roughly divided into four streams. First, the Eurocentric view of the nineteenth century which held that a single standard of rationality could be used for evaluating human institutions, and since contemporary West European society was said to have achieved the highest expression of a rational thought, people of the European colonies could achieve a higher quality of civilization in the manner of Europeans by imbibing what the Western intelligentsia valued as rational. According to this view, all the existing forms of culture in the colonies were to be evaluated in terms of their similarity or dissimilarity to the culture of Europe. The main nineteenth-century proponents of this Eurocentric view in the Indian context were James Mill (in his *History of British India*) and Thomas Babington Macaulay (in his 1835 Minute where he asserted: 'a single shelf of a good European library was worth the whole native literature of India and Arabia'). The education system which influenced the nineteenth-century Bengali elite was in a large measure formulated on the basis of this theory.

The second stream could be described as Orientalist which stressed the study of the ancient classics, religion and linguistics of the colonial societies, and envisaged a development of culture in those societies on those traditional lines. In the Indian context, the main representatives of this line of thought were Warren Hastings, William Jones and H. H. Wilson among others, in the eighteenth and nineteenth centuries. Culture, in their view, was to be studied in its linguistic and religious aspects, detached from questions of its social evolution. The stress was on spiritual as against material reflection in cultural productions.[5]

It should be pointed out that both the nineteenth-century Eurocentric and Orientalist evaluations of culture in India—although apparently pursuing opposite ends—were primarily oriented towards the indigenous elite. The former encouraged 'acculturation' of the higher occupational groups who could afford English education and thus create a culture incorporating the values of the West. The latter encouraged 'conservation' of the products of a traditional courtly culture—Sanskrit and Persian classics, temples, mosques and monuments—the preserves of the old indigenous elite. Neither placed any value on the social worth of the contemporary lower orders and their cultural output. Traditional folk culture, or the new urban folk culture developing in nineteenth-century Calcutta, was out of the purview of theoreticians of both the schools. If at all, the different forms of folk culture prevalent in Calcutta in those days were objects of derision in the eyes of these theoreticians.

Over the years, both these schools lost their sharp edges and blended to evolve a liberal approach towards the interpretation of cultural developments in India. Rammohan Roy's attempts in the early nineteenth century to discover common areas of agreement between contemporary Western thought and the ancient Upanishads were extended in the cultural field by Rabindranath Tagore in the early twentieth century. Expressing the liberal spirit of harmonizing elements from both Occidental and Oriental cultures, Tagore said:

> We congratulate ourselves on the fact, and consider it a sign of our being alive in soul, that European thoughts and literary forms found immediate hospitality in Bengali literature from the very beginning of their contact with our mind. It ushered in a great revolution in the realm of our literary expression . . . And yet, we may go too far if we altogether reject tradition in the cultivation of the arts, and it is an incomplete statement of truth to say that habits have the sole effect of deadening our mind.[6]

The 'great revolution in the realm of our literary expression'— as well as in society in the form of reforms—has quite often been described as a 'Renaissance' by a large number of intellectuals ranging from liberals to Marxists, who sought to draw a parallel with the sociocultural transition and cultural efflorescence in sixteenth-century Italy. But such a comparison does not stand the test of history. Long before the debates which are taking place now about the appropriateness of such a term, an editorial which

appeared in *The Times* of London in 1873 hit the nail on the head
to suggest the falsity of such a comparison:

> There is a certain resemblance between the position of
> Europe about the time of the Renaissance and the position
> of modern India. Both countries, it is evident, have been
> subjected to the influence of a culture far superior to their
> own, and the natural course of their civilization has been
> largely modified accordingly . . . But Europe was more
> advanced than India, and therefore better capable of assim-
> ilating the new order . . .

Referring to the marginalization of the indigenous folk culture
of India under the impact of a foreign culture, and its replacement
by a new elite literature, the editorial then commented:

> The love songs and idolatrous legends which we have in
> great measure displaced are the material out of which a
> native popular literature might, in due time, have been
> evolved. If, therefore, the products of Indian literature have
> an appearance in some degree forced and artificial, we
> must remember that India has not been suffered to follow
> her own course, and that the growth of her literature has
> been set aside as completely as her political development
> by the overwhelming influence of a new power. We find
> ample signs of life, of ferment, of activity, but of quite
> another kind from those which would have followed in the
> natural order of growth and change . . . [7]

The fact that the spontaneous growth of an indigenous culture
was being disrupted by the imposition of ideas and attitudes
borrowed by a new elite from a foreign power escaped the attention of the proponents of the liberal theoretical approach like
Rammohan and Tagore. While trying to draw from both the
Eurocentric and the Orientalist schools suitable perspectives for
the development of an indigenous modern culture, Rammohan
and Tagore also inherited from the two schools their common
socially exclusive attitude of total indifference to certain socio-

economic and historical factors—the unequal access among the indigenous population to Western education, which was bound to make 'European thoughts and literary forms' a jealously guarded preserve of the privileged few; the hierarchical features of the indigenous traditional culture separating courtly culture from folk culture, the esoteric from the popular in the religious and ideological movements of the past; the occupational division of labour in nineteenth-century Calcutta which gave birth to two separate streams of culture.

In Bengal the glorification of the history and cultural achievements of the past Hindu era, set in motion by the nineteenth-century Orientalists, contributed to the awakening of national self-consciousness among the Bengali Hindu intelligentsia at the turn of the twentieth century. But the cultural nationalism which became an ally of the political movement against British colonial rule took the form of a return to the past—the past of the feudal kings and nawabs. Besides, its emphasis on the Hindu classics and history drove a wedge between the indigenous Bengali Hindu and Muslim populations.

This absence of a coherent correlation between socioeconomic conditions and cultural output in the theories of development of culture in a colonial society was overcome to a great extent by the Marxist theory of culture, which came into prominence in the colonies during the late 1920s with the growth of an organized working-class movement. In this theory, there was an attempt to trace the growth of culture to the relations of production in the economic sphere. As a result, Marxist critics in the Third World turned to the lower orders of their own countries. In Bengal, from the 1930s, Marxist cultural criticism began to lay stress on the representation of the working class in cultural productions. To quote an Indian Marxist cultural theoretician: 'Our literature will not acquire reality and vitality unless it broadens so as to include the consciousness of the working masses of our country. The hard realities of their life, their zeal and unselfconscious freshness, their innate practicality and simple courage shall be our weapons to root out the anaemic tendencies in our cultural heritage'.[8] As a result, fiction, songs and plays were composed by the middle-class *littéra-teurs*, with workers and peasants as heroes. But within the framework of the Marxist theory of culture in Bengal, very little was done to evaluate the cultural output of the nineteenth-century lower orders in their own right. Some attempts were made in the 1940s by the Indian People's Theatre Association (IPTA)—a cultural organization influenced by the Marxist cultural theory—to collect folk songs from the villages. But most often, they were urbanized or punctuated with slogans to meet the demands of an immediate political situation or to make them acceptable to the city's middle-class audience.

One of the reasons for the desire of the Marxist cultural theoreticians and workers to improve upon the available specimens of original folk culture by introducing political slogans, or using folk song tunes to compose agitprop songs could have been the conventional Marxist concept of the political party's leading role in the creation of culture—similar to the role of making a revolution in the domain of politics. But this again was another form of imposition of alien ideas and interruption of a spontaneous growth—a danger recognized by some Marxist intellectuals. ('The domain of art is not one in which the Party is called upon to command. It can and must protect and help it, but it can only lead it indirectly'.[9])

Besides, the conventional Marxist concept of a pure feudal–capitalist division, which often influenced the evaluation of cultural forms, did not quite apply to the social and economic situation prevailing in nineteenth-century Calcutta. The tendency to identify the new elite as a bourgeoisie with 'progressive' social and cultural ideas compared to the backward-looking ideology of the rural-oriented feudal society (which encompassed the urban lower orders also to some extent, since in their songs and other forms of cultural manifestations they hit out at social reforms like widow remarriage and women's education) may not lead us to an objective evaluation of the tensions and contradictions that prevailed in the cultural field in nineteenth-century Calcutta. The Bengali elite was not a class of independent industrial entrepreneurs. The patrons as well as the artistes of the elite culture were primarily employees in the tertiary sector of a colonial administrative set-up—deputy magistrates, teachers, doctors, lawyers—and descendants of a class of absentee landlords who were also products of a colonial polity. Even when they championed social reforms like widow remarriage and women's education or asserted political rights like a free press and a voice in the administration, they continued to share certain feudal ideas and habits like strict caste distinctions and religious rituals, as well as subservience to the colonial power.

Similarly, there was no proletariat in the conventional Marxist sense in nineteenth-century Calcutta. The industrial working class which emerged from the middle of the century was numerically small, and did not quite fit into the classic Marxist category of a class sharing the common belief that they had 'nothing to lose but their chains'. Fragmented by caste and linguistic differences, the first generation of the industrial working class in nineteenth-century Calcutta was yet to come out with a distinct cultural output bearing the stamp of its class character.

The rest of the city's lower orders were a working class who had come from a feudal background, and still retained to some extent traces of the past—the pre-capitalist artisans, manual labourers, domestic servants, professional street singers, etc. In the songs and cultural performances which they patronized and participated in, we often come across sentiments that appear to be largely conservative compared with the reformist zeal of the Bengali elite. The male-dominated folk cultural forms frequently came out against reforms like widow remarriage or education of women, perceiving them as threats to their religious tradition. At the same time, Calcutta's folk artistes who came from the lower orders had a better understanding of the human situation than the more sophisticated elite writers. They had learnt the hard way to see through the illusions of property, wealth, power and ambition. Their songs and dramatic performances, their paintings and pantomimes therefore hit out more directly against the habits of both the nouveau riche and the orthodox Hindus—the Anglicized customs of the parvenu and the hypocrisy of the priests. Thus, in one sense, their cultural expressions could be interpreted as a more radical manifestation of social protest coming from the bottom, directed against both the new colonial influence and the old feudal customs, in a language that was more earthy and authentic than that cultivated by the educated gentry.

Any attempt at an analysis of the cultural history of nineteenth-century Calcutta therefore must reject a unilinear interpretation and take into account the complexities and contradictions that prevailed in the cultural attitudes and manifestations of both the elite and the lower orders. In relation to the latter, it is essential to recognize the fragmentation in their experiences. Orthodox Marxist convictions about 'working-class consciousness' have often been based upon the assumption of a degree of homogeneity, or at least a real or potential essence or core around which a whole culture was organized. The basis was different in nineteenth-century Calcutta. We have to stress here the heterogeneity or complexity of a 'working-class culture', fragmented not only by geographical unevenness and parochialism, but also by the social and sexual divisions of labour, and by a whole series of divisions into spheres or sites of existence.

At the same time, the folk culture of nineteenth-century Calcutta shared certain common features and certain common concerns and faced a common fate, drawing a wide range of cultural forms into a distinctly identifiable category as an alternative to the elite culture.

This brings us to the fourth theory regarding the development of cultural patterns in a colonial set-up.

This theory of culture has coincided with the emergence of the masses into the national political scene of the post-independence era in the Third World. In the sense that it seeks to rediscover the role of the lower orders in the creation of their own culture in a colonial situation and to put it properly in the perspective of the anti-imperialist national struggle, it can be described as an effort to revive the cultural roots of the indigenous masses of the Third World. Frantz Fanon, the most outspoken proponent of this theory, describes how traditional folk culture changes and develops in the colonial situation:

The oral tradition-stories, epics and songs of the people—which formerly were filed away as set pieces are now beginning to change. The storytellers who used to relate inert episodes now bring them alive and introduce into them modifications which are increasingly fundamental. There is a tendency to bring the conflicts up to date and to modernize the kinds of struggle which the stories evoke, together with the names of heroes and the types of weapons.[10]

We shall show in the course of our study how the folk artistes in the new colonial capital—nineteenth-century Calcutta—updated and modernized the stories and characters of the traditional folk songs and plays.

It is this culture, produced by, instead or for, the lower orders, a culture where they are not objects but active participants, that has been totally ignored in all the three theoretical frameworks that we have discussed so far. The unconscious and unorganized development of a new folk culture in nineteenth-century Calcutta stood in contrast with the elite culture which took shape through a deliberate cultivation of the tastes and manners of two civilizations—the contemporary Western and the past Hindu. Through the elitist indifference to the folk culture, it came to be reduced to a 'culture of silence' in the consciousness of the elite.

The theory of the culture of the lower orders, the 'culture of silence', is explained succinctly by Paulo Freire, the Latin American ideologue of pedagogy:

the culture of silence is born in the relationship between the Third World and the metropolis . . . understanding the culture of silence presupposes an analysis of dependence as a relational phenomenon which gives rise to different forms of being, of thinking, of expression, those of the 'culture of silence' and those of the culture which 'has a voice'. . . . The dependent society is by definition a silent society. Its voice is not an authentic voice, but merely an echo of the voice of the metropolis in every way: the metropolis speaks, the dependent society listens. The silence of the object society in relation to the director society is repeated in the relationship within the object society itself. Its power elites, silent in the face of the metropolis, silence their own people in turn.[11]

The present study examines this process of 'silencing' as carried out in nineteenth-century Calcutta, when the culture of the lower orders was 'silenced' by an indigenous elite whose thought patterns and attitudes were shaped by 'listening' to the 'voice of the metropolis' from England. Yet, we must add that the 'listening' was not marked by total obedience to the 'metropolis', but also by tensions between loyalty to the traditional cultural norms on the one hand, and the felt need to adopt the new cultural values introduced by colonial education on the other.

Methodology

The methods employed in the present study are largely the normal methods of historical research in the field of social relations, i.e. the directed search for an evaluation of relevant data, and the construction from these of a picture of the social system of art production at the time.

But, as mentioned earlier, the growing convergence of the arts-based and social science disciplines makes it possible to study and understand both the social structures and processes that shape cultural production, and the aesthetic qualities in those cultural products—their acceptance and rejection by contemporary patrons and the modern audience, following the changing standards of aesthetic evaluation. The underlying approach behind the methodology could be described as a threefold exercise:

It must comprise the understanding (*i*) of the works of literature in their own right and on their own terms; (*ii*) of these works as expressions, in some sense, of a world view or the ideology of a social group or of a society; and (*iii*) of that ideology, here expressed in aesthetic form, as originating in social processes, class relations, and structural features of society.[12]

Thus, on the one hand, the social relations in nineteenth-century Calcutta that governed the production of art have been examined exhaustively. The empirical areas of investigation in this regard are: (*i*) the socioeconomic status of the artistes; (*ii*) the socioeconomic status of the patrons, and their relations with the artistes; (*iii*) the nature of the new technology (e.g. the printing press, lithography, etc.) and its impact on art production; and (*iv*) the role of the art critics (e.g. comments in newspaper articles).

On the other hand, methods from literary and arts criticism have been borrowed to evaluate the quality of the cultural products under review. The changes in one of the main tools of cultural expression—the Bengali language—have been analysed to indicate the differences in style between the literary output of the elite and that of the lower orders. In the visual arts again, stress has been laid on the contrast between the Royal Academy style of neoclassical origin in the paintings produced by the British-trained Bengali artists, and the bold modelling with sweeping brushstrokes which heightened the plasticity of the figures in the Kalighat pats done by the urban folk painters.

Data Collection and Analysis

The data sources have been printed literature, oral records (e.g. songs) and visual reproductions (e.g. paintings, prints, etc.) available in libraries and private collections.

While the culture of the nineteenth-century Bengali elite is well recorded in a host of novels, dramatic literature, songs, etc., that of the lower orders had to be collected from secondary sources. These sources are references and quotations which we found in contemporary newspapers (e.g. a description of a jatra performance, or excerpts from a kobi-wala's songs), articles written by contemporary critics and latter-day research scholars. Another major source is the oral tradition, which still continues in certain old parts of Calcutta (e.g. popular songs or doggerels or proverbs composed in the nineteenth century). An important primary source was located in the *pats* of Kalighat, and the prints (produced by artisans) in cheap illustrated booklets, which used to be popular in those days and were known as Battala publications, some of which are available in private collections, libraries and museums.

Once the data had been assembled, they were subjected to a content analysis. Frequency of certain expressions, images, motifs in the cultural products that betrayed attitudinal beliefs and could be related to the specific socioeconomic origins and occupational habits of the two groups of artistes were measured in the course of the study.

Findings

The results of the survey indicate that notwithstanding contradictions that existed within each group—the elite and the lower orders—and the ambivalence found in their respective cultural expressions, they manifested certain broad social tendencies and artistic styles which set them apart from each other.

Marked by 'dependence' on the metropolitan centre (England) and influenced by the administrative and educational policies of the 'director society' (i.e. the metropolitan centre), the Bengali elite in nineteenth-century Calcutta created a culture which in its form (language, mode of expression, genres) was far removed from the popular forms of folk culture. The highly Sanskritized Bengali language, for instance, made its literature an exclusive preserve of the educated few and inaccessible to the unlettered masses who were used to a colloquial Bengali.

In its choice of content also, the themes and concerns were outside the framework of the memories or experiences of the common Bengali masses. Whether these were exploits of Rajput or Maratha heroes and heroines (celebrated in the epic poems and historical romances of nineteenth-century Bengali writers), or social problems like widow remarriage or the conflict between the older generation and their English-educated sons, they were rarely shared by the lower orders whose social values and cultural tastes were not acquired from a reading of past histories or Western theories, but were born of their daily experiences.

To allay any misgivings that might arise, we should add that no attempt is being made here to counterpose the two literary trends—popular and elite—as superior and inferior, or vice versa, by trying to replace one by the other. We are not belittling the literary achievements of people like Bankim Chandra, Madhusudan Dutta or Dinabandhu Mitra, who were fashioning a new literary language and creating characters and situations that did reflect the social reality of their own milieu. Their treatment of individuals in contemporary Bengali middle-class society did bring forth the subtle nuances of personal relationship between men and women, fathers and sons who were growing up in a society encountering challenges to its traditional norms from the impact of a colonial regime.

In Marxist academic circles, the old tendency to eulogize them as heroes of a 'Renaissance' is recently giving way to a grudging recognition of their limitations—like their alienation from the masses—which are sought to be explained in terms of historically imposed constraints of class and society. This approach permits considerable sympathy for these literary figures of nineteenth-century Calcutta. If the failures of the bhadralok intellectuals can be excused on grounds of historical constraints, if they are to be recognized as a literati which fought as well as they could with whatever limited intellectual equipment that was available to them within the contemporary ideological milieu, why cannot the artistes of the lower orders of nineteenth-century Calcutta claim a similar sympathetic judgement from Marxist critics? Their backward-looking, conservative attitude, their religious beliefs—likely to be dismissed as 'regressive' by conventional Marxist standards—need to be explained in terms of the historical constraints that they suffered in their own way.

The 'culture of silence', or the urban folk culture that was being created simultaneously by these lower orders of the city, demonstrated a style which, in spite of modifications brought about by the urban environment, retained the vigour and spontaneity of its roots—the old rural folk culture. Both in its songs and paintings, it spoke in the familiar language of the common people. While some of their cultural expressions (like the 'sawng' or pantomime shows) were direct onslaughts against contemporary social vices, some of the other manifestations were indirect reflections of prevailing social reality (as in the songs of the 'kobi-walas' and 'jatras'). Humour—which was almost completely absent in the culture of the elite—became an important weapon in the hands of the lower orders, both to lampoon the upper classes as well as to suggest through transparent allusions the changing contours in the surrounding social environment.

One of the questions that we examined in the course of the investigation was how; if at all, the culture of the lower orders was 'silenced' by the elite. In this connection, specific cases were studied. We have seen, for instance, how the once-popular folk theatre form, the jatra, gave way to the modern Bengali theatre with the educated middle class as its patrons and participants. The pat paintings of Kalighat were ousted by the import of oleographs and printed pictures which were bought by members of the Bengali elite who had developed a taste for European works of art under the influence of Western education. The pantomime sawngs were sought to be 'silenced' by police measures. Nevertheless they survived till the 1930s, as the swan song of a virile, socially critical urban folk culture.

A combination of various factors—changes in the taste of the Western-educated gentry, a new set of moral values learnt from the mid-Victorian English mentors, the inability of the folk artistes to compete with a superior media technology, regulation and repression by the state, an ideological campaign by the indigenous elite—led to the marginalization of folk culture in Calcutta by the end of the nineteenth century.

Relevance of the Problem

If the sociological analysis of a particular period in history is not only a means of understanding the past, but also a form of communication to the present, then few historical episodes would better illuminate the strength and weakness of modern Bengali life than the experience of cultural experiments in nineteenth-century Calcutta.

The wide gap that still separates the urban Bengali intelligentsia from the Bengali masses, the unlettered poor, can be traced back to this period. The former's inability to understand the latter's needs and thought pattern has led to repeated failures of experiments in modern times in the political, economic and cultural fields—experiments that might have been altruistic but which were directed from the top by the Western-educated politicians, bureaucrats and intellectual leaders of Calcutta, without involving those who live in the villages and urban slums and are vitally concerned in such experiments of development. The roots of this communication gap go back to the way Bengali culture was shaped by the elite of Calcutta—a city which still remains the centre of modern Bengali culture and a source of cultural innovations that diffuse outwards to the rest of the state. The contours of the elite culture— its language, its style of presentation, form (and content also)— were far from the mode of communication and thoughts of the masses, which remained outside the coterie of the urban elite.

The present study is relevant in the global context also at a time when policy makers are concerned over the existence of First World pockets in Third World urban centres—pockets which demonstrate the continuity of a colonial education system and which determine not only economic policies for development but also the shape of cultural growth. The term 'cultural imperialism' is being increasingly used in the literature of sociology and mass media to describe the way traditional cultures of Third World countries are being swamped by TV programmes, films, advertisements imported from the West by the urban elite of these countries in close collaboration with the First World manufacturers of these cultural ideas and products. Towards the end of the present study, an attempt has been made to throw light on the origins of this 'cultural imperialism', which has been traced from the clash of two cultures in the societal framework of nineteenth-century Calcutta, through the gradual 'silencing' of the parallel culture of the lower orders, to the appropriation and distortion of certain folk forms by the elite-dominated commercial entertainment industry.

An Overview of the Available Literature

A voluminous literature has grown up around the social life and culture of nineteenth-century Calcutta, in both English and Bengali. Contemporary sketches by travellers and inhabitants (H. E. Busteed's *Echoes of Old Calcutta*, 1897; E. Heber's *Narrative of a Journey through the Upper Provinces of India*, 1828; George H. Johnson's *The Stranger in India, or Three Tears in Calcutta*, 1843—are only a few among the vast literature of reminiscences by contemporaries) throw interesting light on the daily lifestyle of both the British settlers and the indigenous elite. The indigenous lower orders loom vaguely in the background in these accounts, and any description of their manners or culture that might appear there is only incidental.

Serious academic studies have been made in the present century on different facets of Calcutta's economic, social and cultural history. Dr Pradip Sinha's *Calcutta in Urban History* (1978) and S. N. Mukherjee's *Calcutta: Myth and History* (1977) trace the growth of Calcutta as a city and the composition of the elite in the early years. These two important studies on Calcutta deal primarily with the urbanization process leading to the physical–spatial differences in the city and the resultant rise of new power relationships. Mukherjee's book in particular draws exhaustively on census reports, archival material, literary works, travel accounts, etc. to analyse the class, caste and political situation in the city during the first three decades of the nineteenth century. But while both the studies frequently draw upon contemporary cultural products— mainly the literary products of the Bengali elite—as sources for studying urbanization, an analysis of the cultural products in their own right and on their own terms, as expressions of social attitudes of certain groups, is outside the scope of their survey framework.

Quite a number of books have been written on the growth and development of the nineteenth-century Bengali elite, with particular reference to their ideological views. Susobhan Sarkar's *On the Bengal Renaissance* (1946) deals with the differences between the so-called 'modernists' and 'conservatives' among the elite and their respective response to British administrative policies. A. F. S. Ahmed's *Social Ideas and Social Change in Bengal (1818–1835)* (1965) is a highly documented account of the impact of colonial economic policies on the emerging elite, the division between the landowning 'conservatives' and the 'liberal' merchants, and the latter's support of free trade and colonization by private British business interests. David Kopf's *British Orientalism and the Bengal Renaissance, 1773–1835* (1969) deals primarily with the educational policies of the British government, passing from the Orientalist phase to the Anglicist phase of Macaulay, and how the Bengali intelligentsia responded to them. In these books too, the cultural products are referred to only as sources. Although Kopf's study throws some light on educational experiments directed at the lower orders and how such experiments were abandoned because of various socioeconomic reasons, the culture of the lower orders as a separate entity is absent from the purview of the study.

Benoy Ghose in his Bengali books—*Banglar Samajik Itihaser Dhara* (1968) and *Kalpenchar Rachana Sangraha* (1969)—did pioneering work in drawing attention to the major forms of Calcutta's nineteenth-century urban folk culture and in underlining the reflection of contemporary social developments in those products. Bireshwar Bandyopadhyay's *Bangladesher Sawng Prasangey* (1972) is another original study of an interesting urban folk form—the pantomime, which in nineteenth-century Calcutta was a powerful weapon in the hands of the lower orders for deriding the upper classes. W. G. Archer's *Bazaar Paintings of Calcutta* (1953), and *Kalighat Painting* (1986), published by Kala Bhavana,

Santiniketan, are interesting attempts to collect and interpret the most important form of visual folk art that flourished in nineteenth-century Calcutta.

ECONOMY AND SOCIETY
IN NINETEENTH-CENTURY CALCUTTA

The development of Calcutta as a city has to be understood in the context of the dominance–dependence relationship that exists between the imperial country and its colony. In the post-Industrial Revolution phase, industrialization accelerated urbanization in the metropolitan society of Europe. In the colonial society, the urbanization which took place was dependent on the need of the metropolitan economy. Calcutta, which was one of the earliest colonial settlements of the British, was used by them primarily as a centre for organizing the linkages necessary for extracting from the vast hinterland of the Indian subcontinent the resources required for developing the economy of England. The nature of these linkages influenced the city's pattern of growth.

The city began to take shape from 1698 when the East India Company (set up at the end of the sixteenth century by English merchants to carry on trade with the East), after a series of ups and downs in their relations with the Mughal court in Delhi and with the governor of Bengal, managed to obtain from the latter a *farman* or licence to be 'zamindars' (revenue farmers) of three villages—Sutanuti, Dihi Kolikata and Gobindapur. It was in Sutanuti in the north of the narrow stretch comprising the villages on the eastern banks of the river Hugli that Job Charnock, the Company's chief in Bengal, first established his settlement in 1690, attracted by the indigenous cloth manufactories there. 'Little better than a hamlet that was hardly inhabited by any of the higher castes', Sutanuti in those days was a major centre of handloom weavers who produced exquisite chintz. Rich Indian merchant families— the Basaks and the Setts—who had been trading in the commodity long before the advent of the British, used to operate from the village of Gobindapur, further south.[1]

While the majority of the inhabitants of the three villages were agriculturists or fishermen, the weavers and traders could be described as the first non-agricultural communities whose collaboration led to the emergence of the 'bazaar' or market settlement that was to remain the basic model of the urban development of the indigenous part of Calcutta, or what came to be known as the 'Black Town' as distinct from the European part of the town.[2]

After gaining possession of the three villages, the Company began to build warehouses, improve the port facilities and set up a fort (called Fort William after the name of the then ruling king of England) to protect their interests from the various marauders, both Indian and foreign, who used to rule the roost in the river Hugli in those days.

The three villages were merged into one and began to be commonly called Calcutta. The Company was required to pay the government of Bengal an annual rent and was allowed to collect a certain amount from the inhabitants of the area according to the size of their lands, as also by way of taxes and duties. The settlement hardly bore the features of a town. But the prospects of security (at a time when the Mughal empire was disintegrating) and fortune-making it held began to draw a heterogeneous crowd, rich and poor, from the adjoining area.

Right from the beginning of the eighteenth century, the British began to acquire more lands in the vicinity of Calcutta. The defeat of Siraj ud-Daulah, the Nawab of Bengal, in the battle of Plassey in 1757, placed the British at the helm of affairs in Bengal and made them the virtual arbiters of the destiny of the fast-declining Mughal power. In 1765, the East India Company obtained the Dewani rights of Bengal, Bihar and Orissa, which further helped them to expand their commercial interests. There was a spurt in trade in cloth, sugar, saltpetre and spices—the main items in the list of British exports from Bengal at that time.

I

In those early days of colonialism the British traders and rulers, still unaccustomed to the alien modes of dealing with the Indians, had to depend on interpreters and intermediaries—a role which a heterogeneous group of Bengalis came forward to play. Apart from the original merchant families of Calcutta like the Basaks and Setts, others who came to the city from outside also made fortunes in their capacities as 'banians' or brokers to the British traders, or as 'dewans' (intermediaries in judicial and revenue administration) to the European 'zamindars' of Calcutta, or in various new roles as interpreters and assistants to the foreign traders and rulers. A late nineteenth-century Bengali observer gives a graphic description of the origin and nature of 'banianship' in early Calcutta:

The mode in which business was then transacted, required advances to our workmen for buying the materials for the articles of their handiwork. The country possessed no man-ufacturers or merchants on a large scale, capable of execut-ing extensive orders, and delivering the goods contracted for on the appointed day. The articles had to be collected throughout the country by means of agents . . . there vol-unteered from among our ancestors, individuals willing to stand as securities, and occupy an intermediate position between the strangers and their countrymen . . . Both the 'Dobhash' [interpreters] and 'Banyan' being secured, the English started their business in right earnest and in regu-lar style. They made choice of stations in the country, founded factories, built large warehouses and entered upon the complicated system of operations . . . For purchase of the cargoes of exports to England, there was the European functionary, in the district, who had first his Banyan, or Native Secretary, through whom the whole of the business was conducted. The Banyan hired a species of broker, called a Gomastah, at so much a month. The Gomastah repaired to the aurang, or manufacturing town, which was his assigned station; and there fixed upon a habitation, which he called his Cutchery. He was provided with a sufficient number of peons, a sort of armed servants, and hircarahs, messengers, or letter carriers, by his employer . . .[3]

The banian, who was in charge of procuring the supply of goods and ensuring their despatch to the British traders in their headquarters in Calcutta, resorted to tactics which were far from peaceful. The weavers were forced to sign bonds to produce far beyond their capacities. Unable to meet such excessive demands, silk weavers often refrained from producing the commodity and were compelled to cut off their thumbs. Even Robert Clive had to complain against such extortions in a letter to the Company's Court of Directors: 'The sources of tyranny and oppression, which have been opened by the European agents acting under the authority of the Company's servants, and the numberless black agents and subagents acting also under them, will, I fear, be a lasting reproach to the English name in this country'.[4]

Once the Company obtained the Dewani of the three provinces, such practices increased. The Directors also began to dictate the pattern of production in Bengal. In 1769, they directed that instead of manufacturing silk goods, the natives should be asked to produce raw silk—indicating the growing trend of suppressing indigenous manufacturing industries and concentrating on the production of raw materials for extraction.[5]

A large number of these Bengali banians who operated from Calcutta in the early years of the eighteenth century amassed fortunes through this form of collaboration with the British traders. 'Such people as the famous Setts, and Omichand [a Sikh-Khatri merchant] sometimes acted as Banyans to the Company, by entering into contracts for the supply of cotton goods and saltpetre.'[6]

The counterparts of the banians in the new administrative set-up were the dewans who acted as intermediaries in revenue and judicial administration. They played a major role in the early days of the Company's administration when the rights of property in the soil were being remodelled and the old Muhammadan laws and offices were being gradually replaced by the regulations of the Company and its servants. In that transitional period, when old landed estates were changing hands, these dewans often assumed positions of arbiters of the destiny of the new landlords. Ganga Gobinda Singh, who rose from the position of a local keeper of revenue records to become dewan to the Calcutta Committee of Revenue during the regime of Warren Hastings, was one such powerful intermediary: 'many large zamindars felt obliged to put themselves at his mercy and to pay the price of his favours.'[7]

The new situation opened up unique opportunities even to those from a humble background like the washerman Ratan, who acted as an interpreter for the English merchants by picking up a few English words, and rose to be a man of position and influence in eighteenth-century Calcutta, and came to be known as Ratan Sarkar.[8]

It was these people—the banians and dewans (sometimes the same individual combined the functions of both), the interpreters and intermediaries—who contributed to the growth of the 'Black Town' of Calcutta, by investing in landed property, setting up bazaars in their neighbourhood and settling artisans and labourers of different types in their localities.

II

It needs to be pointed out in this connection that from the beginning, the physical–spatial structure of the growing city was split into two. The White Town was in the south-central part of Calcutta around Fort William where 'English settlers by degrees built themselves very neat, useful, if not elegant houses, laid out walks, planted trees and made their own little district neat, clean and convenient.'[9] How jealously these English settlers tried to guard

themselves from any possible contamination by the black inhabitants of the lower orders—the labourers, the vendors, etc.—is
evident from the frequency of orders issued from Fort William
banning the entry of the natives into the precincts of the White
Town, except at certain hours.[10] This effort at self-segregation—
which became more marked from the early part of the nineteenth
century (in contrast with the comparatively permissive atmosphere
of the eighteenth century when English 'nabobs' often adopted
Indian manners and customs, took Indian mistresses and joined
entertainments on religious occasions of the country)—not only
protected the white minority's monopoly of power, but also influenced the attitude of the indigenous elite and populace. Although
our present study is limited to a discussion of the cultural forms
prevalent in the Black Town, we shall have occasion to dwell on the
impact of the White Town's social and cultural norms on the Black
Town, in the context of the dominance–dependence relationship.

The Black Town developed in the north, around the original
settlement at Sutanuti. Describing its growth, a contemporary
English observer writes: 'The north division between Bow Bazar
and Muchua Bazar comprises perhaps the most dense part of the
native population of Calcutta . . . The houses of the wealthier
classes are brick-built, from two to three stories high, closely constructed and divided only by dirty, narrow and unpaved streets; the
roofs are flat and terraced'.[11]

Members of these 'wealthier classes' among the indigenous
population—the banians and dewans and interpreters—mediated
between the British and the natives in economic and administrative matters. They made use of the available indigenous cultural
resources—both the traditional and the newfangled urban forms—
to entertain lavishly their British patrons in perhaps one of the
earliest public relations campaigns of the modern era. All through
the eighteenth century till almost the middle of the nineteenth, we
read in contemporary newspapers every year of sumptuous dinner
parties and 'nautch' performances (dances and songs by north
Indian performers) organized by the Bengali parvenu class in the
Black Town on occasions like wedding ceremonies or religious

festivals, where the Company's European servants and traders thronged—their thirst for Madeira (the popular wine in those days) and whisky apparently getting the better of their religious prejudices about native customs![12]

III

In the melting pot of the growing metropolis, the rigid caste hierarchy of the Hindu social system underwent a modification, as the parvenus ranging from the upper to the different categories of lower-castes succeeded in gaining positions of power and influence in the new social set-up. There was no levelling down of all castes, but an opportunity of vertical mobility in the caste hierarchy—people from lower castes or of dubious origins being accepted in the folds of the traditionally dominant castes by virtue of their newly acquired wealth. It was thus that the washerman Ratan became Ratan Sarkar, a member of the Bengali elite of eighteenth-century Calcutta. Jayram Tagore, ancestor of the famous Tagore family, was looked down upon as a 'Peerali Brahman' (or a Brahman who had transgressed the traditional norms of the caste because of contamination by a Muslim) according to the conventional Brahmanical standards. But once his son Darpanarayan established himself as a dewan to the then acting Governor-General Mr Wheeler, the position of the Tagores in Calcutta society became indisputable.

In the new social milieu of eighteenth-century Calcutta, money power began to prevail over conventional caste rules or the claims of lineage. This is best illustrated by an incident which occurred towards the end of the eighteenth century when Kaliprasad Dutta, a scion of a wealthy Kayastha family, was threatened with ostracism by a faction of the Hindu parvenu of Calcutta on the ground that he had a Muslim mistress! Dutta approached the leader of another faction—Ramdulal Dey (who himself rose from humble beginnings to the position of a banian of a private English merchant company and later amassed a huge fortune through independent transactions with American business firms)—for mediation.

Dey advised Kaliprasad to placate the city's Brahman priests (who were indispensable for any religious occasion in Hindu households and whose stamp of approval was necessary for a lower-caste Hindu to move up in the caste ladder) with money and gifts. The advice bore fruit and Dey summed up the situation with a laconic comment: 'I keep caste in my coffers!'[13]

Like the gradual changes in orthodox social rigidities about caste and lineage, the conventional norms and values that used to bind rural societies also tended to break down. Bribery, embezzlement of funds, forgery of documents became the order of the day among this new Bengali elite who seemed to be inspired by the single, obsessive motive of making fortunes as fast as possible, and thereby establish dynasties that would be regarded as successors to the old Hindu 'maharajas' and 'rajas'. There was a virtual scramble among the parvenu to obtain these honorary titles from the new rulers—and judging by the proliferation of such appellations in eighteenth- and nineteenth-century Calcutta, it seems that the rulers were quite munificent in granting them.

The British rulers themselves set the example of amassing wealth by all sorts of unscrupulous means. James Hickey, who in 1780 started the first English newspaper in Calcutta, exposed through the columns of his *Bengal Gazette* the corruption of the English servants of the East India Company, including prominent people like Warren Hastings. Excerpts from a satirical catechism published in his newspaper sum up the prevailing English morals in Calcutta:

Q. What is commerce?

A. Gambling.

Q. What is the most cardinal virtue?

A. Riches . . .[14]

Hickey accused the Supreme Court Judge Elijah Impey (who was a friend of Hastings) of securing for his relation a lucrative government job. Hastings himself was alleged to have tried to silence his critics—Phillip Francis, John Clavering and George Monson—

by offering them each 100,000 pounds. Charles Grant, Chairman of the Company's Court of Directors, did not have any qualms to despoil the old kingdom of Gaud in north Bengal of some of its finest marble to build St John's Church in Calcutta.

Hastings and his Indian friends and subordinates exploited one another for their individual interests, fought among themselves and debauched the law to serve their own purposes. The saturnalia of lawlessness could not have been better illustrated than by the affair of Maharaja Nandakumar. Once a dewan to the Nawab of Bengal, and later appointed by the East India Company as a collector of Nadia and Hugli districts, Nandakumar was very close to the British from the days of Clive, whom he accompanied to Patna in Bihar. According to Nandakumar's own admission, he paid Warren Hastings 300,000 rupees to procure a job for his son Gurudas Ray. When he fell afoul of Hastings, Nandakumar brought up this allegation and accused Hastings of bribery. He threw in his lot with Francis, Monson and Clavering in their feud with Hastings. But while the three white men managed to save their skins, Nandakumar had to pay with his neck. An infuriated Hastings brought a charge of forgery against him, and Elijah Impey sentenced Nandakumar to be hanged in 1775—more as an exemplary lesson than as a dispassionate act of justice, to teach the natives what would happen to them if they dared to oppose the British rulers.

IV

In parenthesis we might add here a few words on the attitude and position of the Muslim population of Calcutta in particular and Bengal in general in the eighteenth century. Although the Muslims formed a substantial part of the population of Bengal in those days, available records show hardly any Muslims joining the ranks of the indigenous parvenu who made fortunes through collaboration with the British. In a list of prominent residents of Calcutta, prepared in 1822, we find a solitary Muslim—Moonshee Suderruddeen— described as 'a respectable man and Moonshee [i.e. secretary] of

Mr Barwell, late of the Supreme Council, and John Graham, Esq.'[15] We come across the name of one Gulam Hossain who earned 900,000 rupees as a broker of the Company.[16] In another list, prepared in 1758, of native members of a Commission formed to decide on the payment of compensation to those residents of Calcutta who had suffered because of the city's sack by Nawab Siraj ud-Daulah the previous year, we find only three Muslim names— Ally Boye (Ali Jan Bai), who succeeded in getting two-thirds of the money that was claimed; Mahmud Suddock (Muhammad Sadek), who received only one rupee against his claim of Rs 2,716; and Ayin Noady (Ainuddin), who did not put forth any claim at all.[17]

Explaining the absence of Muslims from the new-rich class of Bengalis that was growing in eighteenth-century Calcutta, one observer notes:

Because of the geographical position of Calcutta, inhabitants of Hugli, Howrah, 24-Parganas, Midnapore, and outlying areas found it easy to travel to the city by foot. These districts were Hindu-majority areas. As a result, an increasing number of Hindus congregated in Calcutta. The Muslims, were in a majority in faraway districts, particularly East Bengal . . . The majority of the Muslims were agriculturists; there were few who were in service. Muslims did not want to leave the economic security of land for the city where life was full of financial uncertainties. Those who were engaged in services and administrative work (during the Mughal regime) turned to agriculture after the loss of ruling power . . . while the Hindus advanced towards their improvement through seeking opportunities in services by collaborating with the British government and receiving English education, the Muslims lost similar opportunities by turning away from the British government and English education and suffered decline.[18]

It is quite possible also that the English colonialists looked down with distrust upon members of an erstwhile ruling community from which they had snatched power. The attitude comes out clearly from Clive's observation: 'You may lay it down as a maxim that the Musalmans will never be influenced by kind treatment to do us justice. Their own apprehensions only can, and will, induce them to fulfil their own agreements.'[19]

V

The men who gave shape to the Black Town in north Calcutta were therefore primarily Bengali Hindu parvenus, although in their cultural tastes and social habits they often continued to display traces of influence of the former Muslim ruling powers. Leading among these people was Raja Nabakrishna Deb, who was a typical representative of the new political norms and social values that were developing in Bengal in those days. Nabakrishna started as a Persian teacher to Warren Hastings as early as 1750. He was used by Clive as an intelligence agent in 1757, when Siraj ud-Daulah on his way to sacking Fort William was encamping in Halshibagan in the northern extremity of Calcutta. Nabakrishna went to the camp, collected all the necessary information regarding Siraj's plans and conveyed it to Clive. He earned further gratitude of the British by supplying them with provisions when they were beleaguered near Calcutta after it had been sacked by Siraj ud-Daulah the same year. As a faithful ally of the British, he was amply rewarded when the British reconquered Calcutta. In 1767, he was appointed the political banian to the Company, serving mainly as an intermediary between the Indian princes and the Company. We must also mention the name of Darpanarayan Tagore, ancestor of one of the branches of the famous Tagore family. He made his fortune as a dewan to the then-acting Governor-General Mr Wheeler. Another personality, Nemaicharan Mullick of Burrabazar, acquired a fortune through 'an extraordinary efficiency in our [English] laws, so much so that he had for many years been the adviser of all those who had anything to do with courts of Justice'.[20] Ramdulal Dey, who began his career as a bill collector at the very low salary of Rs 5 a month at the office of a Bengali dewan in Calcutta, rose to be a millionaire as a banian to Fairlie, Fergusson and Company.[21]

The names of these individuals are important in the context of the present discussion, since they and their descendants laid the foundation of the culture of the Bengali elite. Describing their development, one scholar writes: 'By the end of the eighteenth century . . . the banians and dewans had combined to give a definite shape to Calcutta's comprador elite as the topmost layer in the "native" economic community in the city and as a more or less homogeneous group, consisting predominantly of families of fortune-makers.'[22] As for the social shape into which they were moulding the city, they were

> re-enacting a role expected of the 'zamindar' in the little *rajyas* [chiefdoms] of the earlier period. These little *rajyas* accommodated centres where a kind of urbanism, at a level other than that of commercial cities or great politico-military centres, persisted through the centuries . . . The comprador purchased land and settled it with tenants. Rent was his primary concern. He had, however, to distribute patronage on an elaborate scale—he had to acquire prestige and status . . . [23]

Thus developed the 'bazaars' and clusters of hutments where the artisans and labourers lived. 'The opulent households or prominent family residences tended to draw clusters of people around them. These people were needed for service . . . '

Modelled on small villages, these localities became replicas of the old landed estates owned by feudal chieftains, their contours changing in response to the urban needs. Calcutta thus became basically a city of hutments, palatial buildings of opulent Bengalis surrounded by bazaars and slums. 'The hutments formed the great slums of Calcutta. The urban landlords, acting with a frame of mind influenced by both traditional and new notions, created in the slums of Calcutta a powerful trend towards urban heterogeneity.'[24]

The inhabitants of these slums and the vendors in these bazaars came from a varied range of castes and occupations. It is to them that we have to look for the cultural output of the lower orders, which formed an alternative trend parallel to the Bengali elite culture that was being shaped by their landlords and employers—the banians, dewans and other categories of the new class who invested in land and business.

Describing their living conditions, a contemporary observer writes:

The mass of labouring classes live in huts, the walls of which are of mud, or of matted reed or bamboo, roofed with straw or tiles, according to the means of the occupant; these would not be so bad, but that they are uniformly placed on the bare ground, or on damp mud, but little raised, which continually emits injurious exhalations . . . A man who procures a rupee monthly, with his wife and two children, eat two maunds of rice in the month, the price of which is one rupee; they eat twice in the 24 hours . . . such a day-labourer must have some other resource, otherwise he could not live; if he is a Mussalman, he rears a few fowls; or if a Hindoo he has a few fruit trees near his house, and he sells the fruit. If by these or any other means, the labourer can raise half a rupee or a rupee monthly, this procures him salt and a little oil, and one or two other prime necessaries; though vast multitudes of the poor obtain only from day to day boiled rice, green pepper pods, and boiled herbs; the step above this is a little oil with the rice.[25]

VI

By the end of the eighteenth century there was a growing trend among this new class of the Bengali rich to gradually withdraw from business and invest instead in urban and rural real estate. It 'was a manifestation of weakness in the long run, but from another angle as a sociohistorical process related to more immediate realities, it might be regarded as withdrawal in favour of a more immediately meaningful urban framework.'[26] The banians of the early eighteenth century left, when they died, large landed estates, where rents from bazaars and slums yielded a constant income to their descendants. While some of these descendants squandered the inheritance within the span of one or two generations on wine, women and expensive pastimes,[27] a few others managed to sustain a degree of opulence and aristocratic status till the end of the nineteenth century, like the Tagores, the Debs and the Mullicks, who played an important role in the development of the elite Bengali culture.

Their concentration of investment in landed property led to the expansion of the city and increase of its population. The urban part of the town area showed a rapid increase between 1756 (on the eve of the battle of Plassey after which political power passed over completely to the East India Company) and 1794, from 704 acres to 3,714 acres. The number of 'pucca' houses (which the well-to-do could afford to build) went up from 498 to 1,114 during the period. In 1800, the population of Calcutta stood at 500,000.[28]

According to one statement made in the twenties of the nineteenth century, which refers to Calcutta's population in the previous century, 'the large estimates made of the population of Calcutta at former periods may be owing to the crowds of Artisans, Labourers, Servants and Sircars and to the numerous strangers of every country which constantly meet the eye in every part of the Town.'[29]

It is quite possible that the first labouring class to settle down in the new city were the artisans, as the names of the various localities in Calcutta indicate. Still in use, these names are after the trades practised, by the original residents there, as Kumortuli (from 'kumors' or clay modellers); Sundipadah (from 'sundis' or liquor vendors); Kansaripada (from 'kansaris' or braziers); Chhutarpada (from 'chhutars' or carpenters). Kumortuli, in north Calcutta, which continues to be the main centre where the clay modellers mould images of Hindu gods and goddesses for the various religious occasions, is one of the oldest settlements. Gobindaram Mitra, who was the dewan to the zamindar of Calcutta and was known as the 'black zamindar' because of the undisputed power he wielded over the indigenous inhabitants in the mid-eighteenth century, built a number of temples, for which purpose he imported clay modellers from the nearby village of Banshbedey. They came by boat and settled down in Kumortuli. Soon after this, clay modellers began to arrive from Nabadwip, Krishnanagar and Shantipur—old towns of fame which were well known for this particular art. Leading among the first settlers were Madhusudan Pal, Kangalicharan Pal, Kashinath Pal, Haripada Pal and Annadacharan Pal.[30]

Throughout the eighteenth century, these artisans and labourers faced a precarious existence. In 1737, a devastating cyclone and floods swept away their hutments and about 300,000 of them died. In 1752, an increase in the rate of taxation on foodstuff imposed by the Company led to an unprecedented rise in its selling price. Unable to buy food, thousands died in the streets of Calcutta. John Zephania Holwell, the Company 'zamindar' of Calcutta, reported 'walking skeletons' and parents selling their children in the city. His dewan, the 'black zamindar' Gobindaram Mitra, however, expressed satisfaction that the company had earned more revenue that year because of the increased tax rates. The handloom weavers of Sutanuti—whose chintz attracted the first British merchant settlers to the area—started fleeing from the middle of the eighteenth century because of extortions by the Company's agents.[31]

Since the Company introduced the system of payment of revenue in cash, the poor farmers were forced to make distress sales of their produce for cash to be able to pay the revenue. In 1769, the Company's agents bought off the entire stock of harvested crops, hoarded it and created an artificial scarcity in the market. This, among other factors, led to the famine of 1770 which wiped out one-third of the population of Bengal—about 10 million people. In Calcutta itself, 76,000 died. The new Fort William was being constructed in the city at that time, and describing the plight of the workmen, the Rev. James Long wrote later that there was 'great difficulty in obtaining food' and 'children died at their mothers' breast—the Ganges stream became corrupt from the corpses . . .'[32]

Even 15 years after this terrible famine, poverty stalked the Bengal countryside, forcing villagers living near Calcutta to walk down to the city in search of jobs, or even to sell their children. Writing in 1785, Sir William Jones, the famous Orientalist, who was then a judge in the Calcutta High Court, tells his readers: 'Many of you, I presume, have seen large boats filled with . . . children coming down the river for open sale at Calcutta. Nor can you be ignorant that most of them were stolen from their parents, or bought perhaps for a measure of rice in time of scarcity.'[33]

The stark poverty, otherwise dispersed in the city, used to converge in a massive shape of horror and malnutrition in front of the houses of the Bengali rich, whenever there was a *shradh* or obsequial rites performed for anyone in these homes. The city's poor were given alms on such occasions—the custom being known as *kangali-biday* or distribution of alms among the poor. Reports in contemporary newspapers describe in vivid detail the clamour of the hungry masses.

Thus, when Maharaja Nabakrishna Deb's mother died, during the *shradh* ceremony, people travelled 14–20 days from distant places. 'As presents were given per head the very babies were brought and when many of them died of suffocation, the parents preserved them for the occasion and exhibit[ing] them as if they were alive, added to their incomes . . . '

When the widow of the well-known banyan Ramdulal Dey died and his son Ashutosh Dey held a *shradh*, 'for three or four days . . . the poor continued to pour into the town from every venue, like so many files of ants . . . . Among these, one hundred and nineteen thousand four anna pieces, and forty thousand eight anna pieces were distributed . . . but still one-fourth of the poor went away empty-handed . . .'[34]

At the death of the widow of Nilmoney Mullick, a scion of the well-known merchant family of the Mullicks, there gathered

> a great number of poor people each of whom expected to have had one rupee . . . The excessive heat together with

the delay that occurred in distributing the money intended for the poor has caused some mortality among them. Several of them alarmed and disappointed have hurled away [sic] home plundering the shops of petty retail dealers of everything upon which they could lay their hands. These circumstances bear sad testimony to the amount of poverty in the country . . .[35]

The expansion and urbanization of Calcutta, which continued throughout the eighteenth century, meant for the poor inhabitants continuous dislocation. In 1757, when the Company decided to rebuild the Fort (after its sack by Siraj ud-Daulah in the previous year), the British cleared Gobindapur in the south of its indigenous population to set up the Fort there. 'Much ground was cleared to make room for a new fort; many thousand huts thrown into the holes from whence they had been taken, to form roads and an esplanade . . . '[36] The ousted people were however given land in exchange for their own, in different parts of the town—mainly in the north, which had already developed into the 'Black Town'. This process of clearing native areas and building establishments for the Company's expanding administrative and business interests obviously resulted in the uprooting of the agricultural population, who, deprived of their cultivable land, had to seek other means of livelihood in the city, or to migrate to nearby villages. The artisans and small traders apparently went north to settle down around the houses and bazaars of the new urban landlords—the banians and dewans. By the end of the eighteenth century, the rural acreage of Calcutta had shrunk by almost half—from 2,525 acres in 1756 to 1,283 in 1794.[37]

VII

By the beginning of the nineteenth century, the outline of Calcutta's economic and social life had taken a clearer shape. The white enclave, which used to be concentrated in a few pockets along the southern stretch of the Hugli river, expanded further westwards and by the end of the century had moved upwards towards the centre—from the original village of Gobindapur to Dihi Calcutta. The changing interests of the British settlers influenced both their own norms and customs and the economic and social trends among the city's Bengali elite.

The British had emerged from the role of traders and were now firmly entrenched in that of administrators. This required a new breed of Englishmen. The old habits of the Company 'nabobs' of the previous era—their adoption of native customs like smoking the hubble-bubble, keeping an Indian mistress, and offering puja to the goddess Kali at the ancient temple of Kalighat in the south of Calcutta[38]—had to be discarded so that the new rulers could maintain their separate identity and thereby the prestige of the imperial culture. Explaining the reasons why a college had to be established at Fort William in Calcutta in 1800, Marquis Wellesley, the then Governor-General of India, said: 'The age at which writers [the term used for young English civilians] usually arrive in India is from sixteen to eighteen . . . Once landed in India their studies, morals, manners, expenses and conduct are no longer subject to any regulation, restraint, or guidance. Hence, they often acquire habits destructive of their health and fortunes . . . '[39]

Not satisfied with the prospects of training in India, the authorities decided in 1805 to open a college in England itself so that the civilians could arrive in India fully prepared for their responsibilities. The new mood of the rulers in which they were indoctrinated in Haileybury College in Hertfordshire in England comes out clearly from the reminiscences of one of the civilians trained there:

It was there [Haileybury College] that we first became cognizant of the fact that we were members of the Civil Service, a body whose mission it was to rule and to civilize that empire which had been won for us by the sword; it was there that we first became firmly impressed with a conviction that, as members of such a body, there were certain traditions to be kept up . . . and a code of public and private honour to be rigidly maintained . . . [40]

The insistence on rigid norms of behaviour which led to a sort of self-segregation of the British ruling elite in Calcutta from the local Bengali society (in marked contrast with the social bonhomie of the previous century) was not only a means of establishing the image of exclusiveness of the ruling class, but was also a reflection of an ascendant ideology in England, the two important components of which were Utilitarianism and Evangelism. With its emphasis on a well-laid-out organization of civil society to protect the interests of the propertied individual with which it equated the overall progress of society, Utilitarianism turned to India to remould it in accordance with these ideas.[41] The axis around which the plan of remoulding rotated was not, however, the Indian individual, but the commercial, administrative and cultural interests of the Englishman.

A major ally of Utilitarianism was Evangelism. 'The three most important features of the Evangelical mind . . . were its intense individualism and exaltation of individual conscience; its belief that human character could be suddenly and totally transformed by a direct assault on the mind, and finally, its conviction that this required an educative process'.[42] Equating the material superiority of the West with the moral superiority of Christianity, Evangelism evaluated all existing forms of religion and culture in India in terms of their similarity or dissimilarity to the Western culture. The religious customs and cultural tastes of the 'backward natives' were from now on denounced vociferously as 'superstitious', 'obscene' and 'unnatural'. The conclusion from this was that the natives needed to be emancipated socially and culturally. Charles Grant, who was the Chairman of the East India Company's Court of Directors, and an ardent Evangelist, set the tone of the future British attitude towards the Indians at the end of the eighteenth century in his 'Observations on the State of Society among the Asiatic Subjects of Great Britain, particularly with respect to Morals and on the Means of Improving it, 1797', where he said:

we cannot avoid recognizing in the people of Hindostan, a race of men lamentably degenerate and base; retaining but a feeble sense of moral obligation; yet obstinate in their disregard of what they know to be right, governed by malevolent and licentious passions, strongly exemplifying the effects produced on society by a great and general corruption of manners and sunk in misery by their vices . . .

Grant then stressed the need for civilizing these 'degenerate and base' people through the spread of Christianity. His missionary zeal, however, did not blind him to the basic interests of the industrial society of his homeland. He wrote: 'In every progressive step of this work [of civilizing Indians] we shall also serve the original design with which we visited India, that design still so important to this country—the extension of our commerce.'[43]

In 1813, on the occasion of the renewal of the Company's charter for India, the Evangelicals in England launched a campaign for permission of missionary work among Indians. They finally obtained it and India was thrown open to the missionaries from that year. Although churches had been built in the past for the Christian population of India (ironically, it was a Hindu—the famous Raja Nabakrishna Deb—who donated a plot of land in Calcutta, then valued at Rs 30,000, for the erection of St John's Church in 1787), in the early years of the Company rule a policy of non-interference in native religious customs was rigorously followed, and scrupulous care was taken not to hurt the religious sentiments of the indigenous people, to avoid any possible retaliation by them against the still uncertain position of the fledgling British enclaves. But with the growing self-confidence born of the gradual consolidation of colonial rule in most parts of India, and with the ascendancy of Utilitarian and Evangelical ideas in nineteenth-century England, it was felt that the time had come for stamping the image of the Empire upon India by 'transplanting the genius of English laws and English education'.[44]

The flow of Christian missionaries to India also helped the authorities to impose a rigid standard on its own men—the Company's writers, the British merchants and other members of its racial category—whose 'moral degeneration' through their social intercourse with the indigenous population had been a constant source of worry for the Christian missionaries all through the eighteenth century.[45]

Hand in hand with Utilitarianism and Evangelism emerged the demand for free trade in the early years of nineteenth-century England. The stability of the Empire in India had opened up the possibility of exploiting the vast Indian market for the needs of the expanding British industry. Free traders were demanding an end to the monopoly of the East India Company to enable private enterprise to have a share in the import and export business of this country. The Company's monopoly was abolished in 1813. The trade of the British being duty-free from the time of the acquisition of the Dewani in 1765, their goods had already ousted India-made articles of commerce from the market in the country. Soon after the abolition of the Company's monopoly, there was a rush of eager British adventurers into India to take part in the import and export business. In a few years several houses were established in Calcutta with London and Liverpool connections. The local Bengali banians found again a new opportunity to make money through collaboration with these private traders. This was a time 'when some half-a-dozen Banyans managed all the mercantile business of Calcutta and accumulated vast fortunes'.[46]

Describing how such collaboration worked to ruin indigenous manufactures, one contemporary observer reminisces:

I can speak from my personal knowledge that Mr David McIntyre . . . busily employed himself for some years in collecting information regarding the cotton fabrics most in use and demand among the natives, and through the assistance of his Banian the late Baboo Bissumbhur [Biswambhar] Sen . . . procured samples of all kinds and species of cloths in use among the various classes of Natives both in Bengal and Upper Provinces . . . his efforts did not end in vain, as within a few years he not only reaped a rich harvest for himself, but paved the way of all Indian merchants for following his example. White jaconets, cambrics, long cloths . . . Dhoties, Scarfs, Chintzes, Lappets, Japan spots, and Honeycombs were then imported on large scales which would find a market as soon as landed, at highly remunerative prices, and the imports were multiplied as the consumption increased.[47]

With the accumulation of wealth, the consumption pattern of the Bengali propertied class also underwent a change, paving the way for an increasing import of luxury items from Europe. Explaining the motives of his own class, an English protagonist of free trade wrote:

We should not only see the palaces of the Rajahs, and the houses of Vakeels, Aumils [sic], Sherofs, and Zamindars furnished and decorated with the produce of English arts and manufacturers, but the Ryots who form so large a part of the Indian population may, like the British farmers, have a taste for foreign produce, as soon as they can acquire property enough to procure it . . . Under these circumstances a trade might suddenly grow up beyond the Cape of Good Hope to take off all the surplus manufactures that Britain can produce.[48]

Already as early as 1805, Bengal had imported Rs 4 million worth of goods from London, the bulk of which consisted of boots and shoes, carriages, looking-glasses, hats, jewellery, perfumery, saddlery, wines and spirits, malt liquors and miscellaneous items described as 'treasure'.[49] A large part of these imported goods found their way into the newly built houses of the opulent banians, as evident from the following description of one such house in the thirties of the nineteenth century:

The drawing room was the most splendidly furnished . . . pictures the imitations of Raphael and Claude with some originals, which seemed living realities, diamond cut wall shades with brilliant drops were arranged with art, two tables of solid marble, white as morning snow, with two large chiming clocks . . . The retiring chamber was also beautifully adorned . . . French prints were hung round the room, and a large portrait of Venus in all her loveliness, was placed at the front so as to be visible to a person reclining on the bed . . .[50]

The phaetons, the bogies and broughams which used to carry these Bengali gentlemen during their promenade in the evenings, the French wine which flowed in their houses during festivals, the paintings and furniture which adorned their homes—all bore the marks of British manufacturers.

With the indigenous industries destroyed by the import of cheap commodities from England and a growing market within the country for imported consumer goods fashionable among the rich Indians, the country by the end of the century was reduced to an exporter of raw agricultural produce:

> our Exports to Foreign Countries showed that eighty-five per cent of them were represented by the bulky agricultural produce,' which gave no employment to local skill and capital, except such as was represented by the rude methods of Agriculture, while in the Imports we did not know how to supply our wants in regard to seventy-two per cent of the articles we received from foreign Countries.[51]

VIII

What was to have an important bearing for the indigenous cultural life of Calcutta from the second and third decades of the nineteenth century was the Government's policy regarding the social norms of behaviour of the British inhabitants of the city and the system of education for its indigenous population.

The desire to elevate the British administrators of the city to a position of distinct identity as members of a ruling class, which began with the establishment of Fort William College in Calcutta and Haileybury College in England, led to a marked change in their social relationship with the Bengali population. We have seen earlier how the entry of Indians in certain parts of the White Town, near the Fort, was banned during specific hours of the day. The policy of such segregation was extended to the members of the Bengali elite too. In an effort to reproduce and institutionalize in Calcutta the social features of their own national life in England, the British population of the city established the Bengal Club in 1827. A latter-day English writer speaks approvingly of its exclusiveness: 'Even when judged by the more exacting standard of London, the Bengal Club can fairly claim a respectable antiquity.'[52] To protect its respectability, the Club refused membership to Dwarkanath Tagore (the poet's grandfather), in spite of his lifelong loyalty to the British rulers, his grand balls at his Belgachhia garden house in the northern suburb of Calcutta where all the British gentry of the city were invited, and the audience granted to him by Queen Victoria during his visit to England. A cousin of Dwarkanath's—Prasanna Kumar Tagore, who was the grandson of Darpanarayan Tagore—was refused admission to Bengal Club in 1855, on the ground that 'the personal habits of Bengallee gentlemen cannot in the relaxing moments of convivial intercourse be found agreeable to the rest of the members.'[53] The training imparted at Haileybury College was obviously bearing its fruit. Commenting on the event, a contemporary Bengali-edited newspaper said: 'Few members of the Bengal Club can be ignorant of the fact that, for months and years, sometimes, the only regular guest at Baboo Prosunno Coomar Tagore's table is some English gentlemen [sic] of the best class of those who resort to the Bengal Club.'[54]

Although members of the local British population of Calcutta still attended parties thrown by the Bengali elite during religious festivals or wedding ceremonies, the Company authorities and the English missionaries discouraged the habit. Partly as a result of the campaign against such social intercourse, from the thirties of the nineteenth century onwards there was a fall in the attendance of Englishmen in such ceremonies. Partly because of the ruination of many old Bengali aristocratic families caused by long-drawn-out expensive litigations over inheritance claims, the number of gala parties on as lavish a scale as in the eighteenth century had also gone down. Further, quite a few English mercantile houses in Calcutta started collapsing in the 1830s because of 'over-trading, improvident enterprize, extravagant miscalculation and excessive expense in living',[55] bringing down with them the fortunes of the Bengali banians who were associated with them. Describing the poor show at the Durga puja in Calcutta in 1832, one contemporary newspaper reported:

> In the past in this city during the Durga puja festival, there were songs and dances and other shows of a similar pleasant nature. To watch the nautches of the Baijis and the dances of the clowns, even many Englishmen used to get invited and swarmed in such massive crowds that other people could not enter those houses where these performances were held. This year, even women from the lower orders could easily get in and stand before the image [of Durga]. The Baijis moved from street to street, yet no one hired them . . . There has been a marked decline in the pomp of Durga puja this year, and many explain it by saying that men of this country have lost their wealth . . .[56]

Some years later, the same newspaper reported: 'Very few from among the Christians came to watch the nautches and pantomimes this year during the Durga puja festival.'[57] Referring to such performances, an article in an English journal (written by an Englishman) of the period said:

> none [among the English gentlemen], by attending such exhibitions at the house of the native gentry, raise themselves much in the estimation of their brethren . . . The holiday and other nautches now given by some native gentlemen are attended only by natives, and such less reputable Europeans as have little or no character to lose . . . [58]

IX

The attempt to bind the city's English population to a code of behaviour was followed by plans to 'educate and reform' that section of the Bengali inhabitants who could best serve the interests of the colonial administrators. From their earlier role as intermediaries in business they were now to be transformed into that of intermediaries in the expanding tertiary sector which was coming up as an ancillary to the colonial rule—the vast network of administrative and judicial services, the Calcutta Municipality, the education department, etc.

Earlier attempts to 'reform' the natives through the spread of education to the lower orders (mainly by Christian missionaries) had not yielded much result, as it was found that the pressure of household chores prevented children of poor families from attending schools.[59]

On the other hand, members of the Bengali upper and middle classes had been showing an inclination to learn English from the beginning of the eighteenth century, purely from the need to be able to do better business with the English merchants and administrators. We come across the names of several enterprising Bengalis like Andiram Das, Ramram Misra and Ram Narayan Misra in eighteenth-century Calcutta who set up schools for the teaching of elementary English so that the banians and other inter-mediaries could converse with the British. Nabakrishna Deb was supposed to have picked up English from Warren Hastings, who in his turn learnt Persian and Bengali from Deb. Dwarkanath Tagore learnt English at a school run by one Mr Sherburn. Several such schools came up in Calcutta during the eighteenth and the early part of the nineteenth centuries, primarily through the efforts of individuals—both Englishmen and Bengalis.[60]

By the turn of the nineteenth century, as the Bengali upper class of Calcutta came to realize that the British were firmly entrenched as rulers in the country, they sought to improve their prospects under the patronage of the new rulers and were ready to adopt their language (as their predecessors had accepted Persian and Arabic under Mughal rule) for official purposes. The first organized effort by this class to educate their children in the 'literature and science of Europe' was made in 1816, when some 'respectable Hindus' of Calcutta met at the residence of the then Chief Justice Sir E. Hyde East, following which the next year the Hindu College was established in Calcutta. It is significant that among the members of the committee set up to run the institution, along with English administrators and judges and prominent Bengali citizens of Calcutta there were five eminent Sanskrit pundits. According to E. Hyde East, during his earlier meeting with these 'most respectable Hindoo inhabitants' at his house, these pundits 'deplored their national deficiency in morals' and requested him to include the 'English system of morals' in the curriculum of the college.[61]

It suggests that in those early years of the nineteenth century when conversion to Christianity was not yet perceived as a threat, in their ardent desire to further the prospects of their sons under the new regime, even the conservative religious elements of Bengali Hindu society were willing to depreciate their own social mores in favour of an alien system.

The Bengali students of Hindu College—and other schools set up around the same time with the objective of educating the natives in European science and literature—were quick to gain proficiency in subjects like the intricacies of the British political and legal system, the history of England and Greece and Rome, the European classics and the plays of Shakespeare, as evident from the appreciative reviews of their performance during the annual prize distribution ceremonies of these schools in contemporary English newspapers. Noting the change in their cultural tastes while reviewing the performance of Shakespeare's plays by the Hindu College students, one paper commented:

the mere language of the English has been hitherto their principal, if not exclusive object; but now, in these scenes, the habits and manners of Europeans become to them matter of familiar study and acquirement. This is certainly a grand step towards enlarging the sphere of their

understanding, and freeing them from the spell of preju-
dice, which had so long bound them to their primeval
notions and customs . . . [62]

The purpose for which such education was being encouraged
by the government was quite clear. The East India Company's
Court of Directors, in a despatch in March 1825, asked the government of Bengal to give 'a very efficient stimulus to the cultivation
of the English language and useful knowledge in general among
the natives—by a marked preference to successful candidates at
College in the selection of persons to fill those situations in service
which can advantageously be conferred upon Natives' (quoted in
D. P. Sinha, *The Educational Policy of the East India Company in
Bengal to 1854* [Calcutta, 1964] p. 85). Three years later, Lord
Amherst, the then Governor-General of India, in an address to the
Company's Court of Directors felt that the training imparted
through these institutions had made 'Natives of education and
respectability of character eligible to higher grades of the
public service that are at present open to their fair and honourable
ambition . . . '[63]

The policy to employ educated Bengalis in junior posts in
the administration was dictated by the expanding network as also
by the need to reduce the expenditure on high salaries required to
be paid to their English counterparts. A Parliamentary Select
Committee appointed in 1832 to look into this aspect asked Holt
Mackenzie, the Secretary to the Government of India: 'The result
of your opinion is that the finances of India would be much
improved by the employment of natives?'

Mackenzie replied: 'I think so; I think the natives are quite
equal to Europeans in intellect.' Following this, the Charter Act of
1833 opened newer opportunities for Indians in the administration.
The same year the office of Deputy Collector was created for
Indians, in 1837 that of Principal Sudder and in 1843 that of Deputy
Magistrate. But the Indians appointed to these posts provided
cheap labour to the Company. Out of 2,813 Indians employed
in 1849 as uncovenanted servants, only 493 received salaries above

the £240 grade, while the rest were below it (cf. Mukherjee, *Calcutta*, p. 11).

Encouraged by the results of the training scheme which was bringing forth a new generation of efficient intermediaries (the number of Indians employed by the Company's government went up from 49,322 in 1800 to about 100,000 in 1930—vide Mukherjee, *Calcutta*, p. 10), the government decided to streamline the educational experiments into a single, comprehensive programme that would unfailingly supply the personnel for the various departments of the legal and administrative institutions of the colonial society. The government decided to withdraw support from the missionary schools, and resolved instead to teach 'respectable classes' in preference to the indigent classes.[64]

The Calcutta Council of Education recommended that 'efforts should be at first concentrated to the chief towns of Sudder stations of districts, and to the improvement of education among the higher and middling classes of the population.' Thus, the authorities made up their minds as to the class of Bengalis that should be trained up. C. E. Trevelyan described this class as 'a creature of our own . . . [with] no notion of improvement but such as rivets their connection with the English and makes them dependent on English protection and instruction'.[65]

But in trying to formulate a comprehensive educational policy, the new generation of British rulers had to contend with a section of their own community—the English Orientalists in Bengal. Still attuned to the Company's earlier policy of non-interference in native religious customs and social practices (dictated by the Company's preliminary need in the eighteenth century for collaboration with the local banians and dewans to consolidate its control over the country's economy and political system), these Orientalists in the Committee of Public Instruction, which controlled education in the country, emphasized the cultivation of their own respective religious scriptures, laws and literature by the Hindus and Muslims. They could be described as the lingering representatives of the British attitudes towards India of an earlier century, whose

philosophy and policies were no longer relevant to the new generation of rulers in nineteenth-century Calcutta (although their
contribution to an understanding of India's past was a source to
which Indian nationalists harked back occasionally in later years).
The tendency of the English merchant and the Company's servant
to fraternize with the local Bengali gentry in the eighteenth-century
Calcutta social scene had its parallel in the cultural field in the
studious endeavours of Orientalists like William Jones and Horace
Hayman Wilson to discover the past heritage of Indian music and
literature. Interaction often led to a sort of acculturation, as in
the weird case of Major General Charles Stuart (1758–1828) who,
having made a close study of Hinduism, was said to have conformed to its practices. He used to walk down from his residence
in Wood Street in Calcutta to the Ganga for his daily bath, and
made a collection of Hindu idols. Although 'Hindu' Stuart (as he
was known among his contemporaries) was buried with Christian
rites in a cemetery in Calcutta, his tomb was modelled on a Hindu
temple with a carved gateway.[66]

But such days were over. The coexistence of two distinct cultures was perceived by the nineteenth-century British rulers as an
annoyance in the way of smooth administration and economic
domination. To man the various services, it was necessary to have
a class of Bengalis who were attuned to the cultural and social values of the contemporary administrators, and to the requirements
that followed from such values. Their education had to be brought
completely under the control of the government. The teaching of
Oriental classics was absolutely irrelevant in this framework: 'In
professing to establish Seminaries for the purpose of teaching
mere Hindoo, or mere Mahommedan literature, you bound your-
self to teach a great deal of what was frivolous, not a little of which
was purely mischievous.'[67]

What was considered 'mischievous' by the government was
obviously the pride in national culture that could have been fostered among the natives by a study of their ancient languages and
classical texts. Such a pride would have obviously stood in the way
of their subservience to the foreign administrators in their daily

operations. It was necessary therefore to invade the native mind, destroy its foundations and reshape it so that it learnt to depreciate its own cultural roots and stood ashamed of them. Only such a mood of self-denigration among the natives could have made them look up to the English as a superior race and ensure the rulers a steady supply of loyal functionaries.

X

The intellectual basis of the British government's education policy in India in the nineteenth-century lay embedded in two important texts: first, the *History of British India* by the Utilitarian James Mill, which came out in 1818; and second, the famous 'Minutes of 2 February 1835' by Thomas Babington Macaulay, who was then the President of the Committee of Public Instruction. Mill's general argument was that Asiatic societies existed in the depths of degradation, and the absence of Christian 'enlightenment' had produced art and culture which were 'unnatural, offensive and not infrequently disgusting'. To emancipate such a society Macaulay, in his Minutes seventeen years later, proposed a dissemination of knowledge of English literature and English science in preference to the science and literature of the East, so that there could develop 'a class of persons, Indian in blood and colour, but English in taste, in opinions, in morals and in intellect'.

Macaulay's educational 'Minutes' sealed the fate of the Orientalists. Under the provision of the India Bill of 1813, a sum of £10,000 was being spent every year for the 'cultivation of learning' among the Indians. The expenditure had to be diverted now from Oriental studies to English studies: 'the sum available for English education was but the pittance that could be saved by reductions in the Oriental assignments'.[68] Explaining the need to eliminate the indigenous culture from the educational programme for the natives and to replace it with Western culture, Macaulay in his 'Minutes' said:

The question now before us is simply whether . . . when we can teach European science, we shall teach systems

which, by universal confession, whenever they differ from
those of Europe, differ for the worse . . . In India, English
is the language spoken by the ruling class. It is spoken by
the higher class of natives at the seats of Government. It
is likely to become the language of commerce throughout
the seas of the East.[69]

The need for a firmer official control over education, as empli-
fied in Macaulay's 'Minutes', was dictated by another development
also. The teaching of young Bengalis in institutions like the Hindu
College was in the hands of private individuals. Although they were
producing useful candidates for the services, there was a danger
lurking behind. Exposure to European history had led these
impressionable minds to respond to radical ideas current in the
West at that time. A Calcutta-born Eurasian, Henry Louis Vivian
Derozio, started teaching in the Hindu College in 1826 at the very
young age of 17. He was very popular among his Bengali students,
who were also in their teens. In 1827–28, under his patronage and
often in his house, debates and discussions used to take place on
political issues. In 1829–30, Derozio and his pupils brought out a
number of journals where they not only attacked Hindu orthodoxy,
but sometimes raised questions about the legitimacy of British
colonization in India.[70]

Kashinath Ghosh, a student of Hindu College, during
Derozio's teachership there, came out with a critique of James
Mill's *History of British India*, protesting against Mill's attempt to
prove that the Indians were not a civilized people.[71] Although
Kashinath's critique was from an Orientalist point of view in
defence of the past glory of Hindu kingdoms, and the other intellectual forays of Derozio's Bengali pupils were confined at that time
to debates and articles in journals, and hence did not pose any
immediate threat to the authorities, the latter were quick to detect
the ominous signs. They took the cue from a warning sounded by
Marquis Wellesley at the beginning of the nineteenth century with
regard to the young British servants of the Company who were
coming to India: 'It cannot be denied that during the convulsions

with which the doctrine of the French Revolution has agitated the continent of Europe, erroneous principles of the same dangerous tendency had reached the minds of some individuals in the Civil and Military Service of the Company in India.' He, therefore, stressed the need for the setting up of a college in Fort William to 'establish sound and correct principles of religion and government in their minds at an early period of life'.[72]

A similar need was felt in the field of higher education of the Bengali youth, by the government as well as by its supporters. The Rev. Alexander Duff, a Scottish missionary who arrived in Calcutta in 1830, opened an educational institution with five pupils to start with. One of his achievements was to persuade the pupils of Derozio to accept the Reformation as their model in place of the 'terrible issue of French illumination and reform in the last century'.[73]

Macaulay completed this process of weaning away the vocal, dissident sections of the English-educated upper and middle-class Bengali youth with promises of self-government for the natives at some future date. In the meantime they were expected to prepare themselves for that distant goal by educating themselves into a 'capacity for better government', by becoming 'instructed in European knowledge' so that they could perpetuate the 'imperishable empire of our [i.e. English] arts and our morals, our literature and our laws'.[74]

Within a decade or so, the radical Derozians had changed into loyal subjects of the British Empire, some among them were even ready to retract their former atheist beliefs and become Christians (like Krishnamohan Banerjee) or join the Brahmo Samaj (like Tarachand Chakrabarty, Ramtanu Lahiri and Sibchandra Deb among others). Ramgopal Ghose, the one-time stormy petrel among the Derozians, addressing the opening session of the Bengal British India Society in Calcutta on 20 April 1843, said: 'The Society shall adopt and recommend such measures only, as are consistent with pure loyalty to the person and government of the reigning Sovereign of the British Government and the laws of this country.'[75]

XI

In the meantime, the composition of the Bengali gentry in the Black Town was also undergoing a change through the first three decades of the nineteenth century. As we have indicated earlier, from the close of the eighteenth century there was a tendency among members of the gentry to withdraw from business and invest in land. The Permanent Settlement of 1793 gave it a further impetus when the old zamindars of Bengal, unable to pay the revenue, had to put up their estates in the various districts for auction. These estates were bought by the nouveau riche banians and dewans of Calcutta who came to be known as 'absentee zamin-dars', staying in Calcutta in pomp and collecting rents from the estates through a vast network of 'gomastahs' (rent-collecting agents) and 'paik-barkandajs' (armed footmen).[76] The wealth that accumulated in the hands of the banians and the various categories of intermediaries in Calcutta was thus diverted from any possible investment in business and industries to land.

By the beginning of the nineteenth century, members of the old generation of Bengali intermediaries, who had made their fortunes in collaboration with Hastings and other Englishmen, had passed away one by one. Darpanarayan Tagore died in 1793, Raja Nabakrishna Deb in 1797. Businessmen who started as bani-ans but had a flair for independent trade and commerce, like Nemaicharan Mullick, who died in 1807, and Ramdulal Dey, who died in 1825, were also on their way out. Their descendants contin-ued an affluent lifestyle primarily out of the income from the landed estates left by their forefathers. Some among them, how-ever, tried their hands at commerce and business, like Dwarkanath Tagore who, besides adding estates to the landed properties left by his ancestors, set up a merchants' office called Carr, Tagore and Company. Ashutosh Dey, Ramdulal's son, was a director of the Union Bank. But by the end of the 1840s such ventures had flopped. Tagore's firm had to be wound up in 1848. The same year the Union Bank crashed. It was the junior posts in the colonial administration and judicial services which provided opportunities to some of these descendants of the old families. Prasanna Kumar Tagore, a grandson of Darpanarayan's, became a lawyer. Commenting on the failure of the Bengalis in trade and commerce, as well as on their inability to occupy senior positions in the administration, a Bengali newspaper ruefully said:

They [the Bengalis] are ill-trained to improve their positions through widespread trade and commerce, and inefficient in earning enough money from superior industries, and equally ill-equipped to occupy any senior administrative post . . . There are no signs whatsoever that men in Bengal will receive important positions of prestige and honour from the English as did Raja Rajballav, Raja Nabakrishna and Dewan Ganga Gobinda Singh.[77]

We get an interesting picture of the economic composition of Bengali society in the middle of the nineteenth century from an account in a contemporary newspaper:

There are now in Bengal only two, perhaps three, families which can boast of a clear annual income of above fifty thousand pounds, or five lacs of rupees a year. The source of their incomes is, of course, property in land . . . [As for] families of incomes ranging between ten and fifty thousands a year . . . in Bengal . . . the number at the outside would be a hundred. The major part of this class . . . are, we may assume with confidence, landowners . . . about half a dozen of that class which combines banking with trade may be found in the list, but not one salaried or professional man. The next class, namely of those in receipt of incomes ranging from five to ten thousands a year . . . in Bengal, their number may be a little above a hundred . . . the landowners form a still larger majority in this class; there are a few bankers and merchants in the list, and we know of but a single income derived from professional sources that exceeds five thousand pounds or fifty thousand rupees a year. The fact that there is not a single salaried income which amounts to that figure has not only an economical but a political signification.[78]

Although these landed interests continued to play an important role in Calcutta society in the early years of the nineteenth century, a new generation of Bengalis was coming up as the ruling elite of the Black Town from the 1830s. They had very little to do with the city's economy and growth (unlike the Setts, Basaks, Debs and Tagores of the previous century), their main contribution being confined to the Company's administrative services and the social changes that were taking place in Calcutta. The majority of the young people who flocked to Hindu College and similar educational institutions of the city were sons of petty clerks in the judicial and administrative services, or of the various sub-contractors, leaseholders, tenure holders and small landholders who came up in the countryside as a result of the Permanent Settlement.[79] While the eighteenth-century Bengali intermediaries took part in the colonial scheme of overhauling the country's economy and political system, this new generation of English-educated intermediaries played an important role in the government's attempts to remould the Bengali society of the 'respectable Hindus'.

XII

Till almost the third quarter of the nineteenth century, attempts at social reforms like the ban on the customs of 'sati', child marriage and Kulin polygamy and measures favouring changes like widow remarriage and women's education split Calcutta's *sambhranta* or respectable society into several fighting factions. Debates on these issues were often interlinked with controversies over the interpretation of Hindu religion, the need to adapt it to the changing circumstances, the virtues and vices of Christianity, etc. A number of organizations and journals cropped up to rally the supporters of the respective groups. The Brahmo Sabha was founded by Rammohan Roy in 1828 which was preceded by his publication in 1818 of a Bengali tract against sati. Although Rammohan's ancestors had established themselves as rich people during the Mughal days, their influence was confined to Khanakul in Hugli where

Rammohan was born. Unlike the forefathers of many among the Calcutta elite who came to the city in the early eighteenth century, Rammohan arrived in the metropolis sometime in 1815 only, and was comparatively an obscure outsider in Bengali society at that time. But his ideas on religion and social reforms brought him closer to the English administrators, and in a very short time he emerged as an indigenous leader of the programme of reforming Bengali society.

While Rammohan was able to enlist the support of Dwarkanath Tagore from among the city's old *abhijata* or aristo-cratic families as well as of the new English-educated Bengalis from the middle strata, his opponents, who were against any ban on sati, gathered round the leaders of the landed aristocracy like Radhakanta Deb and Gopimohan Deb of Raja Nabakrishna's Shobhabazar Raj family, Narasimha Ray of the Posta family, and traditional businessmen like Vaishnavdas Mullick of the Pathuriaghata gold merchant family. They established the Dharma Sabha in 1830.

In the meantime, in 1827–28, the pupils of Derozio, who were also in favour of radical reforms, had set up the debating society called Academic Association. Their demonstrative gestures against the conservative habits of traditional Hindu society, like eating beef and drinking wine in public and taunting the image of Kali with the greeting: 'Good Morning, Madam'[80] shocked the orthodox section of Bengali society. Although the orthodox Hindus forced the ouster of Derozio from Hindu College in April 1831, Alexander Duff's efforts to curb the radicalism of the Derozians by converting them into Christians posed another threat to the Hindu conserva-tives. In 1832 a number of young Bengali Hindus were baptized, including Mahesh Chandra Ghosh, Krishnamohan Banerjee and Gopeenath Nandi.

The dual threat of dilution of the ideological basis of the Hindu religious system from Rammohan and his Brahmo Sabha on the one hand, and of the erosion of younger people from its ranks under the influence of the Christian missionaries on the other, reinforced the traditional conservatism among the old families of the city. The permissiveness of the early eighteenth century which allowed people from lower castes to be absorbed in the *abhijata* Hindu society gave way to a tendency to guard jealously the newly revived caste hierarchy. It was ironical that Ashutosh Dey, whose father Ramdulal Dey scoffed at caste niceties by bribing Brahman pundits and claiming, 'I keep caste in my coffers', became in the 1840s the leader of the orthodox Dharma Sabha to impose sanctions on anyone violating the traditional caste norms. In 1842 one Madhusudan Mitra got his son married to the daughter of a person from a different caste, having been 'deceived by the intrigues of a matchmaker'. He was forced by Ashutosh Dey to make his son forsake the bride and do penance to be able to gain re-entry into the Dharma Sabha.[81]

We should hasten to add, however, that both orthodox Hindus like Radhakanta Deb and reformists like Rammohan Roy and Dwarkanath Tagore were agreed in principle on the need to accept some of the new changes, such as the education of the Bengali 'respectable classes' in English and the spread of modern education among the women of these classes. They were also united in their demands for better prospects for the educated Bengalis in the administrative services, and for the protection of their economic and political interests. Unitedly they held meetings and signed petitions to protest against the Jury Act in 1826, stamp duties in 1827 and to demand a free press in 1835.[82]

As for traditional Hindu customs and practices, some of the reformists were no less loyal than the orthodox Hindus in following those rituals. Dwarkanath Tagore, for instance, who adhered in his beliefs to Rammohan's campaign against idolatry, regularly observed the Durga puja and other Bengali religious ceremonies of image worship. He had no qualms in conforming to the old convention of feeding Brahmans during the *shradh* ceremony of his mother.

What then divided them? According to one historian of modern days, Rammohan Roy believed that 'the organization of society' depended on religion. Since Hinduism had imposed unnecessary restrictions on the Hindus, which denied them 'social comfort' and disqualified them from entering into 'difficult enterprises', he insisted that some religious reform was essential at least 'for the sake of their [Indians'] political and social comfort.' . . . The 'conservatives', however, did not find any necessary connection between 'political and social comfort' and religious reform. They were eager to separate their religion from secular activities.[83]

The debates and disagreements on reforms had a lot to do also with traditional rivalries between various factions of Calcutta's Bengali gentry rather than with the intrinsic merits of the proposed reforms. Known as *dals*, these factions competed among themselves for positions of power within the Bengali community, and later for control over schools and other institutions that were cropping up in nineteenth-century Calcutta. Several such *dals* were led by scions of important old families like Radhakanta Deb, a grandson of the famous Raja Nabakrishna Deb; Ashutosh Dey, a son of the millionaire Ramdulal Dey; Dwarkanath Tagore, of the Jorasanko Tagore family.

The jockeying for positions of dominance among these various Bengali groups, often parading under differing labels like 'reformists', '*sanatani* Hindus' (orthodox Hindus), or Derozians, kept the Black Town astir during the nineteenth century. By the 1840s the Derozians, already a minority of young radicals, had been outmanoeuvred, and those who were left in the field were the followers of Rammohan and the Brahmos on the one hand, and the Dharma Sabha adherents on the other—both seeking some form of social stability and economic security. There emerged a tacit understanding between them on the need for accepting the reforms at a gradual pace and in modified forms as part of the general inclination towards a social cohesion of the Bengali *sambhranta* people, based on a set of values born of a compromise between the old and the new, the traditional norms and the influences from abroad. The needs and requirements of their survival and further progress under an alien rule allowed the rejection of certain customs that were too demonstratively obnoxious to be practised in public in the eyes of the authorities (like sati), and the adoption of certain new manners and mores that were felt to be conducive to the advancement of the Bengali 'respectable' classes. As a result, some innocuous but expensive religious rituals and conventions, however irrational they might have looked to outsiders (like idol worship, following the almanac, or feeding Brahmans), continued to survive in peaceful coexistence with reforms that were meant to emancipate the followers of these rituals from unscientific beliefs. Over the years Calcutta's Bengali society accommodated all the erstwhile warring groups—the original adherents of the Brahmo Samaj (divided into several factions by the end of the nineteenth century), the main body of the orthodox Hindus, as well as the Anglicized gentry, in its folds, as long as they conformed to the mores of the bhadralok.

It was through the debates and discussions on reforms, the competition for gaining influence among their own people, compromises on questions of rejection and adoption, and bargaining with the foreign rulers for a better deal for themselves that the Bengali 'respectable' classes moved towards the development of certain common standards of behaviour and cultural norms which were to mark them out as bhadraloks. It was a social category embracing different strata of upper and middle income groups, landed interests as well as administrative employees and professionals. The outward manifestations of the bhadralok (to which members of the group had to rigorously conform), which were made possible by a basic standard of income, were (i) residence in a 'pucca' house, either through ownership or renting; (ii) attention to one's sartorial style in public; (iii) use of a chaste Bengali that was being shaped from the middle of the nineteenth century; and (iv) a noticeable knowledge of English language and manners.

Thus, the efforts at proselytization by Alexander Duff and the missionaries, and at Anglicization by Macaulay and his English disciples, did not quite succeed in creating a totally new community of transmuted Bengalis. The hold of the Brahmanical tradition on society, which rigidly controlled the cultural and social behaviour of the 'respectable' classes, prevented a wholesale transformation of the community. The compromise worked out by these 'respectable' classes in the shape of the peculiar Bengali pro- totype—the bhadralok—is described by a modern historian as a 'combination of Mill and Manu, the latter largely expurgated of its priestly and patriarchal excesses . . . While the English utilitarian afforded a tool for intellectual analysis, the Hindu sage offered a key to social cohesion.'[84]

XIII

Contemporary journals, newspapers and government despatches of nineteenth-century Calcutta quite often give the impression that the entire city throughout this period was engrossed in debates over the subtle points of Hindu and Christian religious scriptures, controversies over sati and widow remarriage, and meetings in the Town Hall and other places to press the demands of the educated Bengalis.

But one should remember that the vast majority of the city's population was completely out of the picture evoked by these reports. As mentioned earlier, these people were mainly artisans who came from the lower castes, labourers who worked as domes- tics or low-paid employees in the city's numerous shops and other establishments, and non-Bengali migrants from nearby states who manned certain services (like the palanquin bearers who came from Orissa, or the watchmen employed to guard the palatial buildings of the well-to-do Bengali families, who came from Bihar and the eastern part of the then United Provinces). The issues that stirred the imagination of the *sambhranta* Bengalis were of no consequence for these people who formed the bulk of the city's population.

For instance, Kulin polygamy—which was one of the objects of reform in nineteenth-century Bengal—affected only the upper- caste Bengali families. As for the problem of widow remarriage, among the lower-caste and lower-class Bengalis the remarriage of a widow, or her cohabitation with a man, was often accepted in these communities. *Sanga* or *sangat* appeared to be a recognized

form of marriage among the lower orders, as evident from a contemporary saying popular among them:

Ghar podley chhagoley maday,
Rand holey sabai eshey sanga kortey chay.
(When the hut collapses, even the goat tramples on it.
When one becomes a widow, everyone comes to arrange a
sanga with her.)[85]

In cities like Calcutta, widows from the lower classes were
often known to be cohabiting with men of their choice, as revealed
by the evidence of a woman textile worker before the Indian Factory
Commission, who said she was a widow and was living with an
'adopted husband'.[86]

The system of child marriage also might not have been as
widespread among these classes as among the upper-caste Hindus.
A research scholar working on the nineteenth century notes:
'poorer class or lower-caste women were married usually a bit
later in life . . . The training that they got helped them in life after
marriage to stand beside their husbands in their labour and not
become parasites on them.'[87] This is corroborated by a comment
in a nineteenth-century Brahmo newspaper. Opposing the pro-
posal to make respectable Bengali women self-reliant through
education, the writer said that they did not have to be self-reliant
since they were being looked after by their menfolk, and then
added: 'Only among the women of the lower classes in this country,
we come across some sort of self-reliance.[88]

The debates over education and religious issues also did not
cover these lower orders of Calcutta. As the early missionary experiments proved, poverty prevented their children from any access
to the new education. The controversy over religion between Rammohan and his Brahmo followers on the one hand, and the
Dharma Sabha on the other, was monopolized by the upper and
middle caste well-to-do Hindus—the Brahmans, Kayasthas and
Vaidyas, and descendants of the eighteenth-century lower-caste
millionaires like the gold merchant Mullick family or the Basaks

of the weaver caste. Even though the majority of the Brahmans and Kayasthas in nineteenth-century Calcutta were poor and illiterate,[89] since they were not considered bhadraloks, they were not drawn into the religious debates.[90] The importance attached in these debates to the observance of rituals and adherence to certain provisions of the scriptures was basically a manifestation of the Bengali gentry's attempt to codify a set of norms for the bhadralok, so that the 'respectable classes', those who had risen to the top during the eighteenth century, and the others who were joining them in the nineteenth, could preserve their distinct identity different from the English as well as from the lower orders of their own community. Gone were the days of Ratan the washerman, who could climb up to the top of the social hierarchy by being an interpreter for the newly arrived Englishman, or of Piritram Marh, who came from a lower-caste and humble origins, but through speculation amassed a fortune to become the founder of the Janbazar Raj family in Calcutta. There was no need for people from such humble origins in nineteenth-century Calcutta. There was no scope for them in the firmly established administrative and commercial capital of the British empire. Once having consolidated their positions in the economy and society of Calcutta, these Bengali parvenus were determined to protect their domain. The socio-religious norms that they codified were based on education and money—the two props which marked them out from the lower orders. Continuation of Hindu rituals like feeding Brahmans at ceremonies, the employment of 'ghataks' (matchmakers) to determine the caste alignments for marriages, the social duty to arrange sumptuous feasts during occasions like a wedding, a *shradh* or the adoption of the sacred thread (for upper-caste Hindus), as well as the more modern obligation of sending children to schools and colleges, learning the English language and manners to win the confidence of the rulers, furnishing the homes in accordance with the newly acquired tastes—the customary observance of all these was agreed upon by both the orthodox and the reformist sections of the Bengali Hindu gentry. Neither these nor even the less ostentatious religious and social practices of the Brahmo Samaj (marked by the singing of highly Sanskritized hymns at prayer meetings with divine service on abstruse topics, and a rigorous cultivation of refined manners) could be afforded by the poorer classes.

The short-lived Derozian rebellion against the establishment in the 1830s brought into being an ephemeral world which was also distant from the framework of references of Calcutta's lower orders. The Derozian defiance of traditional Hindu rituals was marked by demonstrative gestures like drinking foreign liquor, eating beef and holding forth (mainly in English) on radical politics—gestures that, however well meaning they might have been, could never be shared by the lower orders. When one of their leading advocates, young Krishnamohan Banerjee (who later became a Christian), during a brief stint with atheism, went around the streets of Calcutta with his friends, parodying the quaint Bengali used by the English Christian missionaries, they might have struck a sympathetic chord in the minds of the populace.[91] To be fair to the Derozians, however, some among them tried in their own way to understand the problems of the downtrodden. Radhanath Sikdar, who was a direct pupil of Derozio and was later to discover the highest peak in the world (though his claim was appropriated by his white boss, Sir George Everest), protested against the assault on hill porters by European officials.[92]

But for the most part, Calcutta's lower orders remained an invisible mass for the bhadralok society. They found their way into newspaper columns only when they posed a threat to the economic and social comforts of the bhadralok. Thus, in 1827 the Oriya palanquin-bearers

> assembled on the plain of the Fort [William], others at Chandpal Ghaut [a landing place on the banks of the river Hugli], in separate bodies. They say, these confounded Firingis [Englishmen] have been at their usual tricks of taxing our bodily labour! . . . They have refused, accordingly, to bear palanquins for these few days . . .[93]

In 1834 the salt workers of Calcutta, known as 'khaladis', demonstrated before the house of the governor-general protesting against the custom according to which each of them was forced to offer a free gift of a vessel load of salt to the then Salt Dewan— Dwarkanath Tagore.[94] In 1851 the drivers of bullock-carts (which were the main means of carrying freight in those days) went on a strike against the proposed imposition of a tax, and succeeded in getting it repealed. Noting their success, the editor of a contemporary Bengali journal made the snide comment: 'Had I known before, I would have left the job of an editor and become a bullock-cart driver, and could have become the King's object of favour![95] In 1859 again, we find the bhadraloks complaining about a strike by the city's milkmen as a result of which the Bengali's favourite sweetmeat—'sandesh'—had disappeared from the market.[96]

Although education was the privilege of the upper and middle classes, some from among the lower orders in Calcutta seem to have sought advantage of the several free schools that were established in the city in the nineteenth century. A bhadralok writer in the 'letters to the editor' column of a contemporary Bengali newspaper complains:

> The respectable classes of this country are pained to find that there are hardly any barber or washerman in Calcutta; their sons have become clerks . . . The lower caste people like sadgops, dealers in spices, cowherds used to work as servants for the brahmans, kshatriyas and baishyas. Now they have learnt English and do not want to work as servants . . .[97]

It is difficult to get an idea of the exact numerical strength of the poorer classes—the artisans, domestic servants, low-paid employees doing menial jobs, workers in construction jobs and clearing operations (new areas were being cleared and houses built in the city till almost the end of the nineteenth century), labourers in the docks and the workers employed in the manufacturing industries that were coming up from the middle of the century. An occupation-based census was not taken till 1876. But for the period before that, we can form some estimate on the basis of the number and types of dwelling units that were counted by the city authorities at certain intervals during the century, although there are glaring inconsistencies since they were not all compiled on the same system. The dwelling units in these estimates are usually divided into two categories—houses, or 'pucca' (i.e. solid buildings with brick and cement), and huts, or 'kutcha' (i.e. built with mud and thatches or tiles). Judging from accounts by contemporary observers, we can safely assume that the poor people lived in the huts, while the better off in the houses.[98]

The number of huts fell from 53,289 in 1821 to 50,871 in 1837. In that year the erection of huts with thatched roofs was prohibited because of fire hazards. Thatch was replaced by the more expensive tiles. The number of huts fell further to 22,860 in 1876, the year of the census.[99] During the same period, i.e. from 1821 to 1876, the number of houses had increased from 14,230 to 16,896. Noting that the falling off was 'entirely restricted to native huts', Mr H. Beverley, who was in charge of the Calcutta census in 1876, while acknowledging that there might have been some miscalculations in the earlier estimates, admitted that 'huts have largely made way for the erection of pucka buildings and the construction of tanks and new roads'.[100] In other words, the displacement of the poor people from their original settlements in the city, as mentioned earlier, continued well-nigh into the last quarter of the nineteenth century. Mr Beverley adds later: 'Every street that is widened, every new square opened, means so many persons displaced, and as the limits of the Town are fixed, many of them doubtless remove outside it altogether.'[101]

From an estimate made in 1831, we find that at least one-fifth of the servants and other workers employed in the town itself were residing outside its limits.[102]

The bulk of those living within the precincts of the town were concentrated in the north between Mechhuabazar at the top west and Bowbazar at the bottom east, accounting for more than half of the total population which was 409,036 in 1876. Here lived the old artisans like potters and clay modellers (in Kumortuli, where they were first settled during the days of Gobindaram Mitra, the

black zamindar). Beverley found here, in 1876, 'several large bustees [slums] peopled by shopkeepers, boatmen and courtesans'.[103]
While the clay modellers were lucky enough to be able to stick to
their original settlements, the oil-pressers who settled down in
Coolootola in the north-western part in the eighteenth century were
'compelled to recede eastwards' and were found by Beverley in
Sookea's Street (named after a famous Armenian trader) in 1876.
The north-eastern part of the town, including Sookea's Street, comprised 'large bustees, more than half the population living in
kutcha huts'. Further south in Moocheepada, 'about 57 per cent of
the inhabitants still lodge in kutcha huts', according to Beverley,
who also discovered 'unsightly collections of native huts' like
Colvin's Bustee and Hill's Bazaar even in the southern part of the
city 'occupied by the palatial mansions of Chowringhee'. According
to Beverley's estimates, a little over half the city's population were
living in 'kutcha' houses. If we add to them the labouring population residing outside the town but employed within its precincts,
and the floating population entering the city every day by the river
Hugli from the suburbs (estimated at 10,000 persons in 1876
against 100,000 in 1821, indicating the growing tendency among
these suburbanites to settle down in Calcutta), we can assume that
the bulk of the city's daily population consisted of the lower orders,
comprising domestic servants (of various categories like 'khan-
samahs' or butlers, cooks, 'punkah-pullers' or those who pulled
the elaborate hanging fans, and gardeners, employed by the
Englishmen and the rich Bengalis); barbers, water-carriers, washermen; labourers engaged in transport like palanquin bearers, coach-
men, boatmen and porters; artisans like potters, bangle-makers,
clay modellers, braziers; persons employed in traditional manufactures like oil-makers and sellers, salt workers; the first generation of the industrial proletariat—the jute and textile mill workers;
and, what is important for our present discussion, the numerous
types of artistes from these lower orders who were popular enough
to be enumerated in the 1876 census—street musicians and
singers, actors, dancers and jugglers.[104]

In these occupations of the lower orders, the Bengalis, forming about three-fourths of the city's population, were primarily engaged as artisans and domestic servants, and in caste-based occupations like those of barbers and washermen, fishermen and boatmen, and also as street singers and dancers.

XIV

The majority of these poorer Bengali citizens of Calcutta, who migrated from nearby villages, transplanted the dwelling style of rural life to Calcutta. 'The tiled hut or mud "baree" that in the mofussil would be occupied by a single family, is in Calcutta the constant home of some eight or ten households; while the sanitary precautions that would render such a state of things wholesome are altogether wanting.'[105] While condemning these people for transplanting their dwellings—unsuitable for the growing and crowded metropolis—into Calcutta, the English official who made the above comment did not care to point out that these inhabitants of the city's slums and hutments could not afford, even if they wished, the 'pucca' houses, often rising to five storeys (reported to be owned by a native in north Calcutta in 1850) built by the well-to-do bhadraloks.

We can form an idea of their living standards from a missionary's account in the 1820s. The highest paid appeared to be the khansamah working in some English household or a Bengali rich man's house, getting Rs 8 a month, or 6d. a day. The lowest paid was the coolie or day labourer who would earn Rs 4 per month, or 3d. a day. The earnings of sweepers, gardeners and water-carriers varied from Rs 4 to Rs 5 per month. None of the domestic servants received any food.

Artisans are paid a little better. Carpenters, bricklayers, blacksmiths, etc. get about 6d. or 8d. a day and consequently are enabled to enjoy a few luxuries denied to their humbler brethren . . . The coarsest rice, even in a good harvest season, cannot be purchased for less than one rupee per maund . . . Wheaten bread is never seen in the

houses of the poor, nor any animal food whatever, except
a little fish, principally shrimps, which are caught in great
numbers in the numerous nullahs and rivers in Bengal.[106]

But towards the end of the nineteenth century, even the artisans appeared to be facing problems. Writing about them in 1888,
an observer says:

> as their occupations are hereditary, and are changed with
> difficulty, they suffer much when any alteration in trade
> renders their particular handicrafts unremunerative. Such
> a change occurred when native cotton stuffs were generally
> superseded by English goods, with results very injurious
> to weavers . . . some [of the weavers] have sent members
> of their families to work in the mills on good wages.[107]

The 1876 census of Calcutta refers to the 'small number of
artisan castes (12,864)' in the city, and speculates that 'caste is
fast dying out in the town as an exclusive system of hereditary
occupations.[108]

Primarily inspired by the experiment of the 'mechanics insti-
tutes' for the upgrading of skilled workers in England in the 1820s,
the English rulers here along with the Bengali social reformers
established a Mechanics Institute in Calcutta in 1839, apparently
to educate the artisans and improve their skillls. The Derozian
leader, Tarachand Chakrabarty, was an important member of its
executive committee. But such an effort proved self-defeating when
the English authorities themselves were flooding the indigenous
market with imported manufactures that were ousting the goods
made by the artisans. A Bengali newspaper commented some
years later: 'in the absence of general interest among the people,
this institute wound up after some time'.[109]

Again in 1871, a free evening school was established in Calcutta
to educate shopkeepers, carpenters, blacksmiths, goldsmiths,
weavers, masons, etc.[110] by the Bengali Brahmo reformer Keshub
Chandra Sen. The idea this time also came from England. Miss
Mary Carpenter, an English educationist and social reformer,

visited Calcutta in 1868, and while driving along Chitpore in north Calcutta noticed the poor people in the streets. Writing about them later, she said: 'What I saw of the lower orders led me to think their existence a joyless one, devoid of any desire to ameliorate their condition.'[111] When Keshub Chandra Sen visited England in 1870, he was made an honorary member of the National Indian Association there, set up by Miss Carpenter for the 'amelioration of the condition' of the Indian people. On his return to Calcutta, Sen informed the Association that he would be launching a campaign of reforms, including education of workers and publication of a journal for the lower orders.[112]

But the school which was set up following this appeared to be aimed at improving the economic lot of the middle classes rather than that of the lower orders. It had two wings. The morning classes were meant to train the sons of the bhadraloks in sophisticated skills based on English and European technology, like carpentry, tailoring, watchmaking and printing among other things. The other wing comprised evening classes for the artisans, shopkeepers, domestic servants who were to be taught mathematics, geography, science, etc.[113] Explaining the objectives of the morning classes, the organizers referred to the dearth of jobs in the overcrowded clerical posts for the middle classes, and urged the latter to learn instead tailoring, carpentry and watch repairing, to be able to start independent business in these areas.

> [W]ho has not suffered because of the carpenters, tailors and watchmakers?—they are always up to cheating us . . . the bhadraloks have to suffer losses often by giving them advances (and yet not getting the work done) . . . We are therefore requesting our people to send jobs of the above three categories to the school and help it, as also to get rid themselves of carpenters, tailors and watchmakers and resort to honourable business enterprises . . .

As for the city's lower orders—the artisans and domestics— the organizers of the school regretted that they did not care to educate themselves and wasted their evenings in drinking sessions or 'abominable entertainments'. They therefore requested these people to attend the evening classes and listen to 'advices in simple language', so that they could converse with the bhadraloks.[114]

The bhadraloks' campaign to improve the lot of the lower orders at the end of the nineteenth century thus boiled down to efforts to make the middle-class youth self-reliant by turning their attention from the already overcrowded tertiary sector to petty trades like tailoring and carpentry. That the success of such efforts would ultimately lead to the ouster of the traditional carpenters, tailors and similar other poor people, and therefore defeat the professed aim of helping the lower orders, did not apparently strike Keshub Chandra Sen and his enthusiastic bhadralok followers. For them these lower orders still remained an invisible mass, their actual problems beyond the comprehension of the educated Bengalis who were convinced of the simplistic solution that education alone would help the lower orders to better their situation. Since the bhadraloks themselves had had the privilege of education which had helped them to rise in society, they recommended the same panacea for the artisans and other poor classes, without for a moment recognizing the hard facts. It was the fortune from bani-anship, the income from the landed estates, the access to the English rulers, the opportunities for social mobility that helped the bhadraloks to take advantage of education and improve their status. On the other hand, bereft of these basic economic privileges, the poor people, mainly from the lower castes, were unable to cope with the new demands being made on them. The artisans, who formed one-eighth of the total population of Bengal in the sixties of the nineteenth century,[115] were losing their occupations because of the stiff competition from the machine-made goods. Learning mathematics and geography, or listening to 'advices in simple language' as recommended by Keshub Sen's school, would not have helped them in their economic distress.

The response of the lower orders to such misleading philanthropic efforts of the bhadralok class comes out clearly in a letter written by a 'shopkeeper', apparently with his tongue in his cheek, in colloquial Bengali mixed with attempts at chaste Bengali (which was adopted by the bhadralok for literature). The letter was published in *Sulabh Samachar,* the newspaper that, priced at one pice, was brought out by Keshub Sen ostensibly for the lower orders. Referring to the mushrooming of several such cheap magazines following the publication of *Sulabh Samachar,* the letter writer says:

> I've also decided to give up my shop and start a one-pice paper. If you fling back and tell me—you are illiterate; how can you bring out a paper?—I can retort: Why? You people write drinking liquor is bad, don't drink! I'll also write— yes, drinking liquor is bad; but what else am I to drink? People all over the country are drinking, and you expect me alone to give it up? Well, I'll write something like this, and then fill up the paper with this or that, plays, Ramayana, Mahabharata, etc. etc. I won't have to run my shop then; I'll be able to earn my livelihood, and people will respect me as the editor of a newspaper . . . [116]

The sarcasm obviously went over the heads of the editors of the magazine who published the letter.

XV

Whatever little recorded material we get about the lifestyle and mood of nineteenth-century Calcutta's lower orders does not suggest that they were a mass of ignorant creatures steeped in darkness, unaware of their rights, indifferent to a sense of right and wrong, waiting to be emancipated and lifted up by the bhadralok who, after having secured his position, economically and socially, found time towards the end of the century to 'educate' and 'reform' the lower orders, partly out of a genuine sense of guilt, and partly under the influence of the English philanthropists.

We have already noted how certain groups from among the lower orders, right from the 1820s, got themselves organized on their own to protest against their exploitation and other unjust practices. Unlike the Bengali gentry who managed to overcome their internal differences and emerged into a more or less homogeneous group of bhadraloks by the third quarter of the nineteenth century, enabling them to articulate and campaign unitedly for their political and other rights, Calcutta's lower orders were a fragmented lot, owing to linguistic origins (the palanquin-bearers who went on a strike in 1817 paralysing the city's transport system were Oriyas) as also to caste-occupation loyalties. The 1859 strike of milkmen, mentioned earlier, arose out of a dispute between them and the sweetmeat makers—the two belonging to different castes.[117] Even when they were brought together in a common production relation in the latter-day manufacturing industries from the mid-1860s (the first generation of workers in the jute industry came from the agricultural and fishermen communities and the displaced weaver and artisan groups in Bengal), it took them a long time, through a process of individual actions of protest, recourse to law, inchoate group activities, to finally emerge into an articulate, organized class. Traditional clan loyalties as well as the influx of a large number of workers from outside, speaking a different language, often stood in the way of organization.[118]

Motivated by opportunities for making money and improving their social status through banianship, and education leading to employment in the Company's administrative and judicial services, the city's ambitious upper- and middle-class Bengalis tided over their traditional differences and shaped themselves into the bhadralok community in the nineteenth century. But such opportunities were beyond the reach of the agricultural labourers and artisans who flocked to the city in search of employment, with a few notable exceptions like Ratan the washerman, or Piritram Marh.

The possibility of collective resistance against oppression and persecution was yet to be perceived as a viable option by the city's lower orders. Their counterparts in the Bengal countryside, however, were already on the warpath. From the 1760s (when peasants under the leadership of Hindu sannyasis, Muslim fakirs and petty landlords exploded into rebellions in different parts of Bengal), a series of peasant jacqueries shook the rural areas for more than a century. Most important among the rebellions of this period were those of the Garo tribal peasants of Mymensingh in north Bengal early in the century, the Wahhabi rebellion under Titu Meer's leadership in 1831 in Barasat in 24-Parganas, the Faraizi rebellion in Faridpore in east Bengal in 1838–48, the 1855–57 uprising of the Santal tribals in the Bengal–Bihar border, and the resistance mounted by the indigo cultivators against the English planters in 1859–61. Although the great rebellion, known as the Sepoy Mutiny of 1857, had its beginnings in the soldiers' barracks near Calcutta, it did not embrace the peasantry in Bengal to the extent it did in northern India.[119]

These peasant rebellions do not appear to have raised any sympathetic echoes among Calcutta's lower orders, although some of these uprisings were taking place in the same villages from where these artisans and agricultural labourers had migrated to Calcutta. But their changed and uncertain status in the city had probably destroyed their sense of identity and solidarity with their erstwhile peasant comrades who were fighting in the countryside the same system that was pauperizing them in the city. The Bengali bhadralok community, which either remained silent, or condemned these rebellions (barring the indigo cultivators' rebellion, which moved some intellectuals like Harish Mukherjee, editor of *Hindoo Patriot;* Dinabandhu Mitra, the playwright; Madhusudan Dutta, the poet, and Kaliprasanna Sinha, author of the famous satire *Hutom Penchar Naksha,* to take an active part in the campaign of protest against the indigo-planters), often sought to brainwash the lower orders into believing that these rebels were savages, and deserved to be crushed by the British. Thus, *Sulabh Samachar,* which was addressed to the half-literate members of the lower orders, reported the tribal Kuki uprising in Tripura in north-eastern Bengal in 1870 in these words:

Their [the tribals] customs are extremely savage; they indulge in dacoity. The English tried to bring them under control by giving them a lot of good wine and toys; as a result they remained subdued for some time. But they have again resumed their old form; they have started burning the houses of people and are trying to kill everyone . . . The English have sent their troops. They will soon be given a good beating and will learn the lesson . . . [120]

Uprooted from the social and economic base of the villages, cut off from their original homes by lack of communication, and still to discover a new identity for themselves in the nomadic existence in the alien metropolis, Calcutta's lower orders in the nineteenth century were groping towards a collective self-consciousness through their own distinct forms of self-expression. Religion was one such form.

Beyond the world of the religious debates and reforms of the Bengali 'respectable' classes lay a sub-culture of popular religion which found its numerous adherents among the city's lower orders. This underworld of popular religion consisted of various heterodox religious sects which had cropped up in eighteenth-century Bengal. Started by lower-caste religious leaders, these sects were often joint Hindu–Muslim ventures in the tradition of the earlier Bhakti movement, represented in Bengal by Chaitanya's Vaishnavite religion. Running almost parallel to the Bengali bhadralok community's hesitant attempts to reform Hindu society, this underworld stream of plebeian religion often went far beyond these reforms. These sects renounced polytheism, idol worship and formal observance of caste regulations. They gave a status of equality to women in their society. [121]

The various groups of Auls and Bauls (wandering minstrels), who used to roam around the streets of nineteenth-century Calcutta, [122] decked in their flowing saffron robes and strumming at the single-stringed 'ektara' and a small kettle drum ('dugi') tied to their waists, were some of the earliest followers of lower-class religious radicalism. While Calcutta's *sambhranta* people were belching an orgy of printed exhibitionism in newspaper columns and verbal histrionics in the Town Hall, debating over the subtle points of the caste system and how to protect their religion from contamination, these Bauls made fun of such pedantry in songs like the following composed by the well-known nineteenth-century folk poet, Lalan Shah:[123]

If you have to make out a Muslim man (from circumcision)
How are you to identify a Muslim woman?
If a Brahman man is to be recognized
By his sacred thread,
How are you to identify a Brahman woman?

The Bauls were roaming mendicants without any settled homes. But numerous other sects provided moorings to the house-holders among the poor people. One such popular sect that raised a lot of controversy in those days was the Karta-bhaja group. Although its headquarters was (and still is) in a place called Ghoshpada, a few miles away from Calcutta, it drew a lot of people from the poorer classes of the city, who used to converge there during festivals. Commenting on the reasons for its popularity among these classes, one contemporary newspaper said: 'This religion holds sway particularly among the *itar* people [i.e. the lower orders] ... According to Hindu scriptures and practice, women do not have any freedom. In all situations and at all times they have to remain dependent on their parents, husbands and sons. But in the Karta-bhaja religion, they enjoy a great amount of freedom ...'[124] Another earlier account,[125] written apparently by an upper-caste Bengali, expressed surprise at the fact that 'Brahmans, Sudras and Yavanas [i.e. Muslims]' sat together at the Karta-bhaja festivals and ate the same food—a practice which even the educated bhadralok reformist did not dare to follow publicly in nineteenth-century Calcutta. According to a modern researcher, 'For the *kaivartas* (agriculturists and fishermen), *tilis* (oilmen), dealers in spices, shell-workers, grocers, weavers and other similar lower-caste Hindus of Calcutta of those days ... the "Ghoshpada" precepts were perceived as a simple, straightforward religion ...'[126] Their leader in Calcutta was one Raghunath who stayed at Shyambazar.[127]

It was obvious that the stress on equality of all people irrespective of caste or religious origin, and a simple interpretation of right and wrong, drew the lower orders to the Karta-bhaja sect in such large numbers—estimated to be 100,000 according to one contemporary account.[128]

Interestingly enough, Calcutta's bhadralok society was quick to condemn the Karta-bhaja sect as a religion of 'itar' people and prostitutes, who were promiscuous in their habits and customs and who violated the norms of Hindu religion. Leading personalities from the Bengali 'respectable' society, ranging from the Brahmo reformer Sivanath Shastri to the Hindu sadhu Ramakrishna, joined the chorus of denunciation.[129]

Like the Karta-bhaja and similar sects which sprang from the Hindu lower orders, the 'pir' cult developed from the Sufi movement among the Muslims, which emphasized again the equality of human beings and condemned the elaborate performances of rituals insisted upon by the orthodox mullahs. In nineteenth-century Bengal in general and Calcutta in particular, festivals at the 'dargah' (burial places) or 'nazargah' (imaginary burial places) of famous pirs were occasions for the congregation of both Hindu and Muslim poorer people. Manik Pir, regarded as the protector of cattle and milk, was a favourite of both Hindus and Muslims, and his dargah at Circular Road in Calcutta used to draw huge crowds during festivals.[130]

It is difficult to gauge the extent of influence of these various heterodox Hindu–Muslim sects. It is quite likely that the attacks launched by the bhadraloks drove some of these sects into the underground and compelled them to evolve secret codes in later days. Secrecy could have encouraged the licentious rituals with which some of them came to be associated. But during their heyday, their membership constituted a religious element among the lower-class Bengalis who were untouched by the religious debates and reforms that were being conducted by the upper-class Bengalis. In these sects and their congregations they found something that they needed and which they could not find elsewhere in the bhadralok society. The membership of a familiar community could make them feel that their talents—whether as singers, or as accompanists in the religious songs sung during the congregations, or as cooks of the community meals served on such occasions—were fully valued.

The contrast between the two sets of values, the two worlds—the world of the heterodox religion of the Bengali lower orders and that of the Bengali bhadralok's religion—comes out clearly from two contemporary accounts. A mid-nineteenth century report of a congregation at Ghoshpada describes in detail the bustling atmosphere and carnival spirit of the devotees:

> men and women, sitting in groups under trees, on the banks of lakes, playing on the Gopi-yantra [a one-stringed musical instrument] and singing, clapping to the shouts of the name of their founder—Aulchand. In another corner, a Muslim Fakir, waving a brush-fan, narrates in a song the history of the Karta-bhaja sect listened to by an enraptured crowd. Inside the house of the 'karta' [the present leader of the cult] piles of rice are being cooked for the devotees . . . [131]

On the other hand, Rajnarayan Basu describes a Brahmo Samaj service at about the same period in the Calcutta prayer hall where a *shloka* from the *Kathopanishad* is being sung to the notes of the newly fashionable Western instrument, the accordion, with men (women in those days were not allowed to sit with men in public Brahmo prayers) sitting with solemn faces.[132] A leading Brahmo intellectual, Rajnarayan was to regret later: 'In [Brahmo] Samajes of Bengal, the majority of the members are English-educated natives. From this it is evident that the Brahmo movement is a superficial one, and has not penetrated into the very depths of Hindu Society'[133]

For Calcutta's lower orders, the arid dissertations on the form of God in Brahmo Samaj meetings were of no relevance whatsoever. While the grand Durga puja festivities in the houses of the

Debs, Tagores, Sinhas and Mullicks no doubt offered them spectacles to watch from a distance, they themselves hardly had any part
in them. The poor therefore fashioned their own gods and
godlings, 'thakurs' and 'pirs', and organized their respective modes
of worship, which reflected the daily concerns of their social environment. Thus, the goddess Shitala was worshipped to avert small-
pox, Ola Bibi to ward off cholera, Satyapir for cure from ailments,
Manik Pir for protection of cattle. Some among them were represented by small images, some merely by a piece of stone. As the
mixture of Hindu and Muslim names suggests, they were worshipped by members of both the communities, as well as by people
from all castes, the site of their worship often being courtyards of
households, or slums. The rigid adherence to Brahmanical rules
was replaced here by a primitive liberal community spirit.

Thus, the Black Town, itself a division of a split metropolis (the
other division being reserved for the whites), was in its turn further
split into two societies—economically, politically, socially and in
religious matters too. The stratification was ideologically buttressed
by the bhadralok concept of 'itarjan' and 'chhotolok'—the pejorative terms used to describe the lower orders and evoke the picture
of a lifestyle that was to be scrupulously avoided by the educated
and privileged Bengalis. The traditional upper-caste attitude of contempt towards the shudras was reinforced by the new values and
norms acquired from collaboration with the English rulers and the
education imparted by them. Those from the, lower castes who
made good and climbed up in the social hierarchy in the eighteenth century were eager to distance themselves from their
brethren who were still sunk in poverty. The junior clerks in the
administration and the numerous middle strata landed interests
(who rose from humble beginnings in their villages to become
leaseholders, tenure-holders and small landlords) also wanted to
enter the *sambhranta* circle by cutting themselves off as fast as possible from the social associations of rural community life which
involved both the rural rich and the rural poor in collective functions. The typical Calcutta Bengali term 'geinya' (meaning a rustic

simpleton) became current during these times among this new middle class who felt that education in English language and norms alone could set them apart socially from their humble rural origins and associations. The perseverance with which the Christian missionaries, English administrators and educationists drummed into their ears that the Bengalis were a degenerate race, that their social habits and religious practices needed to be discarded and that only the adoption of English language and manners could regenerate them, also motivated these rising Bengali middle classes to dissociate themselves from the lower strata of their community, who, being incorrigible as they were, were still following such degenerate practices![34]

When from the middle of the nineteenth century the educated Bengalis began to formulate an ideological basis for their identity as a social class, they turned, significantly enough, to the Sanskrit religious scriptures of the past (the Brahmos, for instance, delved into the Upanishads), trying to work out a compromise between the traditional social norms of Hindu society and the requirements of a modern society. Yet, at the same time, among the lower orders of Bengal a reformist trend was prevalent, manifest in the various heterodox sects, and derived from local Vaishnavite and Sufist traditions rather than from the Hindu scriptures composed by the upper castes. In their social and religious practices they often succeeded in overcoming the traditional abominations of Hindu society like caste discrimination or exploitation of women— objectives which the educated Bengali reformists professed in their utterances and writings in nineteenth-century Calcutta. But available records do not suggest that either Rammohan Roy or the more radical Derozians ever cared to seek inspiration from these contemporary reformist movements among the lower orders of Bengal.

Even later, when some among the bhadraloks attempted to educate and 'reform' the poorer classes of Calcutta (like Keshub Chandra Sen through his evening classes in the 1870s, or Shashipada Banerjee through his journal *Bharat Sramajibi*, the first newspaper in Bengali for the labouring classes, brought out in 1874), their philanthropic efforts appeared to be inspired and

coloured more by European concepts than by indigenous requirements, leading to the floundering of such plans.

But even when the bhadraloks were becoming increasingly
articulate about their grievances against the colonial rulers towards
the end of the nineteenth century, and forming various organizations to press their demands, they rarely thought of incorporating
the causes of the city's lower orders. Their political agitations were
confined to issues concerning their own class only: more positions
in the higher posts in the administration; a free press; demands
for reduction on house taxes, etc.[135] In the early phase of the newborn spirit of patriotism in the 1860s, they turned back to the
ancient history of Hindu kings and their exploits to derive inspiration and self-confidence in their politics of bargaining with the
English rulers. The stories of heroism of Rana Pratap of Rajasthan
or Shivaji of Maharashtra, to which they kept harking back, had
never been a part of the cultural heritage of the Bengali lower
orders. The latter, on the contrary, had been reared upon historical
legends about Rajput and Maratha depredations in Bengal. In the
sixteenth century, the Rajput general Man Singh invaded Bengal
on behalf of Akbar and overcame the joint resistance put up by
both Hindu and Muslim chieftains. In 1742 again, the Maratha
began their incursions into Bengal, and thousands of villagers
poured into Calcutta for safety, where the panicky citizens—both
the European settlers and the rich Bengalis—started digging a
ditch (known even today as the Maratha ditch) around the fixed
borders of the city to protect themselves. Even today in Bengal
village homes, lullabies are sung evoking memories of the raids by
the 'bargis' (the Maratha horsemen).[136]

But the Bengali nationalist neophytes of the late nineteenth
century needed a myth of heroism based on past history. However,
instead of deriving it from Bengal's own past, where the Hindu
ruler of Jessore, Pratapaditya, as well as the Muslim ruler of
Suvarnagram, Isha Khan—both Bengalis—put up a heroic resistance against the Mughal army led by the Hindu Rajput Man
Singh, the Bengali bhadralok of the nineteenth century chose the
communally surcharged stories of Rana Pratap and Shivaji which

were heavily loaded against Muslims in general. Ironically, this bhadralok discovery of Rajput and Maharashtrian heroism against the Muslims was again a gift of British historians like James Tod, whose *Annals and Antiquities of Rajasthan* continued to inspire a host of Bengali bhadralok poets and novelists to spin out tales with the intention of rousing their followers to a sense of pride in the past glory of Indians, but only Hindu Indians.[137] Such efforts at glorification of anti-Mughal exploits by Hindus with an eye to mobilizing the Bengali Hindu bhadraloks only alienated the Bengali Muslims.[138] This was completely at odds with the trend in the underworld of the lower orders where Hindus and Muslims shared a common heritage of social and cultural habits.

The Hindu Mela (an annual fair exhibiting traditional Bengali crafts and skills) was started in 1867 by Nabgopal Mitra and other enterprising bhadraloks and sought to turn the attention of the educated Bengalis to village handicrafts. But here also it failed to involve or attract the city's poorer classes. One newspaper, *Amrita-bazar Patrika,* compared it to the fancy fair of English country ladies.[139] In 1873 another Bengali newspaper commented: 'Since tickets for entry [into the mela] cost eight annas, the crowd was less than in previous years . . . '[140] By the 1880s public interest in the mela had flagged, and it was closed down in 1881.

In fact, the appeal of the Hindu Mela was directed not to all classes of Bengali Hindus, but only to the 'educated fringe' of the community. Rajnarayan Basu, who was associated with the mela from the beginning, made this clear in the prospectus of a society to be established 'for the promotion of national feeling among the educated natives of Bengal', on the basis of which the mela was started. According to this prospectus, to revive Hindu religion in all its glory it was proposed 'that a society be established by the influential members of native society for the promotion of national feeling among the educated natives of Bengal.'[141]

In turning to the past Hindu royalty of northern India, the educated elite's concept of national feeling excluded the masses of the lower orders of contemporary Bengal. Even the rediscovery of the Hindu past was influenced by the English Orientalists who, in the eighteenth and the early nineteenth centuries, had studied the Sanskrit classics and the court culture of ancient India rather than the popular culture of the common people. Pointing out this lacuna in the bhadralok concept of nationalism, many years later Dwijendranath Tagore (the poet's elder brother), who was associ-ated with the Hindu Mela at the beginning, had this to say about the leaders of the mela:

> their patriotism was 75 per cent Western, and 25 per cent indigenous. The uppermost thought in their minds was— 'I shall be a patriot, just as the English are' . . . [Nabagopal Mitra's] tendency was to invite the English top brass . . . He used to visit frequently the top English administrators and the native princes . . . [142]

For all practical purposes, the Hindu Mela was an effort by the Bengali bhadraloks to rally members of their own class into a coherent social organization. It was paralleled by attempts to organize themselves into an effective political pressure group to persuade the English rulers to bring about reforms in the admin-istration that would open up newer and better opportunities for the educated Bengalis. These attempts passed through various stages—the formation of the Bengal British India Society in Calcutta in 1843, the India League in 1875 and the Indian Association in 1876. 'They all wanted to work within the British India system, had faith in British justice, wanted to create a pres-sure of public opinion in Britain and in India on the British gov-ernment to make political concessions to the Indians.'[143] For more effective pressure, they felt the need for coordinating with similar groups of educated Indians in other parts of the country, and the result was the birth of the Indian National Congress in 1885.

XVI

As the contours of the city's geography changed from the eigh-teenth to the nineteenth century, so did the norms and character of its citizens. The process of change in the relations between the white trader-turned-colonizer on the one hand, the successive black generations of banians, absentee landlords, office subordinates and professionals on the other, was marked by oscillations. The earlier habit of mutual bonhomie of the first generation of dewans, banians and English settlers gave way to the colonizer's assumption of the role of instructor and teacher. English education and English manufactures were welcomed with open arms by the native gentry and the growing middle class. But the proselytizing zeal of the missionaries soon posed a threat to their society and made them retreat. Then followed a period of intense soul-searching for a means that would hold together their social structure and yet enable them to make use of the opportunities offered by colonial rule. Finally, an agreement on the retention and modification of certain traditional religious and social customs in the home, along with the adoption of English education (and manners in some cases) in the world of work, helped them to emerge into the distinct shape of the Bengali bhadralok. Their cohesion as a social class was further strengthened towards the end of the nineteenth century by their ambition to make use of the English political and civil institutions to improve their status and prospects, and thus they became an influential political group which in later days claimed to represent the entire Bengali society.

The bulk of the Bengali society, however, comprised the lower orders, who were simultaneously undergoing a transformation. The client–patron relationship based on caste and custom, which was imported from the villages into Calcutta in the early eighteenth century, between the first native settlers—the traders and banians turned urban landlords on the one hand and the various groups of artisans on the other—tended to break down by the middle of the nineteenth century. The artisans were being ousted from their old occupations by the imported machine-made goods. Many were being forced to move away from their original settlements with the expansion of roads and building activities. Contractual and economic relations were developing between the bhadralok and the numerous categories of urban producers and menial labourers.

The impersonal relationship between the two was further reinforced by the conscious attempt of the bhadraloks to distance themselves socially and culturally from the lower orders, variously
described by the educated Bengalis as itarjan, chhotolok, geinya
and similar pejorative terms.

While the bhadraloks could organize themselves into a cohe-
sive social and political group, the lower orders remained a fragmented multitude—divided into occupational and linguistic
groups. Only a new small fragment among them, the fledgling
industrial working class, could begin to organize themselves to
some extent from the end of the nineteenth century.

The majority of the 'unorganized' labouring classes, bereft of
any chance of vertical mobility in the city's economy and social
environment, either remained stuck in their respective occupational grooves, or often moved horizontally—the artisan's son
joining the jute mill as an unskilled worker for instance.

Their economic and social imprisonment, however, could
neither suppress the basic urge for self-expression which took
interesting cultural forms, nor dampen the spiritual search for values that could give them sustenance in an unstable and alien urban
atmosphere. This search often led them to heterodox religious cults
which, with their liberal and democratic outlook, provided them
with mental solace.

These religious and cultural manifestations of the lower orders
formed a parallel trend to the more publicized sociocultural and
religious movements that were taking place at the top layers of
Calcutta's Bengali society. Reduced to a state of 'invisibility' for the
future by being blacked out by the contemporary elite-dominated
press, the experiments of the lower orders were either ignored or
watched with amused curiosity by the bhadraloks. But at times,
when the culture of the lower orders appeared to pose a threat to
the interests of the bhadralok society, the latter's amusement gave
way to violent denunciation, and even turned into active suppression, as happened towards the end of the nineteenth century.
Such campaigns by the bhadraloks against the cultural forms of

the lower orders could be regarded as one of the many factors that led to the marginalization of the popular culture of Calcutta by the turn of the twentieth century.

NINETEENTH-CENTURY CALCUTTA
FOLK CULTURE

The cultural output of the lower orders of nineteenth-century Calcutta consisted partly of rural folk forms imported by the migrants from Bengal's villages, but adapted to the demands of the urban patronage, and partly of innovations born of the new environment in the city's streets and marketplaces. Though the bulk of this rich popular culture comprised oral literary productions like poems and songs, there were also some interesting experiments in the visual arts, which again displayed the same ingenuity in adapting traditional forms to the new urban tastes and requirements.

The two main trends in Bengali culture prior to the advent of the British were represented first by a host of folk songs, rituals, poetry, verse-plays which had developed through social and occupational customs of the labouring classes as well as through popular religious beliefs; and secondly, by lyrics and songs of a classical nature composed in Sanskrit or highly Sanskritized Bengali, patronized by the royalty.

Among the first group, we can include the different types of songs ('bhatiali', *sari*), love songs and wedding songs, women's doggerels, folk theatre (jatra), and songs about Hindu gods and goddesses. An important example of the last-named type, which was to have a lasting influence on Bengali literature, was the 'padabali kirtan'—a repertoire of songs on the love episodes in the life of the god Krishna. In fifteenth-century Bengal, Chandidas and Vidyapati were the leading composers of these songs, in which the loves of Krishna and his consort Radha were described in human and homely romantic terms. These songs were highly popular among the unlettered masses as well as among the educated gentry. The domestication of the divinities and the narration of their exploits in the familiar language of the people stood in sharp contrast with the earlier lyrics of Jaydev, the Bengali poet who composed in Sanskrit.

Jaydev could be described as a typical representative of the culture patronized by the Hindu royalty. According to a modern critic:

He [Jaydev] was appreciated in the court, or in the temple along with the dances of the *devadasis* [girl dancers attached to Hindu temples]. They [his songs] used to be sung as parlour songs. The *kirtans* about Krishna were also meant to be sung. But they were sung in gatherings, in open space in the midst of the public. The scriptures which used to be understood only by the Sanskrit-knowing pundits were now accessible to all [through the *kirtans*]. The wall that separated the scriptures from the common people thus began to crack . . .[1]

A similar popularization of another Hindu mythological story—of Rama and Sita—took place at around the same time in the fifteenth century with the composition of a Bengali *Ramayana* by Krittibas Ojha, a village poet.[2]

Royal patronage reached its peak under Maharaja Krishnachandra Ray (1710–82) of Nabadwip, which by then had become a major centre of learning, religious movements and art and culture. The leading poet of his court was Bharatchandra Ray (1712–60), who composed *Vidya-Sundar*. The story revolves round the love of Vidya (literally 'knowledge'), daughter of the king of Bardhaman, and Sundar (literally 'beautiful'), son of the king of Kanchi, with Malini (an elderly woman flower seller) acting as a sort of go-between in arranging secret rendezvous for the lovers.[3] Although Bharatchandra set the pace in classical Bengali literature by treating a secular love story (unlike the conventional poems on Hindu gods and goddesses), his language and style were heavily dependent on court culture.

The Bengali folk style, which ran parallel to the court-patronized Bengali literature, however, had a tradition of dealing with both religious and secular topics in the language of the rural masses. We have already mentioned Krittibas Ojha's *Ramayana*. There were also a series of Mangal-kavyas or poetical narratives in praise of Chandi (another form of the goddess Kali), Manasa (a local Bengali goddess of serpents) and similar divinities, composed by village poets, in which we often get realistic pictures of daily life in the Bengal countryside in those days. There was also an old oral tradition of romantic songs about ordinary human characters (as distinct from the romantic songs about the divine pair Radha and Krishna). In Mymensingh (now in Bangladesh) there were two such popular ballads—one on 'Andha-Bondhu' (about a blind flute-player with whom the wife of a prince fell in love) and the other on 'Shyam Ray' (about the prince Shyam Ray who wanted to marry a low-caste Dom woman).[4]

It needs to be added, however, that the patronage of the rural gentry in early eighteenth-century Bengal was not confined to the poets of the classical, Sanskritized lyrical style. Maharaja Krishnachandra of Nabadwip appointed Bharatchandra as his court poet on a monthly salary of Rs 40, allotted a house to him and gave him the title *Gunakar* (repository of all poetic qualities). At the same time, he recognized the talents of a folk poet, a devotee of the goddess Kali—Ramprasad Sen, who was a contemporary of Bharatchandra. Ramprasad, who started as a clerk in the office of a Bengali dewan in Calcutta (Gokulchandra Ghoshal of Kidderpore, or Durgacharan Mitra of Sutanuti, according to others), used to write verses in the office accounts book, and thus caught the attention of his employer. Impressed by his abilities as a poet, the employer advised him to quit the job and write poetry, promising him a monthly allowance of Rs 30. Although the allowance was meagre for Ramprasad's large family, he refused Maharaja Krishnachandra's offer to appoint him as his court poet as he wanted to be independent. Ramprasad, however, accepted a small plot of land from the Maharaja, who also gave him the appellation *Kaviranjan* (the poet who charms).[5]

Although both Bharatchandra and Ramprasad often dealt with the same topics (like the story of Vidya and Sundar, or hymns in praise of Kali and Shiva), in their use of language, style and treatment they reflected two different trends—the former leaning more towards the traditional romantic vein of Sanskrit classics, and the latter more to the down-to-earth tradition of the colloquial Bengali folk songs. As a result, they had two different types of audience. Even today, while Bharatchandra's appeal is restricted to a handful among the educated, Ramprasad's songs are sung and listened to all over Bengal by a variety of people ranging from peasants in the countryside to mendicant friars in the streets of Calcutta. A nineteenth-century observer, writing about the popularity of Ramprasad in his own times, said that even Muslim boatmen of Dhaka, Sirajgunje and Pabna in East Bengal were fond of singing his songs.[6]

Since these two poets, among others, exerted a strong influence on the growth and development of urban Bengali culture in nineteenth-century Calcutta, and since we shall frequently have to refer to them in the course of our discussion, it may not be out of place to briefly compare their styles.

Fond of alliteration, Bharatchandra chose Sanskrit or Sanskritized Bengali words (known as *tatsama*, as distinct from *tadbhaba*, words which are derived from Sanskrit but considerably changed into Bengali) for their sounds. The following couplet from *Vidya-Sundar* describes the goddess Kali with a necklace of fierce-looking skulls and her mass of matted locks flapping around her head:

Chanda-munda munda khandi khanda-munda maliké,
Latto-patto deergha jatto muktokesha jaliké.

Surrounded by the luxury of Krishnachandra's court, Bharatchandra chose his imagery from this environment. His description of the Hindu goddess Annapurna (who is supposed to feed the world) is that of a queen surrounded by celestial nymphs, decked in meticulously carved ornaments of gold, dressed in finely woven garments, and worshipped by panegyrists playing on a variety of musical instruments.[7] It could be an ethereal version of the Nabadwip royal court.

Ramprasad on the other hand uses both the colloquial *tad-bhaba* words as well as Arabic terms which were in common use in Bengali business and trading circles in those days. In one of his early poems composed when he was a clerk in Calcutta, he makes innovative use of these terms in a hymn praising Kali:

Amaye dao ma tahbil-dari
Ami nimak-haram noi Shankari

(Make me your cashier, O mother
I'm not ungrateful, O Shankari!)

As a clerk in the office of the Bengali dewan, the poet often ran into trouble with the cashier, who was his direct boss, and who was in all likelihood embezzling the office funds. In an amusing trans-position, Ramprasad puts himself in the position of a clerk in the heavenly abode of Kali whose treasure is guarded by the absent-minded Shiva: 'Everyone is looting your treasury; I can't stand it any more. The man who's in charge of your treasury is the forgetful Shiva. Yet, he's paid a lump sum while I, the servant without salary, only get the dust of your feet!'[8]

The goddess Kali in Ramprasad's songs quite frequently resembles typical female characters in a Bengali home—some-times a shrewish housewife, sometimes a careless mother, or a hoyden romping around shamelessly. The poet's poor circum-stances often intrude in his songs and they become bitter com-plaints against Kali instead of hymns in her praise. Thus one song accuses the goddess: 'Who calls you a merciful, compassionate soul? For some people you provide sweet for their milk. And here am I who can't even get rice to go with the pot-herbs . . . '[9]

The feeling of intimacy with which Ramprasad sings about Kali is interpreted as an expression of his mystic communion with the goddess. But whatever the inspiration might have been, Ramprasad's domestication of the divinities (as distinct from Bharatchandra's elevation of them into ethereal realms) is in the typical tradition of Bengali folk songs on Hindu gods and goddesses, where they are treated as ordinary mortals with human feelings like love and jealousy, gratitude and vengeance, lust and selfishness.

An important trait which Ramprasad shared with many other folk poets of his times was the ability to versify extempore—a convention in oral literary tradition which gave birth to the form known as the 'tarja', where two poets or groups of poets are engaged in poetic duels. In eighteenth-century Calcutta such verbal duels between well-known songsters and poets (who were known as 'kobis' or 'kobi-walas') were a popular form of entertainment.

An idea of the nature of exchanges that used to take place between these poets can be had from the following slanging match—the first verse composed impromptu by Ramprasad, and the second as a repartee by his contemporary Aju Gonsai:

Why go on drifting, my soul?
Dive deep into the sea of ideas of Kali.
Your pulse is weak, my friend.
Don't dive too deep.
If you catch cold,
You'll give up the ghost![10]

Verbal desecration of highfalutin and mystical theories in the above fashion, or the coupling of serious myths with their earthy, abusive parodies of gods with their comic doublets in rhymed ripostes, were an important part of Bengali folklore. They offered a sort of non-official, extra-ecclesiastical version of the world, as seen by the lower orders of society who had no access to the Brahman-dominated, Sanskritized society of the upper-caste 'respectable' people.

Interestingly enough, parallel to the court culture this alternative stream of folklore was allowed to run its distinct course in medieval Bengali society. It was appreciated by both the upper-class patrons and the lower orders even in the new metropolis of Calcutta in the late eighteenth and the early nineteenth centuries. Folklore from which Calcutta's later street literature and popular culture derived was essentially a shared experience. There was not yet any sharp distinction of high and low. Just as Maharaja Krishnachandra Ray of Nabadwip patronized Ramprasad, so did Maharaja Nabakrishna Deb of Shobhabazar in Calcutta's Black Town in the late eighteenth century support a host of urban folk poets—the kobi-walas whose performances drew a wide range of Bengalis, from the rich banians and dewans to the artisans, day labourers and different types of workers who came to the city in search of a living.

A schism in this cultural homogeneity began only from the middle of the nineteenth century when, with the spread of English education and Western cultural ideas, a new generation of educated bhadraloks appeared on the scene. Determined to distinguish themselves from the lower orders, they sought to exclude the traditional folk culture and their later urban variations from the common heritage.

I

The migrants who came to Calcutta from the villages brought with them a rich repertoire of entertainments which they had inherited from the traditional rural folk culture. They not only kept alive the old folk culture in the squalor of the growing metropolis of Calcutta, but enriched it with new motifs borrowed from the surrounding scenes.

The manifestations of this folk culture can be divided into three distinct forms. First, verbal compositions, like the various types of songs, recitations of rhymes during rituals (known as bratas, which were performed by women with a view to fulfilling their aspirations) and poetical contests (e.g. kobi-gan). Second, spectacles like theatrical performances called jatras, and comic shows of the streets and marketplaces in the form of pantomimes, known as the 'sawng'. Third, various genres of folk humour, like proverbs and doggerels.

The earliest specimens of urban folk culture in Calcutta can be found in the humorous doggerels and proverbs, jokes and rhymes about contemporary society that used to make the rounds of the city's streets. The rat race among eighteenth-century Calcutta's English traders and their Bengali banians and dewans to make fortunes by every conceivable means was a target of raillery on the part of the city's lower orders. The following couplet popular in mid-eighteenth century Calcutta sums up their social mores:

Jal, juochuri, mithye katha
Ei tin niye Kolikata.[11]

(Forgery, swindling and falsehood.
These three make up Calcutta.)

Even almost a hundred years after this, things had not changed much in the city as evident from the following lines of a song popular in mid-nineteenth century:

Ajob shahar Kolketa
Randi badi judi gadi michhey kathar ki keta![12]

(A strange city is this Calcutta.
Whores and houses, carriages and cars abound. And how fashionable it is to lie!)

The habit of lying and deceiving which had become ingrained in the city's moneyed circles was a running theme in popular jokes. One such story which travelled from mouth to mouth is about the arrival of a: boat loaded with 'European lies' at the banks of the Ganga. The gomastahs, Company officers, banians, moneylenders, traders—all came and took their respective shares of 'lies'. The hero of the story reached the spot late, by which time the boat had been emptied. Sorely disappointed, he was about to drown himself in the Ganga when the goddess of the river appeared before him and asked him to take heart. She granted him a boon that he would be a 'one hundred per cent liar' and would never speak the truth![13]

The men who made money through dubious means—the banians and dewans of eighteenth-century Calcutta—were also made the butts of ridicule in popular verses. The following is an interesting who's who of the period:

Banamali Sarkarer badi,
Gobindaram Mitrer chhodi,
Amirchander dadi,
Hajuri Maller kodi.[14]

Banamali Sarkar, whose house is mentioned in the first line, was the East India Company's Deputy Trader of Calcutta. His palatial building in Sutanuti fell into ruins by the twenties of the nineteenth century. Gobindaram Mitra, the 'black zamindar' of Calcutta, who was dewan to John Zephania Holwell, was notorious for his 'chhoti' or club which he wielded over the poor to collect and swell the Company's revenue (see Chapter 2). Amirchand (also known as Omichand in contemporary records) was a Sikh contractor of the Company's merchandise. More important than his 'datji' or beard was his 'kotji' or money, which was inherited by his brother-in-law Hajuri Mall (Hoozuri Mull).

Watching the pomp and splendour in which these Black Town 'zamindars' lived and entertained their acquaintances, their poor neighbours who lived in the slums surrounding the palatial buildings intoned rhymes lampooning them. Many among these rich people wasted their fortunes on lavish rituals and expensive pastimes like kite-flying contests or setting birds to fight for sport. One such popular doggerel records their habits:

Bells ring at Durga puja,
Drums beat at the birth of a son.
They let fly the parrot from the cage
And bring in the crow.
Their business goes to the dogs,
And the only warriors are their fighting cocks.
Thus they die—
Their nature knocked out of shape![15]

Hemp smoking had become institutionalized among some members of the idle rich by the beginning of the nineteenth century. Shibchandra Mukhopadhyay, whose father made money as a dewan to several English officers, set up a hemp smoking club in Baghbazar in north Calcutta, where members were given names of different birds and were expected to warble accordingly. The floor of the club house was carpeted with tobacco leaves and the walls made from hemp leaves. Members were divided into three classes, according to how much hemp they could smoke. Shibchandra served them sumptuous meals along with hemp.[16] Some years later, drinking in public became fashionable with the young students of Hindu College who wanted to ape Western manners. Their centre was further south of Baghbazar—in the Battala area. The traditionalist hemp smokers of Baghbazar spun rhymes deriding the neophyte boozers of Hindu College:

Deber durlabh dugdha chhana, ta na holey guli rochey na,
Kochu-ghechur karmo noy rey jadu!
Shundir dokaney giye, tak tak phele diye
Dhuk korey merey diley shudhu.[17]

(We drink milk and take butter coveted even by the gods. Otherwise we don't enjoy hemp. This isn't the pastime of the riff-raff, dear friends! You go to a wine shop, shell out money, and merely gulp down the drink!)

Subtle class distinctions seem to have been developing around addictions and intoxication habits also. The leisurely and elaborate mode of smoking hemp, accompanied by expensive meals, which only the idle descendants of the old banians and dewans could afford, stood in sharp contrast with the new habit of taking a few drinks fast for a quick kick that was prevalent among the young students of middle-class families.

For the poorer classes of Calcutta, however, such niceties were of little concern. The habits of the rich and the educated middle classes were generally sources of amusement for them. Mocking their indulgences, they composed a rhyme in the form of a street-guide supposedly directing pilgrims to religious spots:

Baghbajare ganjar adela, gulir Konnagaré.
Battalae mader adda, chondur Bowbajaré.

Ei sab mahatirtha je na chokhey herey,
Tar mato mahapapi nai trisangsarey.[18]

(Baghbazar is the centre of hemp smoking, Konnagar of opium pills. Battala is the centre of drinking, and Bowbazar of opium smoking. If anyone fails to visit these places of pilgrimage, there can't be a worse sinner than him in heaven, earth and hell.)

Among other targets of urban folk humourists was the expensive habit of the rich to throw parties. When Maharaja Nandakumar during his heyday (before he fell foul of Hastings and was hanged) invited 100,000 Brahmans to a grand feast to fulfil some religious obligation, the poorer classes ridiculed the scramble among the invitees and described their plight in a verse:

Keu khele machher mudo, keu khele bonduker hudo.[19]

(Some were treated to the delicacy of fish-heads, others to the thrust of the musket-butt.)

Later, in the 1840s, when Dwarkanath Tagore established the Carr, Tagore and Company, he used to throw sumptuous dinner parties for the city's English top brass at his garden house in Belgachhia in north Calcutta. The lower orders used to go around the streets mocking at these parties:

Belgachhiar bagané hoy chhuri-kantar jhanjhani,
Khana khaoar kato maja,
Amra tar ki jani?
Jane Thakur Company.[20]

(Knives and forks are clanking in the Belgachhia garden house; what fun with all that food around! But what do we know of it? It's all an affair of Tagore Company.)

The competition among the city's nouveau riche in the eighteenth century to rise in the caste hierarchy earned the scorn of the lower orders who, having had no opportunities of economic gains in the metropolis, were without any stakes whatsoever in the social race. When Piritram Marh, the low-caste millionaire, lost in the race and failed to buy his way into an upper caste, Calcutta's street wags spun the following verse, putting the words into Piritram's mouth:

Dulol holo Sarkar, Okkur holo Dutta,
Ami kina thakbo je koibotto sei koibotto![21]

(Piritram is here complaining about his fate: 'While Dulol [Ramdulal Dey, who came from humble origins] had earned the title of 'Sarkar', and Okkur [Akrur Dutta who amassed riches as a contractor to the Company] had acquired the caste surname of Dutta, why should I remain the same 'kaibarta' [the lower caste of fishermen and agriculturists] as I was before?')

Social developments in the upper-class strata of Calcutta, like educational reforms, proselytizing attempts by missionaries, or cultivation of Anglicized habits by the young students, were viewed by the lower orders with amusement, occasionally tinged with a faint concern about the future of Hindu religion. We come across a couple of doggerels where Rammohan Roy is ridiculed for setting up a school that would destroy families and caste loyalties. Christian missionaries like William Carey and Alexander Duff are accused in another rhyme of corrupting Bengali boys by teaching them to use knives and forks to eat mutton and chicken.[22] Yet another verse of the same period refers banteringly to the aping habits of young Bengalis:

Honoured Calcutta, all glory to you!
You are the birthplace of all that is new.
Casting aside his native customs
The Bengali babu hankers after European fashions.
Leaving his home he goes to Calcutta
And dreams of becoming rich overnight.[23]

Some of the sayings of those days gained currency as proverbs like 'Companyr latgiri, parer dhoney poddari' (usurping the wealth of others, the Company servants have become aristocrats), indicating a surprisingly accurate perception of the process through which the Company's traders and officials became 'nabobs'. The nineteenth-century Bengali babu was fond of lounging, dressed in an expensive dhoti with its front tuck (called 'koncha' in Bengali) flowing in folds. This familiar sight in the streets of Calcutta gave rise to the proverb:

Baire konchar patton, bhitore chhunchor ketton

(While he parades his koncha outside, in his home there goes on a musk-rats' chorus, i.e. the shrews' screech).

Women dancers from the lower orders, known as khemta-walis, whose swinging steps, swaying hips and flashing limbs were in contrast with the slow movements of the north Indian 'bai' dancers or 'baijis' (whose nautch performances graced aristocratic Bengali homes in the nineteenth century), were looked down upon by the educated Bengali gentry as 'obscene'. But they became heroines of a contemporary proverb—'Ghomtar adaley khemtar nach'—which flung back at the hypocrisy of the gentry. 'A khemta dance hidden behind the veil of a saree', which is the literal meaning of the proverb, is the bhadralok's way of indulging in 'improper' acts under cover of refined manners.

The authors of these 'blasons populaires', doggerels, rhymes and proverbs were mostly unlettered and anonymous. Their style is marked by a few common characteristics which indicate their collective and rural origin. First, like nursery rhymes, we find different versions of the same doggerel or rhyme, which suggests that while the rhythmical structure remained the same the words changed from mouth to mouth according to the mood of the composer or the relevance of the situation. Thus, we come across several versions of the four-line verse about Banamali Sarkar and other personalities of eighteenth-century Calcutta. One replaces the last two lines with

Noku Dharer kodi
Mothur Sener badi.

Noku (or Lakshmikanta) Dhar was the founder of the Raj family of Posta in north Calcutta,[24] and Mothurmohun Sen was a shroff of repute who built a large house in Sutanuti.

Secondly, there is a tendency in these rhymes to list a few distinct qualities or some places to express an *idée fixe,* like the one-line description of Calcutta—a city made up of forgery, swindling and falsehood. This is in the tradition of old proverbs about places, current in Bengali and other Indian languages. Thus an ancient proverb about Banaras says: 'Rand, shand, sannyasi, tin niye Baranasi' (widows, bulls and mendicants—these three make up Banaras). The list of the centres of hemp smoking and drinking and opium dens, mentioned earlier, is again a parody of similar traditional rhymes on pilgrimage centres.

Thirdly, there are some interesting urban variations on conventional folk epigrams describing occupations or caste habits. One such epigram runs as follows:

Kalomey Kayastha chini, gonphe Rajput
Vaidya chini tarey, jar oshudh majboot.[25]

(We can know a Kayastha by the power of his pen, a Rajput by the twirl of his moustache, and a physician by the effect of his medicine.)

The Calcutta folk humorists borrowed the style to make a dig at the subservience of their own community—the Bengalis—in the following verse:

Taintir shobha tailtkhana,
Dorjir shobha suto.
Bangalir shobha betraghate
Juto ar gunto.[26]

(The handloom becomes the weaver; the cotton thread befits the tailor. As for the Bengali, he deserves whipping, kicking and butting.)

These earliest specimens of urban folk culture of the fledgling metropolis of Calcutta were mainly aphoristic witticisms in continuation of the rural tradition of maxims and proverbs. They were marked by light raillery directed against the habits of certain individuals in the city, and jesting at the notoriety which certain areas of the city had acquired.

II

Verbal compositions like poetical contests, songs and recitations became a more sophisticated and institutionalized form of Calcutta's folk culture from the end of the eighteenth century. An early nineteenth-century Bengali poet gives a long list of the popular forms of entertainment prevalent in Bengal at that time.[27] Each had a distinct style of its own. The list includes 'panchali' (songs, usually devotional, interspersed with rhymes for fast recitation); 'sari' (boatmen's songs); 'malashi' (songs about Kali); *bijaya* (sung on the last day of the Durga puja festivities to bid farewell to the goddess Durga); 'akhdai' (a contest of songs—but without any exchange of repartees as in 'tarja' or 'kobi' songs—where the participants were required to sing three types of songs: first, on Durga; second, 'kheud' or a humorous piece, often of an abusive nature; and third, *prabhati* or a song in praise of the dawn); jatra (dramatic performances, the dialogues in verses set to music); 'jhumur' (exchange of repartees in the form of songs); 'kirtans' in praise of divinities like Radha and Krishna, Kali and Shiva, as well as the Vaishnavite preacher Chaitanya; and the 'kobi' songs.

Among these types of entertainments, some were basically lyrical like malashi, sari, and some anecdotal like akhdai, kirtan, panchali and the kobi songs. It was these latter types which found a popular audience in Calcutta. In this particular genre there was a tremendous scope for improvisation in accordance with the mood of the audience and the locale, for incorporation of new themes borrowed from the urban environment, and for experimentation in the musical style. We come across daring innovators in the late eighteenth and early nineteenth centuries. Their experiments were in tune with the changes and frequent departures from conventions that were taking place in the fluid socioeconomic life of Calcutta in those early years of its growth, marked by the adaptability of the new generation of Bengali nouveau riche to the demands of an alien ruling power, and changing tastes of the city's lower orders trying to get used to the new urban environment.

The innovations in the traditional popular Bengali musical and literary styles in Calcutta were brought about through a process which was primarily anonymous. But we have come across a few names, like Rupchand Chattopadhyay (1722–92) and Madhusudan Kan (1818–68), who simplified the conventional style of singing of kirtans and developed what came to be known as 'dhop-kirtan'—a style of singing which was adopted mainly by women singers in the streets as well as at gatherings in the houses of the *sambhranta* Bengalis.[28] Similarly, the subtle nuances of the ragas and raginis of the traditional akhdai were replaced by the more popular style of exchanges of quick repartees by an imaginative musician, Mohanchand Basu of Baghbazar in north Calcutta, in the thirties of the nineteenth century, in a new form called 'half-akhdai'.[29]

It is to be noted that most of these innovations were aimed primarily at popularization and simplification—either in the style of singing, or in the treatment of content. It seems that the demands of the common masses of Calcutta, unlettered and unini-tiated as they were in the classical style of literary compositions, to a great extent determined the innovations that took place. The kobis, many among whom came from the city's lower orders, played an important role in the experimentations which trans-formed the traditional rural-based folk style of tarja into the dis-tinctly urban popular 'kobi-gan'.

Among the famous kobis who dominated the scene from the end of the eighteenth century till almost the thirties of the nin-teenth, we come across the names of Gonjla Guin (from a caste of cow owners), Keshta Muchi (Keshta the cobbler), Raghunath Das (variously described as a blacksmith or a weaver), Bhola Moira (Bhola the sweetmeat maker), Kukur-mukho Gora (dog-faced Gora). As their names and surnames often suggest, they came from the lower castes or professions of the lower orders. Praising their com-positions, a latter-day bhadralok poet, Ishwar Gupta (1812–59), who meticulously collected these songs, said: 'If our country's weavers, cobblers, and lower castes can become such excellent poets, just imagine how much better our bhadralok poets would be!'[30] Some among the kobis who came from bhadralok or respectable classes did take lessons from these weaver and cobbler poets. A Brahman kobi, Horu Thakur (Harekrishna Deerghangi) (1738–1808), for instance, accepted Raghunath Das as his teacher. But Horu Thakur came from a poor family in north Calcutta, and did not have any chance to learn either Sanskrit or English, unlike his contemporary Ram Basu (1787–1829), a famous kobi of those days who came from a well-to-do Kayastha family, had his education in Calcutta, learnt some English, and worked as a clerk in the city for some time before becoming a professional kobi. The kobis from the lower orders stuck to their original occupations. Keshta Muchi earned his living as a cobbler and composed songs in his spare time. Bhola Moira used to run a sweetmeat shop on Baghbazar Street in north Calcutta.[31]

The compositions of these kobis reflected the spirit of the old padabali kirtans about Radha and Krishna, and of the various Mangal-kavyas in praise of Durga and Shiva. In these old songs, as we have already mentioned, the Hindu divinities were brought down from their ethereal abodes to the earthly homes of the Bengal countryside and appeared in the familiar figures of truant lovers, or shrewish housewives or idle, worthless husbands. The legends and anecdotes that had grown around Krishna in Bengal and which were celebrated in the padabali kirtans of Chandidas and Vidyapati were at variance with much that is found about the god in the ancient Sanskrit texts. Krishna in the Bengali songs is a cowherd prince who falls in love with Radha. Radha is married to Ayan Ghosh, who happens to be an uncle of Krishna's. Ghosh incidentally is a Bengali surname (not usually found in any other part of India) used by the milkmen caste. Ayan's mother and sister—Jatila and Kutila (literally, the crooked and the wily)—are always waiting to take unawares the two lovers, who go to great lengths in secretly arranging their rendezvous. Radha as a Bengali village housewife involved in the hazards of an adulterous relationship; her visits to the river on the plea of filling her water vessel, but actually to meet Krishna; her pining in her home for the return of Krishna; her starting at the sound of his flute—all these images have inspired Bengali folk poets for ages.

Similarly, the Mangal-kavyas and the various *agamani* songs (sung on the eve of the Durga puja) and the *bijaya* songs recite the woes of Durga in the inhospitable home of her drug addict husband Shiva. The songs become a transparent cloak for describing the palpable craving of a lonely mother for the company of her long-separated daughter married off to a worthless husband, or her sense of loss at the daughter's departure for the husband's home. Human problems of a rural society—the poverty and unemployment of Shiva, the sufferings of the young bride at her husband's home, the few fleeting days of reunion between the mother and daughter, the distance between the home of the bride and that of her husband which makes such reunions difficult— were foremost in these songs, relegating their religious implication to the background.[32]

The transformation of the mighty Shiva of Aryan mythology into a corpulent and indolent hemp smoker in Bengali folklore, or of the elegant Krishna into a truant cowherd philanderer in the padabali kirtans, throws an interesting light on the ingenuity of Bengali folk religion and culture. D. D. Kosambi suggests that pre-Aryan gods or godlings who were popular in certain areas were assimilated to and identified with the established Aryan gods of the Hindu pantheon, like Shiva and Vishnu. While retaining their primitive features, these old gods of the local imagination were rechristened under the new Aryan names. Thus the god of a pastoral tribe could have been reincarnated as Krishna in some areas.[33] It is quite possible that a similar local god associated with a cultivator's lifestyle, marked by work in the fields during the sowing and harvesting seasons, and a sort of languor during the off-season, was incorporated into the Shiva image. A modern Bengali critic seeks to explain the popular image of Shiva in the Bengali mind by suggesting that there was a deliberate attempt on the part of the upper-caste Bengalis to woo members of the Hindu lower castes after the Muslim invasion by co-opting their local gods into the Aryan pantheon. According to him:

> The Muslims came and conquered the country. The Hindus lost their kings and kingdoms. As a result, cracks developed among the warrior communities—the Bagdis, Domes [Doms] Hadis, Lohars, Khoiras, Tiors, etc. [who belonged to

the various Bengali Hindu lower castes]. Temptations for royal patronage, for conversion to the religion of the conquerors, struck at the roots of society. At that moment, there was no other way available to bind them together except some religious identity. They had to be told that they were blessed by the gods, there was nothing ignoble in their occupations. Even if they did not have the jobs of paid warriors, they could live with dignity by following their respective caste occupations . . . They have to be told that the great Mahadeva [Shiva] himself at one time worked on the fields as an ordinary peasant. Annapurna [another form of the goddess Durga, Shiva's consort], who gives rice to the entire world, once had to take on the appearance of a low-caste Bagdi woman to catch fish. For a nation which believes in rebirth, consequences of one's misdeeds, and in gods, these assurances were of no mean value . . .[34]

The domestication of Hindu divinities, which was found in the kirtans, Mangal-kavyas and other folk compositions, was taken a step further by the eighteenth and nineteenth-century Calcutta kobi-walas. They made these characters reflect the surrounding reality. The style was also considerably changed to accommodate secular comments by adding an adjunct called the kheud to the main divisions in a narrative song (the other two divisions in kobi-gan being 'sakhi-samvad', which dealt with the various stages in Radha and Krishna's love affair, and 'Bhavani-bishayak', which was in praise of Durga).

In the songs of the kobis, the complaints of Radha about an elusive Krishna dallying elsewhere with his mistresses could often be a transparent cloak for the bitter admonitions of a Bengali wife of a bhadralok zenana hurled against her profligate husband (a subject which was the staple of numerous social novels, poems, plays and farces in nineteenth-century Calcutta). Let us take, for instance, the following lines from a song by a well-known woman kobi called Jogyeshwari, who was a rival of Bhola Moira, Neelu Thakur and other famous male kobis of Calcutta in the early years of the nineteenth century. The words of the song express Radha's dismay at her lover's infidelity:

... He has now turned into the darling of
his new young sweetheart,
and is floating in eternal happiness!
Well! Let him be happy.
There's no harm done.

The poetess then explains her dilemma in terms of a contemporary socioeconomic situation. Like the revenue collector, the anguish of separation keeps nagging her. But what can she pay as tax? Whatever she had—her soul—had been taken away by her lover. And yet, Madan, the god of love, continues to harass her (by reminding her of her lover) like a tax collector. She then appeals to her lover to take away her anguish.[35]

The recurring theme in the Radha-Krishna songs of the kobis is indictment of Krishna for seducing the married Radha from her home, abandoning her to face the scandal, and forgetting all about the days of his cowherd past and his affairs with the milkmaids in Vrindabana after having left that place to become the king at Mathura. In the various folds of the narrative, the listeners could decipher suggestive allusions to the prevailing trends in contemporary society—the licentiousness of the babus who used to seduce women and leave them in the lurch, the rise of these babus from humble origins and their tendency to forget their past friends and acquaintances as soon as they became rich and powerful.[36]

An interesting example of a description of a contemporary scene under the guise of the Radha-Krishna liaison is the following excerpt from a song by the famous kobi, Ram Basu, about a boating expedition of the two lovers as described by Radha, who used to be addressed by the endearing term 'Rai':

Tuley taranir upor
Natobar karey kato chhal;
Baley dekhichho ki Rai, Jamuna prabal.
Tumi porechho Rai, neel basan.

Megh bhebey badey paban.
Baley taranger majhey, ulango hotey,
Eki lajja, ai go ai![37]

(Taking me up in the boat, the rake started all his tricks.
He said: 'See, Rai! The Jamuna river is turbulent. You have
worn a blue garment. Mistaking it for the clouds, the wind
is getting excited.' In the middle of the river, he then asked
me to strip. Alas! Where am I to hide my shame?)

The account given above sounds like a typical pleasure trip
popular among the nineteenth-century Bengali rich, who used to
hire pinnaces, barges, steamers or boats for a joyride along the
Hugli river to Mahesh, near Calcutta, on the occasion of the
bathing festival (held in honour of the Hindu god Jagannath on
the moonlit night of May–June). Women dancers—either khemta-
walis from the lower orders, or baijis from the richer classes, or
ordinary prostitutes from the red-light areas of Calcutta—were an
essential part of such joyrides. Kaliprasanna Sinha, a perceptive
observer of the manners of nineteenth-century Calcutta citizens,
who wrote in the local Calcutta patois under the pseudonym
'Hutom Pencha' (the owl who keeps his eyes open during night) a
series of sketches on contemporary Calcutta, gives an amusing
description of these pleasure trips of the babus. He writes in one
of his sketches: 'Some of these babus strip the women and make
them dance the khemta. In some places, unless they kiss, they
don't get their due remuneration.'[38]

While the conventional sakhi-samvad part of the narrative
often afforded the kobis a chance to depict contemporary scenes,
like Ram Basu's verses quoted above, the kobis really felt at ease
when they sang kheuds which enabled them to cast away the serious and woeful style of complaints, and to deal with the love affair
of Radha and Krishna in a merry, ribald manner, as well as to speak
more directly about the contemporary reality. Kheuds had their origin in a lively folk style of witty retorts through rhymes or songs,
usually with erotic overtones. According to one Bengali critic:
'Khendu, or kheud, is probably the earliest specimen in Bengali

literature of straightforward expression of the feelings of lovers.'[39] A typical example is the following exchange between a man and a woman. The woman (who is Radha) quips:

Orey amar Kalo bhramar, modhu lutbi jodi aye!

(Come hither, my Black bee, if you want to feast on my honey!)

The bold Radha's unabashed invitation to the Black bee, who is the poetic symbol of the unmistakable, dark-skinned Krishna, is resented by the possessive husband, who retorts:

Ami thaktey chaker modhu panch bhramore kheyejaye!

(How is it that while I am here, all and sundry come to taste the honeycomb!)[40]

In the serious sections of the Radha-Krishna narrative, the kobis used to treat the theme in an effusive, sentimental manner, more conscious of the conventional requirements like alliteration and the rhythmical framework. But through the kheud, they expressed in a rollicking style the 'naughty' thoughts that lurked behind the serious gestures of the divine pair—often openly erotic or suggesting the fun of love in secrecy as in the following kheud composed by Ramnidhi Gupta (known as Nidhu-Babu, who was more famous as an innovator and composer in the classical *tappa* style which was patronized by the Bengali aristocracy, but who also composed songs in the style of the popular kobis):

Goponey jatek sukh, prakashe tato asukh.
Nanadi dekhley pare pronoy ki roy?[41]

(There is as much happiness in having it in secret as pain in making it public. Will love be possible if the sister-in-law comes to know of it?)

The last line is a variation on the perennial theme of keeping the affair secret from Jatila and Kutila—the two in-laws.

The themes of the kheud were borrowed not only from the legends of Radha and Krishna, but from other mythological narratives like those of Durga and Shiva. Lakshmikanta Biswas, who was popularly known as 'Loke Kana' and lived in Thanthania in central Calcutta, composed the following humorous variation on the woebegone *agamani* songs. *Agamani* songs used to describe Menaka's yearning for her daughter Durga. Loke Kana weaves it with the surrounding reality of the city on the eve of the Durga puja, when Brahman pundits with holy vessels of water around them recited verses from the sacred book of *Chandi* in the homes of the Hindu bhadraloks:

Giri, koi amar Anandamoyi, ashbe katokshoney?
Jato bamun karey chhotachhuti,
Ghat niye petechhey ghanti.
Bujhi kar Chandi shune amar Chandi
Atkechhey konkhaney![42]

(When is my darling [daughter] Anandamoyi coming, oh Giri [Himalaya]? All the Brahman pundits are running to and fro, pitching tents with their holy vessels. Maybe my Chandi [another name of Durga] has got stuck on her way, listening to their recitation from *Chandi*.)

The built-in right of improvisation in kheud allowed the kobis to go beyond mythological subjects and take up secular topics like the personal habits or eccentricities of a rival kobi. These songs hurling insults at each other to the amusement of the listeners provided a ribald entertainment with a thin veneer of innocence. They were highly popular with the city's lower orders. Ishwar Gupta, the poet-collector of old kobi songs, writes: 'The respectable people liked to listen to chaste songs and the itarjan [the vulgar masses] were happy with kheud.' He then goes on to recall how at one gathering when the famous kobi Netai Boiragi (1751–1818) was singing sakhi-samvad, members of the lower orders, tired of the long-winded narrative and the alliterations, stood up and shouted at him: 'Look here, Netai! If you again start singing about the cuckoo [a favourite bird of the romantic poets], fie on you! Now, sing a kheud.' To satisfy them, Netai immediately began to sing a kheud.[43]

The exchanges between rival kobis—known as 'kobir ladai' or verbal duels between poets—were the most exciting moments of

a kobi-gan performance, and brought out their talents at extempo-
rizing. Such ripostes were in continuation of the customary witticisms of the old Bengali folk poets, as found in the previously
quoted imptomptu repartees between Ramprasad Sen and Aju
Gonsai. The following excerpts from a similar poetic duel between
two early nineteenth century kobis—Ram Basu and Antony
Firingi—reflect the prevailing popular perceptions of religious
differences. Antony Firingi was a typical product of the late eighteenth century–early nineteenth-century sociocultural melting pot
of Calcutta. Portuguese by birth, Hensman Antony fell in love with
a Brahman woman who left her home to live with him. Under her
influence, Antony adopted the manners of Bengali Hindus, discarded his European clothes, wore dhoti and 'chadar' (scarf to cover
the upper part of the body), learnt Bengali and composed kobi
songs. In a contest, Ram Basu made fun of his Hindu manners:

> It is in vain, white man,
> That you shaved your head
> To show respect to the god Krishna.
> If your Christian clergyman hears of it,
> It will smear your reputation.

Antony Firingi hit back:

> There's no difference
> Between Christ and Krishna, dear brother;
> Haven't ever heard of men
> Running after mere names.'
> The One who is my God
> Is the same Hari of the Hindus . . .[44]

In this attempt at reconciliation of all religions, Antony harks
back to the contemporary Bengali popular religious cults like the
Bauls (described in Chapter 2). Antony was well versed in the
Hindu scriptures and could make ingenious use of the names of
Hindu divinities in his songs. Thus, once in a contest with Bhola
Moira, in a mock-devotional mood he turned Bhola into Bholanath
(another name of Shiva) and sang a hymn in his praise. This

prompted Bhola to come out with a song which gives an excellent description of his profession and beliefs:

Orey, ami shey Bholanath noi,
Ami shey Bholanath noi,
Ami Moira Bhola, Horur chela
Baghbajarey roi.

(Oh no, I'm not that Bholanath. I'm Bhola the Moira, the pupil of Horu [Thakur]. I stay at Baghbazar.)

He then proceeds to describe his occupation:

I cook all the year round. Whether it's autumn, winter, spring or summer, Bhola's pot is never empty. During the [Durga] puja, I fry sweetmeats. Whatever I earn I spend on the kobi contests. Surely I'm not a poet like Kalidasa. But if I meet a kobi, I never back out, however notorious the rascal might be. I don't believe in castes. My only salvation lies in Krishna.[45]

These kobis were popular among both the city's lower orders and the first generation of rich Bengalis—the banian-turned-urban landlords. Among their patrons were such *sambhranta* Bengalis as Nabakrishna Deb of Shobhabazar; Ashutosh Dey or Chhatu Babu, the son of the millionaire Ramdulal Dey; the Dutts of Hatkhola, and other members of the Black Town gentry who used to organize kobi performances in their ancestral houses during the Durga puja, Holi and other festivals. These contests and competitions were open to kobis of all castes and religions, as evident from the records of poetic duels between Bhabani Bene (coming from the lower caste of spice dealers) and the Vaishnavite Netai Boiragi (their contests were highly popular in those days, giving rise to the expression 'Nite-Bhabanir ladai' to describe any debate); Bhola Moira and the Christian Antony Firingi; Horu Thakur, a Brahman, and Nilmoni Patni (from the lower caste of ferrymen). Kobi performances were elaborate affairs, with each kobi having a large troupe of his own, consisting of singers, accompanists and 'bandhandars' or poets specializing in impromptu compositions. Membership of these

troupes also cut across caste barriers. We hear of one bandhandar, Kukur-mukho Gora, or dog-faced Gora, who was unlettered
but could orally compose rhymed repartees full of mythological
allusions.[46] Women kobis also had free access to such contests. We
have already mentioned Jogyeshwari, who was a contemporary of
Horu Thakur, Ram Basu and Bhola Moira. A later kobi mentions
a few other names of women kobis—Swarnamoni, Paroshmoni,
Bidhukamini and Adormoni—who were reported to have moved
listeners to tears by their narrative abilities.[47] In the early nineteenth century, troupes of some women kobis, by sheer force of
their popularity, even threatened to oust the male kobis from
the stage. In a Bengali newspaper, a letter written by 'vagrant
muchi and Dom kobi-walas' (from the lower-caste communities)
complained about some 'nedi' (a term used to describe female
Vaishnavites) kobis who were invited to sing and dance at almost
every festival at the houses of the rich, and were posing a challenge
to their male rivals in the profession.[48]

Although patronized by the rich, these kobis retained their
own independence. When not directed at each other, the humour
of the kobis was focused on their patrons—sometimes in scathing
barbs of satire. Thus, during a contest in the house of a zamindar,
when one sycophant kobi flattered the host and described his
landed estate as Vrindabana (the site of Krishna's carousals), Bhola
Moira retorted:

Orey beta, gabi, poisha lobi,
khoshamodi ki karon?

(Stupid fool! Sing a song, and take your money. Why go
for flattery?)

He then turned to the host and asked him to pardon him if he
did a bit of plain speaking—which he did by describing the host's
avarice and tight-fistedness in these words:

Pimpre tipey gud khaye
Mufater modhu oli.[49]

(He squeezes out molasses from the ant that sticks to it,
and is greedy like the bumblebee hovering over free honey.)

Although among themselves these kobis allowed poetic talents to override caste differences, in their relations with the rich patrons they were quick to assert their caste identity often as a means of snubbing or putting in place the self-opinionated nouveau riche. During a performance in his Shobhabazar palace, Nabakrishna Deb, for instance, in appreciation of some verses sung by Horu Thakur, threw an expensive shawl as a gift to him. Horu Thakur immediately gave it away to the drummer in his troupe, indicating that he as a Brahman could not accept a gift from Nabakrishna who came from a lower caste. Yet, Horu Thakur, whenever he sang, never forgot to acknowledge his gratitude to his teacher— Raghunath Das, who came from the low caste of weavers.[50]

As most of these kobis had no stake in the formal societal structure, they were, in a sense, free to offer their view from the bottom of society with unabashed satire. By demystifying the Hindu divinities and narrating their exploits, often in a facetious vein, in terms of the surrounding society, as well as by engaging in slanging matches of songs which enabled them to speak about their own lifestyles and views, they became the mouthpiece of the masses. Their songs offered the other side of every issue. The licence which they enjoyed in the *sambhranta* households was in continuance of the tradition in Bengali rural society where court jesters were allowed to laugh at the expense of the kings, if their native wit got the better of the royal aplomb.[51] Verbal ridicule through clever language was a sort of equalizer above which no person could rise. Being a part of this tradition, the kobis of eighteenth–nineteenth-century Calcutta were both adored and feared by the privileged rich. Ishwar Gupta tells us that Lakshmikanta Biswas, the poet who was popularly known as Loke Kana, had such a beautiful voice, poetic talents and ready wit, as well as an abusive tongue, that the rich 'loved him and feared him also'. He then adds: 'Out of fear they always gave him money. The reason for this was, they were never sure of the jester's tongue—what he would say and when. So they wanted to keep him happy and obedient by giving him money.'[52]

III

The anonymity of authorship that characterized traditional folk culture was giving way to the individual folk poets with distinctive styles of their own in the new urban environment of the late eighteenth century. The kobis were followed by a number of poets who worked in different genres like the folk theatrical form of the jatra, recitations of mythological stories like 'kathakata' and the traditional popular singing style of panchali. Here also, we come across names of composers emerging from the lower orders and making a niche for themselves in Calcutta's popular culture.

A leading proponent of a new style of the jatra in mid-nineteenth-century Calcutta was Gopal Udey (1817–57). His rise to eminence was phenomenal. Gopal was around eighteen years old when he came from Orissa to Calcutta, possibly in 1835. He used to sell bananas in the streets of the city. His hawker's cry attracted the attention of a rich Bengali babu, a lover of songs, Radhamohan Sarkar, who discovered in Gopal's voice the potentialities of a great singer. Sarkar had his own troupe of jatra performers. Gopal first acted in the role of the flower seller Malini in *Vidya-Sundar* staged by Sarkar, and immediately became a hit.[53]

The form of the jatra originated from the ritual of songs and dances which formed part of the religious festivals in villages. Dramatic elements in the compositions of these songs and dances, like conversations among the various characters of the mythological stories on which they were based, lent themselves to histrionic interpretations by the performers. Jatras were performed in a square or round area of flat ground with the audience sitting all around. There were no reserved entry or exit points, and the actors moved into the square from the midst of the audience. The chorus and the musicians had their places on one side of the acting area. While in a kobi performance the musical instruments used were mainly the 'dhak', the 'dhole' (drums of various sizes and types), the 'kansi' (bell-metal instrument played on with a stick) and the 'mandira' (cymbals), in the jatra during the eighteenth-century drums were the most popular instruments, to which was added later the 'tanpura' (Indian tambourine), and by the end of the nineteenth century a host of Western instruments like the table-harmonium and clarinets had found their way into the jatra orches-tra. While over the years the composers of jatras incorporated new instruments as well as new themes into their repertoire, they rarely departed from the original structure of the jatra form. This was marked by the concert overture, the prologue, the 'judi' or singing chorus (mainly sung by young boys taking the last lines of a dia-logue as their cue), and the comic relief provided by the clowns.[54]

Although there are evidences of the existence of women artistes who used to act in traditional jatras,[55] the prominent jatra troupes in nineteenth-century Calcutta used young boys to act in the roles of female characters, which explains why young Gopal was chosen for the role of Malini.

The jatras of the earlier period were woven around episodes from the lives of Krishna and Radha, or Shiva and Parvati. But the arrival of Bharatchandra's *Vidya-Sundar* on the cultural scene in the mid-eighteenth century encouraged the composition of jatras on this secular romance. A host of popular versions of *Vidya-Sundar* flooded the market, soon after the establishment of the printing press in the late eighteenth century.

The trend of popularizing Bharatchandra's composition and narrating its story in the simple language of the masses provided Gopal Udey with the chance of innovating a new style in the jatra. He formed his own troupe and *Vidya-Sundar* was rewritten. Dia-logues were composed in the form of short, lilting verses. The songs composed for Malini in particular became highly popular, the musical measure used for them usually being 'ad-khemta', a lively tempo. According to one observer: 'By singing them over and over again in fields and streets, markets and squares, people made them almost commonplace.'[56]

Gopal's songs became popular because of his ability to make the characters in the jatra narrate their loves and woes in the famil-iar terms of the social life of the poor people. They could thus immediately touch a sympathetic chord in the minds of the audi-ence. There was a waggish tone with a touch of the wanton in the

songs of Malini whose role was that of the go-between. Her words
and the music which accompanied them immediately evoked the
image of the procuress—a very familiar character in nineteenth-
century Calcutta society, where the foppish rich babus—as well as
their wives—depended on these women for the 'arrangement' of
their extramarital affairs.[57] This is how Malini boasts of her prowess
to Sundar, to whom she promises to bring Vidya:

> Jadu! Chintey to paro nai
> Ami shukno dangaey pansi chalai.
> E noi re tor temon mashi,
> Sarbonashi, nimeshetey Kashi-Macca dekhai.
> Ami jodi money kori, phand petey chand dhottey pari.
> Kuhak diye kuler nari bahir kori.
> Bahir korey bhelki lagai.[58]

(You don't know me yet, my darling; I steer my pinnace
across dry land. I'm no ordinary auntie. I'm dangerous; I
can show you Banaras and Mecca at the snap of my fingers. If I want, I can trap the moon. By my charm, I can
bring out the chaste woman from her sheltered home. I
bring her out and stagger the world.)

Here is a witch and Iago rolled into one—but mellowed by
Gopal Udey's breezy humour.

Gopal also introduced a special type of dancing in his jatras.
This was the famous khemta—a jaunty dance performed by both
men and women. It was said to have originated in Chinsurah, near
Calcutta, from where Keshey Dhoba (Keshey the washerman)
imported it into Gopal's troupe. Having seen the popularity of
khemta as danced by Malini in Gopal's jatra, other troupes also
began to incorporate the khemta style of dancing into their versions of Vidya-Sundar.[59]

Members of the manual occupations, like Keshey the washerman, had a major say in the evolution of the jatra form as a popular
means of entertainment in nineteenth-century Calcutta. The comic
relief which was provided in between the acting out of the main
story consisted of humorous songs and dances performed by

artistes in the roles of these various types of manual labourers who served the Calcutta bhadralok society. These songs and dances were known as 'jatra-duets', since the performers appeared as couples, like 'dhopa-dhopani' (washerman and washerwoman); 'methor-methrani' (the sweeper and his wife); the 'bhisti-wala' (who kept the streets clean by watering them) and his wife; the gypsy and his girlfriend, etc. Often in their songs, these characters poked fun at the habits of the babus whom they served. One such song put in the mouth of Kalua, the sweeper, in Gopal's jatra makes fun of the babu's regular dependence on him (for cleaning his rooms) which makes him almost subservient to the menial:

Babu, nagdi rojgar, sab se guljar
Nokri jhakmari, babu parentazar
 Kam hamari, parentazari (babu) . . .
 . . . Bole kanha raete Kalua jhadudar![60]

(Babu, I work for ready cash. It's grand! The work is difficult, but the babu has to depend on others. The work is
mine, the dependence is the babu's. . . He keeps asking:
Where is Kalua the sweeper?)

Raw wit, expressed in typical feminine idioms, comes out in a funny song sung by a gypsy woman in Gopal's jatra. These women who used to sell herbs and oils were familiar figures in Calcutta.

Ei oshudh more chhuntey chhuntey,
Hudkoe bou jaye aapni shutey,
Baro-phatka purush jara,
Aanchal-dhara hoye uthey![61]

(As soon as these medicines of mine are touched, the truant wife will come back to sleep with her husband, the
profligate will get tied down to his wife's apron-strings.)

Among other jatra troupes of the period, the best known were those run by Gobinda Adhikari (1798–1870); Lokenath Das who was known as Loko Dhoba, or Loko the washerman; and Boko and his brother Sadhu—two Muslims—who were reported to have staged jatras on episodes from the *Ramayana* in the middle of the nineteenth century.[62] Gobinda Adhikari, who came from a poor Vaishnavite family, specialized in jatra performances dealing with Krishna's life. According to a contemporary observer:

> Gobinda Adhikary, even in his old age, put on the gar-
> ments of a woman and came on the stage in the role of
> Brinda, the messenger of Radha, and yet it didn't appear
> unbecoming . . . He could keep everyone spellbound by
> his kirtan-type songs . . . To the beats of the music, he used
> to move forward and backwards by one, two, and three
> steps, which made his singing even more charming . . .[63]

We should add at the same time that jatra was not the exclusive preserve of the lower-class artistes. A number of respectable bhadraloks also set up amateur jatra troupes, drawn by the popularity of this folk form in nineteenth-century Calcutta.

Among them were Srinath Sen, son of a rich Bengali, Gurucharan Sen; Ramchand Mukhopadhyay, who was a dewan of Chhatu Babu; and Swarup Dutta of Hadkata. But it was Gopal Udey who, by the sheer force and spontaneity of his performances, could exert an influence on the Calcutta gentry, affecting, among others, Rabindranath Tagore (during whose childhood, in the 1870s, Gopal's songs continued to be popular even after his death). Rabindranath was later to compose some songs in the ad-khemta style which was the distinctive mark of Gopal's jatra songs.[64] While he never acknowledged his source, his elder brother Jyotirindranath was frank enough to admit: 'It was Gopal Ooriah's jatra that suggested to us the idea of projecting a theatre. It was Gangooly [Satyaprasad], you [Goonendranath Tagore] and I that proposed it'.[65] He was referring to the establishment of an amateur theatre in his ancestral house at Jorasanko in the mid-nineteenth century.

Besides the jatra, the other folk form which became popular in Calcutta was the panchali. The leading exponent of this particular form was Dasharathi Ray, or Dashu Ray (1805–57). Although he was not a resident of Calcutta (unlike the numerous kobis and jatra-walas), many of his panchalis were pungent satires on different aspects of the social life of the metropolis. His popularity also led to the formation of many panchali troupes in Calcutta, leading among the panchali poets being Ganganarayan Laskar, Lakshmikanta Biswas, Kedarnath Basu and Mohanchand Basu.[66]

Panchalis were basically songs interspersed with recitation of short rhymes about the Hindu divinities. Dashu Ray introduced a new style in narrating these mythological stories, which brought him both fame and wealth. Dark and lean, Dashu had curly hair and big, bright eyes. He used to stand up while reciting, surrounded by his listeners sitting on the ground. It was his habit to repeat a stanza thrice—addressing it first to the audience sitting in front, and then turning to the left and to the right. He recited the stanzas while his brother Tinkari sang. The musical instruments used were the Indian tambourine, drums, cymbals, and at a latter stage, the violin.[67]

Although Dashu Ray did not come from a poor background like the kobi Bhola Moira, or the jatra-wala Gopal Udey, he had an intimate knowledge of the lower strata of Bengali social life.

As a boy, he had left home to join the troupe of a village woman kobi, Akshaya Patni of the caste of ferrymen, where he became a bandhandar or a composer of the kobi songs to be sung by Akshaya and her companions. Tired of being constantly abused by his own family and other 'respectable' members of the village gentry for his association with a low-caste woman, Dashu finally left Akshaya's troupe and formed his own troupe of panchali singers in 1835.[68] But Akshaya's influence left its traces in Dashu's compositions, as evident from the raw, lusty style and the colloquial expressions that were the characteristics of the Bengali conversation of the poorer classes of those days.

When treating mythological subjects, Dashu sometimes introduced contemporary characters in his songs to the amusement of the listeners. Thus, in *Rukshmini-Haran* (about the abduction of Rukshmini, Krishna's wife), a Brahman messenger arrives at Krishna's palace gates at Dwaraka, where the gatekeeper addresses him in the language of a Bhojpuri watchman of Calcutta. The environment and dialogues are suddenly transposed from the mythological past to the nineteenth-century Black Town of Calcutta, where rich Bengalis kept musclemen from Bhojpur in Bihar to protect their palatial buildings. In another panchali of his, *Sita-Anweshan* (about Rama's search for Sita after her abduction by Ravana), Dashu Ray juxtaposes the events of the *Ramayana* with contemporary social tendencies:

> Satider anno jotey na, beshyader jaroa gahona
> Raboner swarnapuri, Sri Ramchandra banachari.
> Srishti sab srishtichhada, bajiye pae shaler joda
> Panditey Chandi podey dakshina pan charti ana.[69]

> (Chaste wives do not get food, while whores wear ornaments studded with jewels. Ravana lives in a palace of gold, while Ramachandra is wandering through the forests ... The world is at odds. A music accompanist gets a pair of shawls, while a Brahman who reads the *Chandi* gets a fee of only four annas.)

Like the kobis and other folk poets of the past, Dashu Ray also sought to demystify the Hindu divinities and mythological characters by exposing in a bantering tone their vulnerabilities—like their liaisons which would be glossed over in terms of sophistry by the educated pundits! In one of his songs, women characters called 'kula-kalankinis' (or fallen women) come out with a long list of the heroines of the Hindu epics—the progenitors of the Pandavas and Kauravas (the contending cousins in the *Mahabharata*)—who through several generations gave birth to the future heroes out of wedlock, by mating with a god or a sage.[70] They then ruefully sing:

> When it comes to the gods, it is drummed as mere sport.
> But when we do the same thing, it is called sin.

and lash out at all the so-called virtuous heroines who are expected to be worshipped:

> They all fell in love and got the name of 'sati' [chaste women]
> With ease, they earned both virtue and wealth, as well as
>   love.

But when we fall in love, there's endless anguish for us.
We can't bear it any more. What else can we say?[71]

Dashu Ray did not remain stuck with mythological stories. In many songs, he straightaway took up contemporary topics and social tendencies as a whipping post for his sarcastic wit. The Bengali babus, who were flunkeys to the nouveau riche, were his favourite targets, as in the following song which describes their habits:

Brandy, rendi, ganja, guli, yaar jutey katokguli,
Mukhetey sarboda buli, hoot boley dey ganjaye tan,
Podey thakey parer badi" hoye tader ajnyakari,
Holey tader monti bhari, hunkoti kolketi panti jogan.[72]

(They are immersed in brandy, whores, hemp and opium along with their cronies. Gabbling all the time, and puffing away at hemp, they rot away in the houses of others, carrying out their orders. When their patrons are sullen, they pass on to them their hookah, the tobacco bowl or the betel leaf.)

In his religious views, Dashu Ray was, however, not willing to share the permissive attitude of the heterodox cults of the lower orders of his days. The Karta-bhaja sect (see Chapter 2) was a particular object of his ridicule. He appeared to be as critical of the educated social reformers of Calcutta as of the new urban cultural forms that were developing in the city.[73] There was a streak of conservatism in Dashu's songs, although they often departed from the conventions of style (as in the above quotation from *Rukshmini-Haran*), and challenged traditional beliefs (as in the song of the kula-kalankinis). A sort of dichotomy in his beliefs and attitudes, which Dashu shared with many of his contemporaries among the nineteenth-century Bengali folk poets, could be explained by the nature of his patronage. He was basically a village-based poet. His earlier patrons were the pundits of Nabadwip, to be followed by the rural landlord families of Bengal.[74] As a result, he had to operate at two levels—singing for the traditional upper-caste and upper-class rural gentry on the one hand, and the lower orders of the villages on the other. For the former, he had to speak in a vein of piety, and for the latter, in a simple, half-humorous style. His innovations, like the interpolation of current topics in religious songs, were meant to satisfy the demands of these people. Explaining the dual nature of his songs, Dashu Ray said in the introduction to his panchalis:

> Sadhur santap-door janya
> Jato sumadhur sartatto hoilo jojan.
> . . . .
> Aporey koribey rag, ghuchaitey shey birag,
> Parey kichhu apor prasanga . . .[75]

> (To remove the grievances of the pious, the best and the most essential truths are being brought together here . . . Since others might feel aggrieved, to remove their discontent I have added some other topics . . .)

It was the same compulsion which made the kobi-wala Netai Boiragi shift, while singing at a gathering, from the serious sakhi-samvad to the kheud to satisfy the demands of the restless lower orders.

It appears, therefore, that the secularization of content, the simplification of style, the vivacity in the musical measures, the merry ribaldry and the pungent satire that brought kobi songs, jatras, panchalis and other such folk forms of nineteenth-century Calcutta closer to the surrounding reality and often made them reflect contemporary social trends, were to be ascribed to the prompting of the lower orders rather than the dictates of the rich patrons. The existence of a number of composers who themselves came from the lower orders facilitated the growing proximity of these popular cultural forms to the social reality of the times.

IV

The social environment of nineteenth-century Calcutta left a more direct impact on some other types of verses and songs (some anonymous, some by popular poets) which used to make the rounds in the city. They covered a variety of topics ranging from political events to the city's civic innovations. They could be described as the successors to the eighteenth-century doggerels and rhymes about the city and its inhabitants. They were not as structured as the established folk forms like the kobi songs or the jatra. They were not accompanied by the orchestral paraphernalia of the former. Pithy and pawky, they were sung in the streets and marketplaces.

Women's education, which from the middle of the nineteenth century was spreading rapidly in Bengali bhadralok society with the help of English administrators, educationists and missionaries, was one favourite topic of these versifiers. Unlike the educated reformists and the orthodox Bengali aristocracy (both of whom took up the cause of female education seriously), these popular poetasters looked at their efforts with amusement. Having seen the manners of the English-educated Bengali men, who were only too eager to ape their foreign mentors, these versifiers envisaged a similar future for the English-educated Bengali women. The prospects, as they imagined them, provided them with a host of fanciful, humorous images. A deliberate exaggeration in the description of these newly educated women helped create a stereotype that reappears in numerous songs. Thus one song says:

Housewives no longer have any sense of shame,
They always dress in Anglicized fashion.
They've left cooking and are fond of knitting.
Wearing gowns they move around,
Singing all sorts of nonsense.
Men have lost their power,
They're tied to their wives' apron-strings.
It's a world of women all around.
Feel like dying having watched
The manners of the henpecked men.[76]

Or, take the following lines from a song by an obscure poet called Kanradas:

Haddo-maja Kalikale kolley Kolketaye.
Magitey chodlo gadi, pheting judi
Hatey chhodi hat mathaye . . .[77]

(The modern age has turned Calcutta into a funny place.
The wenches are travelling by cars, phaetons and carriages. They carry sticks in their hands and put hats on
their heads . . .)

We may mention in this connection that such street songs
expressed a mood which was often shared by some bhadralok
poets, who also resorted to a similar style of popular rhetoric while
writing about contemporary urban subjects. Leading among these
poets was Ishwar Chandra Gupta (1812–59), who not only collected
old songs of the eighteenth-century kobi-walas, but himself carried
on the tradition of the kobis.[78] In the next chapter we shall deal
with Ishwar Chandra Gupta and other bhadralok poets who
worked in this particular genre in the nineteenth century.

The misgivings expressed in these popular songs about
women's education were a part of the general distrust and sarcastic
attitude which the man in the street nursed against the Anglicized
gentry. The barbs were directed against both the imitative Bengali
male (as we have found in the doggerels and Dashu Ray's songs)
and his female companion. Nevertheless, in a patriarchal society
(the norms of which prevailed among the lower orders also),
women were special butts of ridicule. The image of an educated
woman, painted in exaggerated colours, provided these poets with
a chance of comic inversion. A reversal of roles, with the woman
on top, helped them also to ridicule the submissive male—often
described in these songs as a *bhedua* or a henpecked husband.

Such symbolic reversals of roles were treated in a different way
in the popular songs composed by women of the lower orders.
Since the educated Anglicized Bengali woman, being alien to
them, could not become their heroine, they turned to the goddess
Kali, whose image as an omnipotent female authority standing on
the chest of a supine Shiva was worshipped all over Bengal. A contemporary observer describes how a jhumur-wali (one of those

women who used to sing jhumurs, variously interpreted as tribal song and dance performances, or as a part of the Radha-Krishna kirtan narrative) sang a song with unabashed glee at the discomfiture of Shiva. His account brings to life a typical Calcutta street scene of those days:

> They [the jhumur-walis] were *chhotolok* [from the uneducated lower orders], dark-skinned wenches who stank when they passed by. They used to wear anklets round their feet when they sang. In those days during wedding ceremonies, jhumur-walis used to dance on peacock-shaped papier mache boats set up on bullock-carts. As they danced, a man from behind used to beat a drum, or strike a bell-metal plate . . . Their language was extremely coarse, but some among them had talents as poets . . .

He then proceeds to give us a sample of a jhumur song about Kali:

> Magi minsheyke chit korey phele diye buke diyechhé pa;
> Ar chokhta julur julur, mukhey neiko ra.[79]

> (The hussy has thrown the bloke flat on his back, with her foot on his chest. Wordless she stands, glaring in anger.)

Among the jhumur-walis of nineteenth-century Calcutta, Bhabani (also known as Bhabarani) came to prominence in the late 1850s. She had her own troupe and moved around the Calcutta streets and other parts of Bengal. One of her jhumur songs describes the plight of a prostitute in words which parody the conventional style used by classical poets to describe a familiar episode in the Radha-Krishna story—Radha's frequent trips to the river, ostensibly to fill her water vessel but actually to tarry there for a glimpse of Krishna:

> Chal soi, bandha ghatey jai,
> A-ghater jaleyr mukhey chhai!
> Ghola jal podley petey
> Gata omni guliye othey
> Pet pheripey ar dhekur uthey heu heu heu![80]

(Come on, friends, let's go to a well-laid-out bathing place.
Fie upon the waters of out-of-the-way *ghats*! As soon as I
take in the muddy waters, I feel like throwing up. My belly
aches and I start belching—heu, heu, heu!)

Having sufficiently deromanticized the situation by describing
in stark, prosaic language the physical hazards involved in such a
rendezvous, the singer now introduces a bitter-sad note describing
her emotional state:

> My tears dry up in my eyes,
> I go around making merry.
> I'm writhing in pain,
> Yet, I act coy
> Swinging my hips.
> The accursed ornaments of mine
> May not remain long with me,
> What with the evil eyes
> Cast upon them
> By the wretched wenches!

Social reforms, which generated heated debates among the
educated gentry, were occasions for good-humoured and light-
hearted merrymaking by the street singers, like the well-known
song beginning with the words:

> Benchey thak Vidyasagar chirojeebee hoye,
> Sadarey koreche report bidhobader hobey biye.[81]

> (Long live Vidyasagar! He has submitted a report to the
> headquarters recommending remarriage of widows).

Or the following song:

> Orey Vidyasagar diberey biye
> Bidhobader dhorey.
> Tara ar phelbey na chul
> Bandhbey benee guiljbe rey phul,
> Shankha saree porbey notun korey.[82]

(Vidyasagar will get hold of widows and make them remarry. They'll no longer shave their heads. From now on, they'll tie their hair in tresses, tuck in flowers and wear shell-bangles and saree again.)

Some of the street songs were about the various occupations pursued by the lower orders, like the following funny lines of a milkmaid:

Banter mukher khariti dudh key nibi go bal,
Ser kora adha-adhi khali kaler jal.[83]

(Tell me, who'll buy milk—flowing pure right from the teats? Only half of it is mixed with water from the tap.)

Epidemics like the plague often led the citizens to parade the streets singing hymns to placate the divinities. Such singing processions were known as 'nagar-sankirtan' (introduced by the Vaishnavite preacher Chaitanya and his followers in Nadia in the fifteenth century). One such song started with the following lines:

Oi dekho ma hatti tuley ditechhen abhoy
Ranga charan sharan niley roy ki maribhoy?
. . .
Chhado krandoneri role, ghuchbe shakol gandogol
Joy Kali Joy Kali balo, mayer koley chheler joy.[84]

(Look! There's mother assuring us with her raised hands. If you take refuge at her red feet, what fear of pestilence remains? . . . Give up weeping. All troubles will be over. Sing 'Victory to Kali'. Victory to the sons in the laps of the mothers.)

It was not only the inhabitants of the city who composed such street songs. Villagers who came for a visit to Calcutta also wrote songs and verses, which again became a part of the urban folk culture. One such song was composed by a folk poet called Kabirdas Gonsai, who used the city, Calcutta, as a metaphor to describe the human body (the convention of describing the human body in terms of a material object to suggest its growth, development and decline is a typical feature of Baul and other Bengali folk songs).[85] Another village poet, Baradaprasad Roy, came to the city, saw the civic facilities like tap water, gas light, and telegraph wires, and wrote the following lines addressed to Queen Victoria:

> Kotha ma Victoria?
> Pet bhorey pai na khete, kaj ki pathey?
> Kaler jaley kaj ki gasey?
> . . .
> Chai na ma tarer khabor
> Dudiner parey
> Kar khabor key korbey deshey?[86]

(Where are you, mother Victoria? . . . I don't even get two full meals; what's the use of roads? What's the use of tap water and gas light? . . . I don't need news through the wire, mother. Who'll hear our news after some time?)

V

While these street songs, continuing the tradition of eighteenth-century doggerels and rhymes, dealt directly with topical events, the kobi songs, the panchalis and jatras, notwithstanding their frequent forays into the contemporary social milieu and transparent allusions to contemporary trends, remained basically oriented towards Bengali Hindu myths and divinities.

Yet Calcutta had a large population of Muslims—both Bengalis and Urdu-speaking. In the thirties of the nineteenth century, the Bengali Muslims numbered about 45,000—one-third of the city's total Bengali Hindu population.[87] They followed occupations like tailoring, masonry, butcher's trade, selling fruits and vegetables, driving carriages, working as cooks and butlers in the houses of the Europeans and rich Bengalis, book-binding, working at tanneries.[88] Thus, a large proportion of the city's lower orders consisted of Muslims.

Did these Muslims of Calcutta have any literature of their own? Did their language differ from that used in the kobi songs or jatras?

It is certain that there was a difference between the language used by the Muslims in Calcutta and that used by their co-religionists in the rural areas of Bengal. Speaking about the vast rural Muslim masses of Bengal, a Christian missionary of the late nineteenth century said: 'They are Hindus who have received a Mussulman varnish and are thus made to pass for Mussulmans. But scratch them and you find the Hindu underneath the Mussulman. So also in regard to their language . . . it is really at bottom Bengali, and this bottom is reached very soon as regards the ordinary common people.'[89]

As evident from earlier Bengali literature, in the rural society Bengali Hindus and Muslims not only shared the same language, but also similar cultural tastes. Since Persian and Arabic were used in official transactions (during the Mughal regime), many terms and words from those languages found their way into the Bengali vocabulary. Just as the Aryan Hindu myths underwent a form of localization in the Bengali religious rituals and literature, so also was Islam adapted to a large extent to local traditions by its Bengali converts. A sort of interfusion of Hinduism and Islam took place in the shape of adoption of Arabic and Persian words in colloquial Bengali as well as in the exchange of Hindu and Muslim themes and motifs in literary compositions. Certain common godlings and 'pirs' (Muslim saints) developed, who were worshipped by both Hindus and Muslims. A seventeenth-century Hindu poet, Krishnaram Das, composed a ballad in praise of Kalu Gazi, a Muslim pir worshipped by all for protection from tigers. Bharatchandra Ray of *Vidya-Sundar* fame wrote a long poem on Satyapir—a very popular godhead who appeared to have emerged from the fusion of an old Hindu god, Satyanarayan, and a Muslim pir. Similar blending of a Hindu guru—Matsyendra—and a Muslim warrior of the seventeenth century, Masnad Ali, led to the formation of Pir Machandali in Medinipur in West Bengal, in whose praise a Bengali Hindu poet, Sitaram Das, composed a ballad.[90] On the other hand, it was a Muslim poet, Sabirid Khan, who was the first to compose a poem on the story of Vidya and Sundar in the sixteenth century. Another Muslim poet of the same period, Mohammad Kabir, composed a panchali called *Madhumalati* about the love of Manohar, prince of the Kangira kingdom and Madhumalati, princess of Mahara, the kingdom of fairies. It was originally a Hindi fable, which was adapted in Bengali by the Muslim poet. Syed Alaol, the famous Bengali Muslim poet of the mid-seventeenth century, chose again a theme from the history of the Rajputs to compose his romance *Padmavati*, celebrating the virtues of Padmavati, the queen of Chitor, who, to escape abduction by the Muslim emperor Alauddin, died on her husband's funeral pyre. In all these ballads and poems, whether by Bengali Hindus or Muslims, Arabic, Persian and Urdu words were used liberally.[91]

The cultural homogeneity of Hindus and Muslims of rural Bengali society, however, seemed to have snapped in Calcutta. One of the main reasons for this appears to be the spatial distribution of the city's lower orders. Although in the Bengal villages also, the different communities had their separate quarters (like colonies of artisans, agricultural labourers, Muslims, etc.)—a custom which continued to be followed in eighteenth- and nineteenth-century Calcutta (see Chapter 2)—the close proximity in which they lived in a small hamlet allowed them to share in the daily social life. Cultural events like a jatra performance, or a kathakata (recitals from religious scriptures) drew members of all the communities. Dinendra Kumar Ray describes his village in Nadia district of West Bengal in the mid-nineteenth century where Hindu and Muslim boys together participated in their respective religious and cultural festivities, like 'ratha-jatra' and Manik Pir's songs.[92]

What with the ever-expanding boundaries of the city, and what with the constant dislocation of the various groups of lower orders, the different communities of artisans, labourers and small traders, who formed the bulk of Calcutta's poorer population, tended to get widely dispersed. Like the other Hindu caste-based occupational groups, the Muslims also were pushed into isolated ghettos. The 1876 census tells us that the Muslims were concentrated south of Dharamtala, in Taltala, Fenwick Bazar, Colinga and Jaunbazar which had 'larger *bustees* than perhaps any other part of the Town, about three-fourths of the population being lodged in *kutcha* huts'.[93] The Hindu artisans and labourers, on the other hand, were mainly concentrated in the northern parts of the town, in settlements which grew around the bazaars and houses of the Bengali banians and dewans. This part of the Black Town was the centre of cultural events like jatras and kobi performances.

The geographical distance tended to drive a wedge between the two communities. (There were some exceptions like the settlement of the Patuas or scroll painters in Kalighat, near the famous temple in south Calcutta, where both Hindus and Muslims sharing the same occupation lived together. See Section VII of the present chapter for a more comprehensive survey of this community of painters.) Further, the Muslim population of Calcutta included a fairly large proportion of immigrants from other parts of northern India whose mother tongue was Urdu. The concentration of a mixed language community in slums invariably affected the conversational pattern of the Bengali Muslims living in such conditions.

Unlike the oral compositions of the Bengali Hindu lower orders of Calcutta, the literature of these Bengali Muslims of the city consisted of narrative poems, elegiac verses and didactic poetry composed in a dialect known as 'dobhashi' (which literally means 'derived from two languages', but actually contained elements from more than two languages, namely, Bengali, Arabic, Persian and Urdu). Although, as we have seen, Arabic and Persian words had been in vogue in Bengali literature since the fourteenth–fifteenth centuries, dobhashi literature was characterized by a preponderance of such words and it became popular among the Bengali Muslims in the eighteenth and nineteenth centuries. As one critic has suggested: 'It is likely that the influence of the growing city of Calcutta and the old port of Hugli had much to do with the growth and development of Dobhasi literature in the eighteenth century'.[94]

In fact, it has been noted that dobhashi literature flourished in political and commercial centres like Dhaka, Murshidabad, the areas around the Hugli port, and the new capital, Calcutta. The regular arrival of foreign traders—mainly from Iran and the Arab countries of the Middle East during the Mughal regime—and the frequent official intercourse of the local people in these centres with the Mughal administrators left their traces in the patois of the Bengalis of these areas.[95]

Explaining the reasons for the increasing popularity of dobhashi literature in the eighteenth century and its diffusion among lower-class Muslims in the next century, some critics feel that Muslim poets during this period tended in their Bengali to avoid the excesses of Sanskritization which were becoming fashionable with certain schools of writers. They were prompted to write in dobhashi as a counterblast to the Sanskritic Bengali which the Hindu scholars were advocating. The popularity of dobhashi in certain quarters could also have been connected with the spread of the Wahhabi and Faraizi movements in Bengal, which advocated a return to the purism of Islam, stripped of all local Bengali contamination.[96]

But however strong the desire for Arabic, Persian and Urdu words might have been, what emerged was again a Bengalized version. Arabic and Persian names were pronounced in a Bengali fashion. Thus, the title of a narrative romance by one of the most popular dobhashi poets of the eighteenth century, Garibullah, was *Iuchaf-Jelekha*. It is the story of the love of Iuchaf, son of a pious rich Muslim, and Jelekha, daughter of a Muslim king. It was borrowed from a Persian story where the hero was Yusuf and the heroine Zuleikha. The narrative in Garibullah's version was tinged with the colour of Bengali society. Like the domestication of divinities such as Krishna, Radha, Shiva and Parvati in the kobi songs and panchalis, here also the Persian princess appears in traditional Bengali dress and ornaments. 'She expresses her feelings, whether of love or resentment . . . in language which might have been used by Radha herself.'[97] But unlike the kobi songs and panchalis, Garibullah's romance is heavily interspersed with didactic messages about the superiority of Islam and the harms of idolatry. A more directly didactic poem was *Bedarelgafelin* by Sekh Munsi Chamiruddin, which consisted solely of Islamic teachings on moral and religious subjects. Elegiac compositions like 'Janganama, Moktal Mochen', also by Garibullah, celebrated events from the history of Islam. The martyrdom of Hassan and Hossain (changed into the Bengali names—Hachan and Hochen) at Karbala was a popular topic. In both the narrative romances and the elegiac compositions on historical subjects of dobhashi litera-ture, the style was marked by a special stress on the supernatural. According to some critics, the description of miracles perpetrated by Muslim saints in these poems could have been prompted by a desire to prove the superiority of Islam over Hindu gods and god-desses, as well as by the need to escape from the turmoils of the surrounding reality and seek refuge in dreams of miraculous changes.[98] Unlike the contemporary folk songs and verses by the Bengali Hindu poets, which primarily sang of common human beings (although often in the guise of Hindu gods and goddesses) and their exploits as well as failures, dobhashi literature tended to be more didactic (even in romances like *Iuchaf-Jelekha*), elevating the pirs or saints to positions of supernatural power. But the dif-ferences in diction and treatment of themes notwithstanding, dob-hashi literature often resembled the contemporary Bengali Hindu folk songs in the expression of certain attitudes. We find echoes of the general distrust about modern women, a common topic of the street songs. Thus, Garibullah (not the author of *Iuchaf-Jelekha*) wrote:

Garibulla kahey ami ki kobibo ar,
Kolikaler aorater likhi samachar.
Phiribare jae jodi padashir ghare
Khachamer gibat karey sabakar tarey.
Dui chari aorat boshia ak sat
Rashto pashto kare tara ei shab bat.[99]

(Garibulla is now speaking about the habits of the women of the modern days. When she goes to her neighbour's house, she speaks ill of her husband in front of everyone. Two or four women sit together and speak aloud all these things.)

The poet ends with an advice to all husbands:

Ar ek katha kohi shuno shabey bhai
Moner katha na kohibe kabilar thai.

(Listen to another word of advice, everyone of you. Never speak your mind to your wife.)[100]

It is interesting to observe that although Garibullah uses Arabic and Urdu words like 'aorat' (women), 'khacham' (husband), 'gibat' (bad words), 'kabila' (wife), when he wants to refer to the modern age, he uses the term 'kolikal' which in Hindu myths is the last of the four ages—Satya, Treta, Dwapar and Kali—and indicates the coming of the Apocalypse.

Although the bulk of dobhashi literature consisted of romantic narratives and religious verses, occasionally there were experiments with current topics in a lighter vein which harked back to the mood of the doggerels and kobi songs. Like the sarcastic rhymes on hemp smoking and opium dens, we hear of a dobhashi poem praising tobacco smoking, composed by one Mokaddas Ali in 1887. It was meant to be a veiled attack on the puritan Islamists like Wahhabis and Faraizis who were against smoking.[101]

'Dobhashi' literature received a boost with the beginning of printing in the early nineteenth century.[102] The narrative poems and religious discourses composed earlier by Garibullah, Syed Hamza and others, began to be printed as cheap booklets from small printing establishments in Battala, in the Chitpore area of the Black Town. Printed in larger types, they came to be known as 'battalar punthi' (although 'punthi' literally means manuscript, it was used to connote printed books in the dobhashi diction in this context). By 1855 we hear of at least 41 dobhashi works, including 22 narrative poems and 17 didactic poems, published from 'Musalman presses in Calcutta'.[103]

These books had a wide circulation among the city's Muslim population, including the lower classes among them. It might seem surprising that printed literature would be popular among a community the bulk of whom were unlettered. According to the 1876 census, of the city's Muslim male population only 16.5 per cent could read and write (compared to 42 per cent among the Hindu males). But we should remember in this context that the habit of listening to the reading out (by literate neighbours) of books, like scriptures or mythological stories, was fairly widespread

in Bengal. As one writer noted in the mid-nineteenth century:
'Compared with the middle and lower classes of other countries—
the European continent not excluded—those of Bengal may be said
to be fond of reading, or at least of listening to the reading of
others'. He then proceeds to give a graphic account of the reading
of a dobhashi book among Muslim boatmen on the Hugli:

the hardy rowers almost invariably form a group of listeners around a man, who professes to read to them . . . .
True, their mouths may be engaged in puffing their
favourite weed, or their hands busy plying the needle to
make some rude garment, either for themselves or for
some members of their distant families; but they are all
ear, and any interruption to their intellectual enjoyment
meets with an instantaneous rebuke. The reader, sitting
on his haunches, with his book laid on the floor before
him, spells out couplet after couplet; for all popular books
are in verse, or are read as if they were in verse . . . It [the
reading] is always carried on aloud and in a sing-song tune,
the modulations of which are not readily acquired. To the
music the head beats time, as regularly as the pendulum
invented for the pianist by the ingenious German.

The writer then describes the types of books read among these
Muslim boatmen:

their favourite books are of a totally different nature from
those of the Hindus. True, they are printed in the Bengali
character, and profess to be Bengali poetry, like all the rest;
but the language contains a large admixture of Hindustani
[i.e. Urdu], and the subject matter usually consists of some
Muhammadan legend. These volumes issue from certain
presses in Calcutta, and are sold somewhat dearer [because
somewhat better got up] than those printed for the Hindu
population; but it is very rarely that a larger sum than half
a rupee is paid for a volume, and when it is so expensive,
it is regarded as a very precious treasure, and kept with the
greatest care.[104]

From another contemporary account we learn that among the 'battala punthis', the book most valued was *Kasasal Ambeya,* 'a history made up of truth and legend embracing the period from Adam to Mahommed'. The next in estimation of the people was *Bedarelgaphelin,* 'a small book containing rules relating to all duties secular and religious . . . '[105]

It was not only the dobhashi romances and elegies which provided entertainment for the Muslim lower orders of Calcutta. Every year the Muharram ceremony was an occasion for a mass turnout. Although primarily organized by Shia Muslims, the Sunnis also participated in the 'tazia' processions. The tazia used to be built like the 'ratha' or chariot, drawn during the Hindu ratha festival in honour of the god Jagannath. The colourful spectacle, accompanied by dramatic gestures like beating of chests by the processionists, was meant to mourn the martyrdom of Hassan and Hussain. But the scope for demonstrativeness allowed the ordinary poor Muslim to abandon himself to an orgy-like dance. During the Muharram procession in Calcutta in 1855, this led the Christian (mainly European) residents of Lower Circular Road to urge the city's Chief Magistrate not to allow the tazia procession to move until church time was over. The magistrate however refused to entertain their appeal.[106]

VI

Spectacles, or visual entertainments, like the Muharram tazia processions, were an important component of Calcutta folk culture. It was provided not only by the various types of dances like jhumur or khemta which were to be seen at marketplaces, fairs and streets, but by numerous other forms. A Malay visitor, touring Calcutta some time around 1810, gives us a delightful picture of street entertainments:

> In every street you will find different sorts of street entertainers; some of them carry dozens of snakes about them which they call upon to dance; there are conjurers who perform all sorts of baffling tricks; there are puppeteers with

puppets representing human beings riding on horseback or on elephants, or camels or various other sorts of puppets, which as a result of the sleight of hand practised by these Bengali Hindus seem as though they can dance by themselves . . .[107]

But the most popular and powerful was the sawng or pantomime, which became a weapon in the hands of the underdog for lampooning the upper classes. These sawngs started as illustrations of common proverbs, but with the development of the metropolis and changes in the manners and customs of its people, the pantomime artistes began to mimick the various types of characters and their habits. Such mimicry was accompanied by special types of songs known as 'sawnger gan'.

Sawngs were also represented by clay models of these urban characters. As we have already seen, clay modellers from Krishnanagar and other places came to Calcutta and set up their colonies in Kumortuli and other parts of the Black Town. Besides moulding images of the various gods and goddesses for the religious festivals (the main being Durga puja and Kali puja) all through the Bengali year, these modellers prepared sawngs or caricatures of urban characters for popular entertainment during Chadak—the Hindu festival of swinging and whirling from the top of a pole in the months of April–May. It was a festival connected with the Shiva cult observed at the Bengali year-end.[108]

We hear of a sawng, a live actor illustrating a proverb, during the Saraswati puja (in honour of the Hindu goddess of learning) in February 1825. The Bengali proverb—'Pathey hagey ar chokh rangaye' (literally meaning, 'He shits in public and yet threatens others')—which was depicted by the sawng was meant to lampoon the civic authorities who themselves violated all laws and yet hauled up the man in the street for the slightest misdemeanour. The display, quite predictably, annoyed the authorities. The police arrested the sawng and his patron and brought them before the English magistrate, who reprimanded them for 'vulgarity' and imposed a fine of Rs 50.[109]

We come across another interesting account by a perceptive English woman of a pantomime performance by Indian servants in an English household in Calcutta in the mid-nineteenth century. The pantomime was enacted by the Indians for their own entertainment after they had finished with a performance for their English employers during a birthday party. The English woman who described the pantomime watched it unobserved by the performers, so that the latter were free to give vent to their feelings. Peeping in, she found that one of the performers

had dressed himself up as an officer, with a white mask, and was . . . showing how a young [English] Ensign treats his bearer . . . He did it admirably, and showed such a perception of European follies as to prove an effectual warning to all present not in any way to commit themselves before these quiet, quick-witted natives. He had laid hold of one of . . . [the] bearers, and was making him walk backwards and forwards for his amusement, bestowing a kick every now and then to quicken his movements. He then sent him for a bottle of brandy, stamped and rampanged [sic] about and finally began to dance, exactly like an awkward Englishman attempting a hornpipe. He then forced his supposed servant to dance, looked at him through an eye-glass, and . . . took a sight at him, and taught him to do the same. He then brought in one of his companions, dressed as a lady, dragged her about by way of taking a walk, and then danced with her in imitation of a quadrille and waltz.

Ashamed of the vulnerabilities of the members of her own community, the English lady added: 'I cannot understand anyone venturing before a native, after seeing this apt caricature of the performance!—It was very droll, and only too true.'[110]

Pantomimes were thus an important means for Calcutta's lower orders of seeking relief from the tensions involved in constant subservience to their masters, whether English officials or Bengali banians. They afforded them an opportunity to caricature the habits of their employers—an indirect way of overcoming their own humiliation by cutting their superiors down to size.

During the Chadak festivals, Calcutta's streets were crowded with these pantomime shows, their main centres being the colonies of the artisans, like the 'jeleypada' (the colony of the fishermen), the 'kansaripada' (the colony of the braziers), etc. Although often patronized by the rich men of these colonies (like Taraknath Pramanik of Kansaripada), the sawngs were acted out by the poor people.

The objects of their satire ranged from the rich babus to the religious hypocrites. A Bengali newspaper describing a procession of sawngs in Calcutta during the Chadak festival of 1833 mentions a sawng caricaturing the bloated rich by depicting an old man covered with flowers, with a foot affected by elephantiasis. Another sawng was worshipping his foot with all the piety of a devotee. This was followed by a wooden platform borne by some sawngs. On the platform sat a religious 'guru' counting the beads of his rosary and muttering prayers. As the bearers moved him round and round, he kept turning his lecherous eyes now to the women watching the procession from the balconies and the next moment upwards in gestures of prayers to his god.[11]

As the years passed, the sawng artistes began to incorporate newer and newer themes from the changing social milieu. The sawng procession during the 1868 Chadak puja is thus described by a contemporary English newspaper:

> Their [the braziers'] procession which extended over more than a mile started at about 6 a.m. and returned to the headquarters at 5 p.m., there being continuous music, singing, laughing, pantomiming and what not for nine hours. The streets, the house-tops, the verandas, every nook and corner of the localities through which the procession passed, were filled with men, women, children . . . Some of the caricatures were very telling, for instance the Indigo vat with its thousand reminiscences, the Hell with its dismal horrors, the Burning Ghat cinerators with a

posse of municipal officers, and the modern Bengali Theatre and concert with their stereotyped airs, songs and discourses . . .[112]

A few years later, describing the sawng procession in 1872, the same newspaper indicated the new additions to the sawngs as butts of ridicule:

> A most phantastic [sic] collection of comicalities was exhibited. A party of water plumbers with tools and instruments, an utter-seller from Persia superbly dressed, a company of bag-menders, an imitation military band playing acoustics upon pipes, drums, and kettle-drums . . . a fast but ruined Babu with a group of flatterers—these were some of the representations, all singing appropriate and humorous songs . . . Some of our social customs and novelties of the day were most effectively caricatured. The Kulin marriage was exquisite. The new form of marriage under Mr. Stephen's Act was beautifully illustrated. The bridegroom was dressed in pantaloons and chapkan, and the bride in the costume of a Hindustani natch [nautch] girl and in top-boots holding a book in her hands . . .[113]

Sawng processions were also accompanied by songs. Here is an example of a sawnger gan taking a crack at the Bengali gentry's craze for titles like 'raja' and 'maharaja':

Ami raja bahadur,
Kochubaganer hujur.
Jomi nai, jama nai,
Naiko amar proja . . .
Andorey abola kande
Kheye amar saja.
Orey baja, baja, baja,
Ta dhin ta dhin nachi ami,
Kochubaner raja.[114]

(I'm a noble 'raja', the king of the garden of trifles. I've no land, no savings, nor do I have any subjects . . . I punish

women in my home and make them weep. Beat the drum!
Let me dance! I'm the king of the garden of trifles.)

While the live sawngs came out in a procession to mimic
various characters, clay models of similar characters were displayed
during festivals and fairs. They were prepared by the 'kumors' (clay
modellers) of Kumortuli and other colonies. Such clay sawngs were
exhibited once in the annual Hindu Mela in Calcutta in 1873. A
newspaper describes some of them:

A Christian missionary is preaching with a Bible in his
hand. A poor man dressed only in a small piece of loincloth with a spade on his shoulders and holding the hand
of his child is listening agape. Another European is hovering around with a bottle of wine. The second sawng—a
thief is escaping with a bundle belonging to a Brahman
priest; the latter is shouting for the watchman. The watchman is focusing his lantern on the face of the priest and
abusing him (instead of going for the thief). The thief is
giving them the slip thumbing his nose at everyone . . .[115]

The Kumortuli clay modellers played an important role in the
visual folk art of Calcutta. They worked almost through out the
year, modelling images of gods (starting with that of Ganesha who
was worshipped in Baishakh, the first month of the Bengali year)
and goddesses for the various religious festivals. Preparation of
these images was a collective affair which involved the participation
of various occupational groups, each contributing its little bit to
the completion. A contemporary critic describes the collective
effort of these artistes who mainly came from the Bengali lower
orders:

Thatched houses (in which the images were placed) are
made by professional thatchers called gharamis; baskets
are made by Doms, a low caste people . . . trees and plants
are made by men who have acquired a proficiency in this
branch of work . . . The potter makes the figures of such
idols, the painter colours them, and the Mali, a member

of the flower-selling caste, adorns them with tinsel ornaments . . .[116]

The tinsel ornaments were made from 'shola' or a parasitic
plant collected from under the waters of tanks. The artistes showed
great ingenuity in carving these plants and making ornaments of
various types known as 'dak' to adorn the idols. A contemporary
poet describes the process of preparing the images which also
included the painting of the 'chalchitra' or the background behind
the images:

First the kumor works,
Then the painter starts.
With earthen colours
He paints numerous figures on the chal (chitra),
Carefully using his brush.
Then the dak artist comes
And makes splendid ornaments . . .[117]

Among all these religious festivals of idol-worshipping, the
Durga puja was of course the most important. Describing the gradual expansion and elaboration of the Durga puja figures and festivities, a contemporary observer noted: 'Gradually the gods and
goddesses came to be furnished with attendants, and in public wor-
ships got up by subscription, more for amusement than for a religious obligation, life-size mythological scenes, scenes from daily
life, portrait figures of athletes and other celebrities, caricatures,
comical subjects and figures representing any scandal current at
the time, were gradually introduced . . .'[118] Thus sawngs also found
their way into Durga puja celebrations.

Such expansion afforded the kumors in particular a chance to
give ingenious expression to their creativity. As in the contemporary kobi songs and panchalis, in the puja images also the divinities
were often moulded according to certain types that were to be seen
in the surrounding society. The god Kartika (son of Durga, who,
along with his brother, Ganesha, and two sisters, Saraswati and
Lakshmi, was depicted as accompanying the main goddess Durga,

who, astride a lion, was poised to kill the demon, Asura) was a favourite character for the kumors. The style of moulding his image changed according to the fashions prevalent among the foppish babus of Calcutta in different periods. Describing the changes, an observer towards the end of the nineteenth century wrote:

> During our childhood, the Kartika we saw was quite a handsome young man, with long and curled hair hanging down to his neck, a thin trace of a moustache, dressed in superfine dhoti, a light plaited scarf thrown around his neck and wearing a pair of gold-embroidered shoes . . . But now, instead of his curly hair hanging down, we find him sporting the Albert fashion of hair style [after Prince Albert, the consort of Queen Victoria]; in the place of the gold-embroidered shoes, he wears English shoes and covers his body in a jacket . . .[119]

Kartika had always been identified with the natty dandy in Bengali imagery. Observing an old-fashioned image of Kartika in a Durga puja festival, one nineteenth-century poet urges him to live up to the fashions of the age:

> Phul pukurey pheley diye paro ohey boot
> Sherry, champagne khao ruti bishkut.
> Bauri kheuri hoye kato Albert-sinthi,
> Shikho ohey hab-bhab adhunik reeti.[120]
> (Throw away your flowers into the tank, and put on a pair of boots. Drink sherry, champagne and eat bread and biscuit. Shave off the hanging curls and part the hair in the Albert-fashion. Learn the manners of the modern times.)

The style in which the images were dressed and decorated with various types of ornaments was of course dictated by the tastes of the patrons—the rich Bengalis who sponsored the elaborate puja festivities. Commenting on the trend to decorate even Kali in golden ornaments (against the conventional style of depicting her according to the old scriptures), a contemporary observer felt that since the rich tended to identify beauty with expensive ornaments, they beautified their tutelary deities with gold and jewellery.[121]

But even within this framework of patronage, the clay modellers never lost the chance of a jibe at the rich and the religious leaders, just like the kobi-walas who never hesitated to hit out at their patrons whenever there was an opportunity. The clay sawngs which were a part of the Durga puja festivities provided them with such a chance. Kaliprasanna Sinha, in his inimitable Calcutta cockney style, describes such sawngs during a Durga puja:

On either side of the image [of the goddess] were sawngs—first, the 'religious hypocrite' and second, the 'pigmy nawab'—both exquisitely done. The religious hypocrite's body was roly-poly—like a cobbler's dog—his belly round like a tomato—the pig-tail on his shaven head tied in a tuft—a garland and a few golden amulets like tiny drums hanging around his neck-amulets tied round his arms—his hair and moustache dyed in black—dressed in a black-bordered dhoti and a vest . . . giving sidelong glances at the housewives and whirling round his fingers the pouch of his rosary beads . . . The pigmy nawab—looks quite handsome—his skin as fair as milk with a drop of lac-dye in it—his hair parted in the Albert-style—like a Chinese pig—short-necked—carrying a red handkerchief and a stick—wearing a fine, transparent dhoti made in Simle [Simulia in north Calcutta], tucked firmly behind . . .[122]

VII

The visual satire on religious hypocrisy, the foppish dandyism of the babus and other trends in contemporary society came out more forcefully in another form of Calcutta folk art—the *pat* paintings of Kalighat, or what among European circles came to be known as 'bazaar paintings'. These were paintings done on cheap paper in water colour, by a community of Patuas (traditional folk-painters who used to draw on canvas scrolls known as *jadan-pat,* or square-shaped canvas known as *chouko-pat* in the Bengal villages) who had settled down in Kalighat in south Calcutta, near the famous Kali temple.

Kalighat had been known since the early eighteenth century, or even before, for the temple of the goddess Kali, where pilgrims used to gather from all parts of the country. The present temple, however, was built in the early part of the nineteenth century by Santosh Roy Chowdhury, zamindar of Barisha-Behala, a southern suburb of the then-Calcutta city. As the city developed, several roads came into existence, such as Nakuleshwartala, Nepal Bhattacharya Lane, Amrita Banerjee Lane, leading to the temple to facilitate the movement of the pilgrims.

Like the other artisans who migrated to Calcutta from the villages, the Patuas also came to Calcutta and settled down near the Kali temple, drawn by the prospects of a thriving market for their talents among the visiting pilgrims. Their original profession was to paint scrolls and display them before an audience, accompanied by singing (known as 'Patua sangeet'). They used to draw figures from Hindu mythology and illustrate their exploits on the canvas scrolls. As they unrolled these scrolls part by part, they narrated in the accompanying songs or doggerels the events illustrated in the *pats*.

But the urban environment changed to a considerable extent their mode of painting, as well as their choice of subjects. First, the canvas rolls were replaced by cheap paper—available from 1800 onwards from Serampore near Calcutta, where the missionaries had set up a printing press. The Patuas found this new medium useful for the purpose of selling their paintings, instead of displaying them. The pilgrims also—primarily from the poor and lower middle classes—who used to buy small wooden or clay toys and figurines as souvenirs from the shops near the temple, added to their list of purchases the cheap paper *pats* that began to be produced in thousands by the Patuas.

Secondly, the subject matter of their paintings also underwent a change. Although they still continued to paint figures of Hindu divinities, they started adding new themes—like the social events in the city and the typical characters like the newfangled, English-educated babu, his wife and mistress, the hypocritical religious guru. Both the demands of the new medium and the selection of the new themes brought about a drastic change in their style of painting. Bold outlines, a few bright colours and sharp, rhythmical sweeps of the brush became essential for a quick turnout to feed the ever-increasing demands of the pilgrims.

The Kalighat *pats* can be broadly divided into five groups: (*i*) pictures of mythological characters and tales; (*ii*) of nature and still life; (*iii*) of historical events—both past and contemporary; (*iv*) description of everyday life and characters; and (*v*) caricatures.

The first group consisted of paintings of Krishna and episodes from his life, like his annihilation of different demons, his carousals in Vrindabana; of Shiva in different roles; and of other Hindu gods and goddesses. The pictures of Shiva in particular, in their style, often hark back to the manner in which the god was described in the panchalis and kobi songs—as an absent-minded, hemp smoking, ne'er-do-well character. A droll drawing shows Shiva with his tiger skin loincloth slipping away from his waist.[123] In the paintings of the young Krishna with his mother Jashoda, while the former is recognizable from the familiar signs (like the black colour in which he is painted, the peacock-feather crest on his head), the latter looks like a typical Bengali village housewife.[124]

The second consists of various studies of fish, birds, snakes and flora and fauna. Here also social satire sometimes peeps out from an innocent-looking picture. A huge cat is shown with a prawn caught in his mouth. But a *rasa-koli*—a longish painted mark on the bridge of his nose, as sported by Vaishnavites—becomes suggestive of social hypocrisy. Many Vaishnavites, who were required to abstain from eating fish or meat, ate both on the sly.[125]

The third comprises paintings and drawings of interesting incidents from history, like the march of British soldiers; a sensational 'crime passionel' from contemporary life (involving the head priest of the temple of Tarakeshwar, a woman devotee of his called Elokeshi whom he seduced, and her husband Nabin Banerjee who

murdered her out of jealousy); scenes of a wrestling match between
a tiger and a famous wrestler of those days, Shyamakanta; and Rani
Lakshmibai of Jhansi, the heroine of the Sepoy rebellion.[126]

The fourth and the fifth groups were the most interesting as
they dealt with contemporary characters and everyday life in a
humorous vein. Here we find the familiar figures of khemta
dancers, and prostitutes carousing with the babus over wine and
music. The babus are sometimes depicted as careless husbands
deserting their wives, sometimes as sheep taken around by their
collar-straps by educated wives or mistresses. Religious gurus are
favourite butts of ridicule. They are shown being beaten up by
angry women. Some of the paintings illustrate proverbs satirizing
the foppish babus like 'Bairey konchar patton, bhitore chunnchor
ketton' (see Section I of this chapter), showing the babu with the
tuck of his dhoti flowing, a flower in one hand, and a stick in the
other, ambling along, while in the background we see an interior
where the musk-rats are engaged in a chorus.[127]

Explaining the value of the paintings of the last two groups,
Dineshchandra Sen, the well-known Bengali critic who collected
Kalighat *pats*, commented:

> The painters [of these *pats*] were usually from the lower
> orders. These pictures were not of any superior quality.
> Yet, they were enjoyed by hundreds of illiterate men and
> women of the Bengali villages. Like a social whip, they
> helped to open their eyes to the morals of society. Like a
> letter, a picture [of this type] used to communicate . . . The
> painters had the superior artistic power to speak through
> lines.[128]

Like most folk art, the production of the Kalighat *pats* was also
a collective affair. The outlines of the figures were first drawn by
the principal artist. The women used to fill up the blank spaces
with colour. Different colours were kept in small vessels, and each
woman was required to lay on a particular colour. In this way four
or five women could complete painting 200 to 300 *pats* within an

hour or so. The equipment at their disposal were few—a piece of paper, a brush and a limited palette of a few colours. The time was also short. By one single sweep of a brush, as long as it carried the paint, the painter had to complete the outline. We seldom find any break in the continuity of a stroke. This explains the excellent rhythm—the brush lightly touching the paper in a thin line and then pressing on to a thick wavy sweep to suggest the swell of a woman's hips, or her falling tresses. A few strokes were enough to indicate the folds of her saree, while a thick black twisting shade stood for the border of her saree.[129]

We should remember that the Patuas were also employed for painting the images of the divinities which were moulded by the kumors. This influenced to some extent the style of their painting the *pats*. The simple oval-shaped face, the large eyes, a slight downward curve to indicate the chin—the fixed features of the Kalighat *pat* faces—bear the traces of the painted images of Durga, Saraswati, Lakshmi and other goddesses. The habit of painting on rounded clay models also led to their drawing rotund limbs on the paper *pats*. The style, dominated by curves rather than angles, created an effect of pneumatic inflation. This technique was extremely evocative in the satirical treatment of contemporary characters like the dandy, the prostitute, the impostor priest. Their bloated limbs and faces conveyed the impression of the hollowness of their society.

The Patuas of Kalighat were a mixed community, consisting of both Hindus and Muslims. As result, their *pats* celebrated both the Hindu divinities and the Muslim pirs. While *pats* portraying Krishna or the Vaishnavite preacher Chaitanya found a ready market at fairs and festivals on Hindu religious occasions all over the city—and even in the villages—those depicting Kalu Gazi (see Section v) were much in demand at the commemoration fairs held at the dargahs of the pir. Known as Gazir Pat, these *pats* showed Kalu Gazi riding a tiger, with his right hand pointing upwards. The bearded pir wears a turban and is dressed in the north Indian fashion.[130] We also learn that 'Muslim pyrotechnicians used to carry these [pats] about and display them at marriage festivals where they would be invited to show their skill in fireworks.'[131]

The names of a few of the Patuas have come down to us. Among them can be mentioned Nilmani Das, Balaram Das and Gopal, who belonged to the early part of the nineteenth century. In the latter half of the century, we come across the names of Nibaran Chandra Ghose and Kali Charan Ghose. The paintings were generally sold at a price ranging from one pice to one anna, and the painters set up their shops along the streets in the neighbourhood of the Kali temple.[132]

The painters, however, began to face a crisis from the last quarter of the nineteenth century. German oleography and photography, with their ability to reproduce pictures at a faster and cheaper rate, posed a challenge to the Patuas. The oleographs used the same subjects, like divinities and contemporary characters, but filled up the outlines and backgrounds with details and ornamental designs. Where the Patua suggested a pillow by one single curve with a few strokes for its folds, or a curtain by two or three lines, the oleograph showed a more detailed and realistic scene. The novelty of photographic realism weaned away from the Kalighat *pats* their original patrons—the poor and lower-middle-class pilgrims and visitors to Kalighat.

Trying to compete with them, the Kalighat Patuas began to produce *pats* in a more elaborate style. Influenced by the realistic portrayal of characters in the oleographs, they introduced ornamental carpets or curtains in the background. This destroyed the boldness and vigour which used to mark the early *pats* of Kalighat. The later paintings degenerated into mere copies of the oleographs.[133]

The Patuas managed to linger on till the early decades of the twentieth century. But the best among them by then had already passed away. We hear about the dispersal of the stalwarts like Paran, who migrated to Rangoon. His contemporary, Balai Boiragi, left for Nabadwip when the industry began to show signs of disintegration. 'Thus the masters of the art were soon scattered all over the country without leaving any trace behind.'[134]

Another interesting visual art form that emerged under the urban influence in nineteenth-century Calcutta was the art of copper engravings and woodcut prints. With the establishment of the printing press in Serampore, and a little later in Calcutta, the need for illustrating the printed publications led to the development of copper and wood engraving among the city's artisan class who found a new avenue in this genre for earning a living. We hear of Panchanan Karmakar, an artisan who helped N. B. Halhed in the casting of Bengali types for his *A Grammar of the Bengali Language,* which came out from Serampore in 1778. We find Panchanan's name accompanying woodcut prints in numerous Bengali books that came out from Battala in the nineteenth century.

When in 1817 the Calcutta School Book Society decided to bring out a Bengali translation of Ferguson's book on astronomy, they employed a number of Bengali artisans to prepare copper plates for illustrations. We come across the names of Calee Coomar Ray (Kali Kumar Ray) and 'the Bengalee Khooshnuvees [Khashnavis] of the College of Fort William' as members of this team of artisans. At around the same time, the Society reprinted Joyce's *Scientific Dialogues* to 'acquaint young persons with the rudiments of natural and experimental philosophy', where the 'highly creditable execution of the plates by a native artist, Casheenath Mistree', drew the praise of the Society authorities.[135] Later annual reports of the Society indicate that Mistree was paid Rs 220 for engraving four plates for the book, and again Rs 25 for another plate to illustrate Pearson's *Teachers' Manual.* Another artisan, Radha Mohan, was paid Rs 90 for engraving 33 diagrams of Euclid.[136]

These engravings were, however, copies of illustrations and diagrams in the original English texts. The copper engraving and woodcut prints that accompanied the text of the Battala Bengali publications were, on the other hand, original illustrations. The books were on a variety of subjects, ranging from Bengali almanacs (*panjika*) and stories about Hindu divinities to secular tales like *Vidya-Sundar.* The illustrations were therefore dominated by pictures of Radha and Krishna surrounded by their companions, Shiva and Parvati, the Rama–Ravana war, the goddess Durga, as well as the ever-popular sports of Vidya and Sundar. Scenes from contemporary social life, like the khemta dancers, the Calcutta

Solvyns: Rasjatra (*above*) and Hari-sankeertan (*below*)

Solvyns: Jhulanjatra (*above*) and Chadak Puja (*below*)

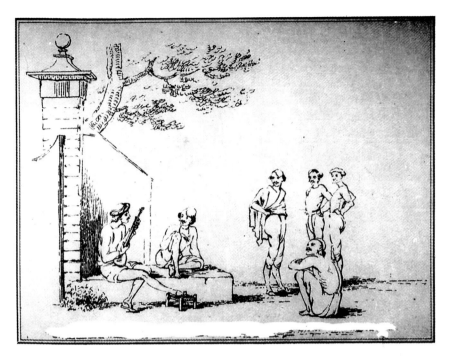

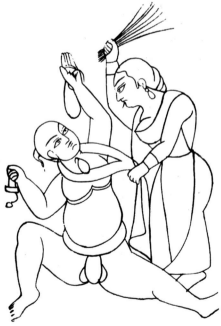

The gatekeeper at the master's gate (*above*) in a sketch by Alex Hunter,
and the Vaishnava disgraced, in a Kalighat *pat* (*below*)

Rat Justice: a Kalighat *pat*

A Muhammadan *pat* from Kalighat

The babu at the lady's feet: a Kalighat *pat*

The barbar examines the lady's ear: a Kalighat *pat*

The babu and his co-wives: in Kalighat *pats*

babus and Anglicized women, were also treated in the style of the Kalighat *pats* in some of the Battala publications.[137]

Like the Kalighat *pats*, these prints too reflect the surrounding reality even when the Hindu divinities are depicted. Glimpses of the contemporary environment can be had in the pillars of the palace of Krishna, the hairstyle and dress of the heroes and heroines. But the resemblance with the *pats* ends there. The prints lacked the spontaneity and mastery of form of the Kalighat Patuas. The strain involved in working in an alien medium is evident in the stiff outlines and the short, mincing furrows, advancing little by little. The characters are without the perfect poise and freedom found in the Kalighat *pats*. Even the social themes and contemporary characters which appear in the prints are painfully executed copies of the *pats*. The latter belonged to the fine arts, while the prints belonged to craft.

The names of the copper engravers and woodcut printers suggest that most of them came from the artisan classes living in Calcutta and its suburbs. We hear of Ramdhan Swarnakar, Gopicharan Swarnakar (both from the goldsmith community), Bishwambhar Karmakar, Panchanan Karmakar, Hiralal Karmakar, Kartickcharan Karmakar (all from the blacksmith caste). There were also Brahman like Nafarchandra Bandujye (Banerjee), and Kayasthas like Netyalal Dutta, who used to sign their name in English, indicating their higher status among these artists.[138]

By the end of the nineteenth century, however, these Battala copper engraving and woodcut artists were facing the same problem as the Kalighat Patuas. The invasion of the market by cheap oleographs and lithographs ousted these traditional artists. Writing in 1888, Trailokyanath Mukherji commented on their plight: 'Some years ago there was a demand for woodcuts among the vernacular newspapers, but at the present moment it is on the decline and the industry is not flourishing.'[139] The annual almanacs published from Battala and title pages of books and ornamental letters and designs for advertisements were the only remaining avenues left for these people for earning a living.

VIII

The folk culture of nineteenth-century Calcutta was built upon the heritage of rural folk literature and art which the Bengali villager brought with him into Calcutta. Both the oral and the visual traditions assimilated much from the new urban milieu, and exercised a selective instinct in adding and discarding what were felt to be necessary to develop a distinct urban folk culture. In this attempt, the artist—the kobi-walas, the panchali singers, the jatra performers, the clay modellers of idols, the sawngs, the Kalighat Patuas—drew upon a fund of imagery which belonged not to the mind of a single poet, but to the collective mind the traditional memories, the topical sights, the religious beliefs, the occupational lifestyles, the attitudes and feelings shaped by both the past and the present, the villages and the city.

Within a span of a hundred years or so, the ups and downs in the history of this urban folk culture reflected the rapid twists and turns that were taking place in the social and cultural life of the city in the course of its urbanization. Although the main forms of the urban folk culture more or less persisted all through the period under review, each had its prime at certain points of time, allowing us to divide its history into four broad phases. The eighteenth century saw the first flush in the shape of the doggerels and popular rhymes about contemporary events and characters. The second phase from the late eighteenth century till the thirties of the nineteenth was dominated by the kobi-walas. Their departure from the scene was followed by the arrival of the jatra-walas and the panchali singers, who were the leading characters during the third phase in the mid-nineteenth century. This was also the period of the flourishing of the visual arts. The last quarter of the nineteenth century was marked by a furious struggle for existence' by these folk artistes in an unequal competition with new cultural artefacts (often of superior technology) and in the face of an organized campaign launched against them by the educated Bengali gentry. While some of their art forms (like the jatra and the Kalighat pats) declined, a few others (like the sawngs) managed to linger on somehow to sing their swan-song at the turn of the twentieth century. The interaction between the urban folk culture and the newly emerging cultural tastes and forms of the educated Bengali society during this last quarter of the nineteenth century will be taken up in the next chapter, where the consequences of such interaction for the urban folk artistes will be discussed.

At the beginning (the eighteenth and early nineteenth centuries), some of the folk forms like the kobi songs and contests could still express a certain form of communal solidarity—a legacy of the feudal rural society. We find the first generation of the urban landlords and nouveau riche like Raja Nabakrishna Deb, or the family of Ramdulal Dey, patronizing the kobis, many among whom came from the lower orders. The latter's performance accommodated the tastes of these patrons, as well as the requirements of the members of their own orders, in continuance of the tradition set by people like Maharaja Krishnachandra of Nabadwip. But a cleavage was already developing in this communal solidarity, as evident from the spatial dispersal of the lower orders in the growing metropolis. The Muslims, for instance, were getting alienated from the cultural mainstream of the Bengali lower orders, being forced to shift to a distant part of the city. Participation in common social festivities, which was possible in a rural society because of its close range, ceased to be a part of their cultural norms. The rise of the dobhashi diction reinforced the cleavage.

Even within the Bengali Hindu society, the spread of Western education and the emergence of a new generation of educated gentry led to the development of different cultural tastes among the upper classes. From the middle of the nineteenth century, the cultural homogeneity that had marked the earlier Bengali society in Calcutta began to snap. The kobi-walas lost their old patrons with the departure of Nabakrishna, Rupchand Mullick, Ramdulal and the other tycoons of the first generation. The folk tradition, however, continued in the street songs and other expressions like the sawngs and the Kalighat pats, which could still depend on steady support from the lower orders.

The oral tradition of the kobi-walas also faced a challenge from the spread of the written word through printed books which began to be published on a mass scale from the early nineteenth century. It introduced a new hierarchy into the culture of the common people. The dominant position of those who retained traditional cultural norms in their memory, who could extemporize (in the kobir ladai or poetical contests) or, when the memory failed, substitute with impromptu innovations (as in the doggerels about the eighteenth-century rich citizens) was threatened by those who had the greatest command over the skills of literacy. Fascination among the unlettered masses for recitations from printed Battala books by the more fortunate literate or half-literate members of their community was not confined only to the Muslims (described earlier in Section v). A newspaper from the mid-nineteenth century reports: 'There is not a peddling shopkeeper who does not spend the hours between his midday meal and his resumption of business in the afternoon in reading something or other, and very few even among the unlettered peasantry are willing to forgo the pleasure of hearing popular books read to them by some fortunate neighbour who understands better than they the mystic symbols of the alphabet.'[140]

By the middle of the nineteenth century, the kobi-walas had almost disappeared. When Ishwar Chandra Gupta began collecting their songs in 1854, he found that they were never written down, and he had to depend on the memory of those who had heard them half a century ago.[141] The discontinuity in the oral tradition which drove the kobi songs into oblivion was partly caused by the proliferation of the Battala books, which offered, in a popular style, the neophyte readers and listeners the same stories of Vidya and Sundar, Radha and Krishna, Shiva and Parvati that were sung by the kobis.

The challenge from the printing press appeared to prompt the innovations that we find from the mid-nineteenth century in the jatras, the panchalis and other audiovisual media, with emphasis on spectacles and elaborate music. The khemta dances and the swinging lilts of Gopal Udey's jatras, the introduction of comic sawngs in Dashu Ray's panchalis, the caricatures through sawngs, both live and clay models, the Kalighat pats—all these helped to attract the audience, as well as to represent more directly the surrounding reality.

It will be observed that humour in all its forms began to be the prevailing mood from the mid-nineteenth century in urban folk expressions. Watching the popularity of Gopal Udey's jatra, an educated Bengali critic ruefully commented: 'In the past, the tragic muse was predominant in Bengal. From these jatras, it seems now that humour has taken its place.'[142]

The boundless world of humorous forms and manifestations offered by nineteenth-century Calcutta folk culture had a special significance for the lower orders. Humour operated at two levels— as their avenue of escape from an increasingly depressing environment, and as a weapon of protest against the humiliations faced by them every day in their professions.

The humorous expressions were subtle as well as robust, bitter as well as bawdy, satirical and iconoclastic. Sometimes they were irreverent and even outrageous. While wordplay with the points of jokes took the place of sword play in the contests of the earlier kobi performances, the street songs and panchalis of later days showed up the follies and frailties of the rich and the privileged. They were a comic exposure of what was condemned in public by the bhadralok, but sneakingly practised by them in private. The ribaldry and sexual jokes in the jatras were often an expression of the common man's desire to thumb his nose at the self-restraints and sanctimonious platitudes of the religious elders of society. Their hypocrisy became special butts of ridicule in the sawngs and Kalighat pats.

As will be seen in the next chapter, the Bengali bhadralok took particular exception to the sexual and scatological suggestions in these folk expressions of Calcutta's lower orders. Double entendres and bawdy quips, which were highly popular with the listeners during kheuds and exchanges of repartees at the kobi performances, were incorporated by the mid-nineteenth century jatrawalas like Gopal Udey and Keshey Dhoba in their compositions and performances. The khemta dances in these jatras with their erotic overtones and stress on suggestive movements of the hips, as well as the dialogues between Sundar and Malini with their overtly incestuous innuendos, evoked amusement among an audience who were not looking surreptitiously for lewd kicks, but were used, thanks to a virile folk tradition, to watching such spectacles and listening to such bawdy exchanges as innocent entertainment. Uninhibited references to certain parts of the human body and jokes about certain bodily functions were a part of the traditional folk culture. In a rare, honest attempt to understand the perceptions of the lower orders, a Bengali bhadralok critic towards the end of the nineteenth century admitted:

In the obscene verses which we today discover in Vidyapati and Chandidas [the fifteenth century Vaishnavite poets who sang about the loves of Radha and Krishna], the common folks of the past could not perceive any obscenity . . . The accepted themes of the poems of those days were all related to the description of the human body and its functions. The ideal of love in those days was based on physical attraction . . .[143]

In a similar rare moment of dispassionate analysis of the differing concepts of obscenity in the West and India, an English observer of India commented: ' European analogy and distinction somehow fail. It is sometimes difficult here to draw the distinction between obscenity and warmth.'[144]

For the man in the street in nineteenth-century Calcutta, it was not therefore a prurient desire for pornography (as we understand it today) that led him to bandy proverbs like 'Pond nangta mathaey ghomta' (a naked arse, and a veil over the head) to ridicule people who had no riches and yet pretended to be wealthy; or to invent a scabrous term for the Scottish Highlander soldier who used to march in the Calcutta streets in his traditional frock which left his legs bare: *Nangta Gora* (the naked white man); or to laugh at his own subservience to his employer in the proverb: 'Kartar padey gandho nai' (There's no stink when the boss farts).[145]

It was in a similar vein of innocent ribaldry that they laughed at Malini in Gopal Udey's *Vidya-Sundar* jatra, when she was trying to seduce the young, handsome Vidya:

Esho Jadu amar badi,
Tomae dibo bhalobasha
Je ashaye eshechho jadu,
Purno habey mono asha.
Amar nam Hire Malini
Korey randi naiko shami.[146]

(Come home, my darling; I'll give you love. You'll get, my darling, what you've come here for. My name is Hira, the flower seller. I've been a widow since my childhood. I don't have any husband.)

For the contemporary audience, Malini's overtures echoed the immediacy of the familiar soliciting heard in the red-light areas of Calcutta in those days. There was also a double entendre implied in the use of the word *randi,* which meant in contemporary parlance both a widow and a prostitute.

The bawdy was also an important weapon in the hands of the lower orders to transfer the sanctimonious to the material sphere, in a gesture of protest against the ethereal world built up by the Sanskrit-educated Bengali Brahman priests and their followers. The goddess Kali thus became a hoyden romping around, stamping on the chest of the all-powerful Shiva, in the jhumur songs (mentioned in Section III of this chapter). Shiva himself came to be depicted as a gawkish hemp addict, forgetful of his slipping loincloth, in a Kalighat *pat,* quite uninhibitedly showing his genitals.[147] The illustration by a sawng in the early nineteenth century of the proverb, 'Pathey hagey ar chokh rangaye' (He shits in public, and yet threatens others), which landed him in the dock (see Section VI), was an earthy expression of such folk humour.

Visual displays like the sawngs or the dances in the streets were a sort of celebration of the world of the senses, a playful expression of primitive sensuality. The occasions on which they were organized—like the Durga puja or Chadak festivities—had a permissive atmosphere about them. They were like the medieval carnivals in Europe—'small scattered islands of time, strictly limited by the dates of feasts, when the world was permitted to emerge from the official routine but exclusively under the camouflage of laughter'.[148] The saturnalia of feasts and songs, seen in the streets of nineteenth-century Calcutta on such occasions, was again a vestige of the feudal rural society.

We hear of a ritual called the 'kada-kheud', or singing of obscene songs while wallowing in muck and slime on Navami, the third day of the Durga puja festivities. At the court of Maharaja Krishnachandra of Nabadwip, this ritual was observed after the sacrifice of a buffalo, when everyone from the king and his sons on the one hand to the commoner on the other had to participate in slanging matches of bawdy rhymes.[149]

Such scatological liberties used to be a safety valve for the conflicts within the existing socioeconomic system, symbolic expressions of the underlying and normally suppressed discontent of the lower orders against the upper. The latter permitted them as a mechanism by which the pressures engendered by social conflicts could be vented without allowing the conflict to become fully overt and threaten the upper orders. But the permissive—and often participatory—attitude of the feudal gentry (which continued to some extent till the late eighteenth century in Calcutta society) was no longer prevalent in the nineteenth century when a new generation of the English-educated bhadralok community was increasingly resenting such displays of saturnalian abandon.

For the city's poorer classes, however, such comical expressions remained an essential part of their social lifestyle. Being at the bottom of the socioeconomic structure, and constantly exposed to oppressions and humiliations, the only weapon they had was verbal ridicule. We must hasten to add, however, that they still lacked any sense of political or trade union organization. Their perception of the causes of their misery was often confused, as evident from the social ambiguity often found in their songs. The male-dominated values, expressed in rhymes and songs, directed against women (as in Dashu Ray's panchalis or common proverbs) secured the subordination of girls and women within their own community itself.

In spite of such divisions and fragmentations among the lower orders (genderwise, Hindu–Muslim), in a general sense humour strengthened the in-group feeling among them as distinct from the out-group—the educated and privileged bhadralok. It is precisely because of this that humorous expressions came to occupy a predominant place in their cultural output.

According to William H. Martineau, humour has a twofold purpose—lubricant and abrasive. It is like oil to keep the machinery of interaction operating freely and smoothly. It can also constitute a measure of sand in interpersonal friction.[150]

By the middle of the nineteenth century, in Calcutta the lubricating role of humour to keep society running smoothly and contain the dormant antagonisms had exhausted itself. The abrasive role was increasingly taking over, to express the conflicts. 'The particular adaptability of humor as a conflict weapon lies in the fact that humor may conceal malice, and allow expression of aggression without the consequences of other overt behavior'.[151] In Calcutta folk culture this conflict function was expressed largely by means of irony, satire, sarcasm, caricature, parody, burlesque, etc.

The expressions arose largely from the need to laugh at things which the lower orders were unable to face and fight. The badinage at the foppish babus in the street songs, or the caricatures of the rich gentry in the sawngs, afforded them a temporary feeling of superiority. These made their adversaries appear ludicrous in their own eyes. An exaggerated account (like the description of the educated woman's habits) was therefore necessary to make the target vulnerable.

When not directly ridiculing topical social events and characters, the urban folk culture offered entertainment through humorous depiction of deities or burlesques of romantic stories (as in Dashu Ray's panchalis or Gopal Udey's *Vidya-Sundar* jatra). The listeners and audience at such performances looked for diversion rather than instruction. It was again another avenue of escape from the squalor of slum life at one level. But at another level, the demystification and deromanticizing of the titular deities and romantic heroes and heroines was a sort of counterculture—an alternative to the bhadralok's genteel culture.

Both in its treatment of mythological and religious subjects and in its dealing with contemporary topics, Calcutta folk culture strove to defeat through laughter the gloomy seriousness that surrounded its economic existence, and to transform it into a gay carnival. In the process, these folk artistes created a second world, a second life outside the official world of the respectable, educated classes. They created an irreverent and iconoclastic world in opposition to the bhadralok world of strict rituals and stiff restraints. Their language became a reservoir in which various speech patterns and words, earthy expressions and muscular gestures, which were scrupulously banished from bhadralok conversation, could freely accumulate. Their linguistic eclecticism again stood in sharp contrast with the literary style of the Bengali bhadraloks, who were trying at that time to shape a language heavily dependent on Sanskrit, and a style borrowed from European literature. Commenting on these literary experiments of the educated Bengalis, a contemporary English journal hit the nail on the head:

> The style of writing, which is now becoming more and more fashionable, is so similar to the more modern Sanscrit that, so far as popular readers are concerned, it might as well be wholly Sanscrit. The English reader may form an idea of it by thinking of the semi-Latin style of Johnson. 'Good' Bengali now-a-day means Johnsonianism run to seed.[152]

We should, however, admit at the same time that the folk culture of nineteenth-century Calcutta was, curiously enough, indifferent to the peasant rebellions and other movements of protest that were taking place in the countryside around the city and in other parts of Bengal. This was a reflection of the general lack of sense of identification among the urban lower orders with their rural counterparts (see Section XVI of Chapter 2). Titu Meer's rebellion in 1831 inspired a few songs in the rural areas—some in admiration, some disparaging. But the Calcutta lower orders seemed to remain unaffected as far as their literary responses are concerned.

The most turbulent event of the century was the 1857 Sepoy rebellion. A popular song current in Calcutta in those days appeared to be more favourably disposed towards the Scottish Highlander troops who arrived in Calcutta on their way to suppress the rebellion:

Bilat thekey ela gora
Mathar par kurti para,
Padobharey kanpe dhara,
Highlandnibasi tara.
Tantia Tapir man
Habey ebey kharboman,
Sukhey Dilli dakhal hobey
Nana Shaheb podbey dhara.[153]

(White men have come from Europe. They wear jackets over their heads. The earth is trembling under their footsteps. They are Highlanders. Tantia Topi's pride will be humbled now. Delhi will be reconquered with ease. Nana Sahib will get caught.)

It seems that the Calcutta lower orders were influenced by the panic that gripped the city's Bengali gentry, who bent over backwards to demonstrate their loyalty to the British in those days.[154]

Surprisingly, however, the heroine of the Sepoy rebellion, Rani Lakshmibai of Jhansi, was a popular figure with the Kalighat *pat* painters. In several *pats* she appears as a courageous woman on horseback. Did these folk artists identify her with their favourite goddess, Durga, the killer of the demon Asura? Or was she just taken up as another interesting contemporary figure worthy of being illustrated, like the wrestler Shyamakanta, or the head priest of Tarakeshwar?

It appears that the indifference to popular revolts evident in Calcutta folk culture stemmed from the same desire to avoid confrontation, which made them seek solace in humour which could 'allow expression of aggression without the consequences of the other overt behaviour'. Like many other expressions of humour, the secret source of the comicality of Calcutta folk culture was not joy, but sorrow and helplessness in an oppressive environment.

Unwilling and unable to adopt the manners of the educated bhadraloks who were cooped up in their schools and colleges and Town Hall meetings, the folk artistes created a culture of their own, a culture of the streets and the marketplace, where expressions ranged from boisterous carnival pageants to satirical take-offs on the high and priggish manners of the white folks and their black flunkeys. Like the Canterbury pilgrims whom Mark Twain's Connecticut Yankee encountered, they were 'pious, happy, merry and full of unconscious coarseness and innocent indecencies'.[155] Unconsciously perhaps, they left behind for posterity a fantastic record of an alternative lifestyle and culture, a humorous expression of their own point of view on contemporary life and manners, religion and society, which was extra-ecclesiastical and non-official, and offered as it were the other side of the picture.

ELITE CULTURE
IN NINETEENTH-CENTURY CALCUTTA

In their cultural tastes and habits, the late eighteenth- and early nineteenth-century Bengali gentry of Calcutta were eclectic. A variety of traditional norms coexisted with the new customs acquired from the Western traders and administrators.

The traditional cultural habits that continued to prevail among the nouveau riche in Calcutta were a melange of Mughal court culture, Sanskrit classics and rural folk culture. The norms of Mughal aristocracy still lingered on to some extent in the eighteenth century and were often taken as a model by the aspiring and ambitious nouveau riche of Calcutta, many among whom (like Maharaja Nabakrishna Deb) started their careers as subordinate employees in the Mughal administration. North Indian classical songs and dances—which were patronized by the Muslim nawabs—thus became a part of the entertainments of the Bengali elite. With the decline of the Mughal empire, musicians and dancers began to leave the north Indian cities and migrate to the new capital, Calcutta, in search of patrons. From the end of the eighteenth till the beginning of the nineteenth century, Calcutta welcomed several dancers from north India, who were patronized by the Bengali rich. Their nautch performances were exotic sources of entertainment for the city's European residents who were invited to the Bengali homes in the Black Town. They were enamoured of the voice of Nikki, Ushuran and a host of other north Indian singers who were employed to sing during puja festivities and wedding ceremonies by people like Raja Sukhomoy Ray (grandson of Noku Dhar, the banian), Rammohan Roy, Dwarkanath Tagore and the rich gold merchant Mullick families. Their favourite was Nikki, who used to be compared with Angelica Catalani (1780–1849) and Elizabeth Billington (1768–1818), the two sopranos (the former Italian, the latter German) who fascinated European listeners in the late eighteenth–early nineteenth centuries.[1] A contemporary Bengali newspaper informs us that, impressed by Nikki's voice and dance, a rich Bengali employed her on a monthly salary of Rs 1,000.[2]

The rich Bengali families of this period also patronized the more respectable Bengalis who cultivated north Indian classical music. Ramnidhi Gupta, more popularly known as Nidhu-Babu (1741–1839), was inspired by an early eighteenth-century Muslim musician of Lucknow, Ghulam Nabi (popularly known as Shori Mian), to compose *tappa* songs in Bengali. Nidhu-Babu's patrons included urban zamindars like Rajkrishna Deb and Gopimohan Deb of the Shobhabazar Raj family, dewans like Shibchandra Mukhopadhyay of Baghbazar (who set up the famous hemp smoking club: see Chapter 3, Section 1), and rich merchants like the Mullicks of Pathuriaghata. Kalidas Chattopadhyay (known as Kali Mirza) (1750–1820) learnt north Indian classical music in Lucknow, Banaras and Delhi. When he came back to Bengal, he got employed as a musician at the court of prince Pratapchand of Bardhaman from where he shifted to Calcutta to become the pro-tégé of Gopimohan Tagore, son of Darpanarayan Tagore, the well-known dewan of Mr Wheeler (see Chapter 2, Section 1).

It was this Bengali elite which for their literary inspiration turned to the ancient Sanskrit classics and got them translated into Bengali. But at the same time they retained their old associations with the rural folk culture. The kobi-walas of the late eighteenth–

early nineteenth centuries were patronized by these landlords,
dewans and banians. Thus, we hear about Maharaja Nabakrishna
Deb: 'Haru [Horu] Thakur and Nitai Das [Boiragi], well known as
composers of songs, were his protégés, and he introduced into
Calcutta Society and popularized the nautch which Englishmen
believe to be the chief of our public amusements.'³ We also learn
about Ramlochan Tagore (1754–1807)—son of Nilmoni Tagore (a
brother of Darpanarayan Tagore)—who in his Jorasanko house
organized classical musical soirees by north Indian *ustads* as well
as kobi performances by Ram Basu, Horu Thakur and others.⁴

They were also keen on adopting some of the Western styles
in their domestic decorations. Although these grandees of the parvenu class did not adopt the European dress, and wanted to show
themselves off in the style of the old Mughal courtiers, the new
houses which they built in the Black Town were 'adorned with
verandahs and Corinthian pillars' and they went around the town
in 'very handsome carriages often built in England'. Harimohan
Tagore (Gopimohan's brother) decorated his garden house in the
style 'of a European villa'.⁵

Thus, we find a peculiar amalgam of tastes in the cultural
behaviour of the members of this first generation of the Bengali
elite at the turn of the nineteenth century. By the middle of the
century, however, the elements of the folk cultural tradition were
to be consciously eschewed. The Bengali bhadralok culture that
was to take shape came to be dominated by the north Indian classical tradition in music, a literature depending for its language on
heavy borrowing from Sanskrit and for its content on both Sanskrit
classics and Western romantic literature from which it derived
ideas. In the visual arts, the painting style that came into vogue
and remained predominant till the end of the century was imbibed
from the model set by the British Royal Academy of Arts during
the Victorian era.

I

Ramnidhi Gupta, or Nidhu-Babu, could be described as the best elite representative of the era of eclecticism. Although he lived long and died an octogenarian, his main output spanned the last quarter of the eighteenth century and the first decade of the nineteenth. With a thorough training in north Indian classical music and familiarity with the contemporary colloquial Bengali, Nidhu-Babu introduced a new style in Bengali music. The coexistence of aristocratic tastes (Nidhu-Babu came from a well-to-do family, learnt Sanskrit, Persian and English, earned a comfortable income from a government job in Bihar for eighteen years before coming back to settle down in Calcutta—all these privileges enabling him to adopt the lifestyle of a fashionable and respectable Bengali in Calcutta) with the easy expressive style of traditional Bengali folk songs (unburdened with Sanskritized *tatsama* words) made his *tappas* the rage of the Calcutta music connoisseurs at the turn of the nineteenth century. His songs on love—without the usual veneer of the Radha–Krishna motif—were straightforward expressions of romantic yearnings of individual souls:

> Bhalobashibe boley bhalobashiney
> Amar shabhab ei toma boi ar janiney
> Bidhumukhey madhur hashi dekhtey badobhalobashi
> Tai tomarey dekhtey ashi dekha ditey ashiney. [6]

> (I don't love you expecting you to love me. It's my nature—
> I don't know anyone except you. I love to watch that sweet
> smile on your beautiful face. So I come to see you—not to
> be seen.)

Although there was no reflection of the tumultuous events of the period (the invasion of Calcutta by Siraj ud-Daulah, the 1757 Battle of Plassey that changed the political situation of the province radically, the disastrous famine of 1769, the political changes in the administration) through which he passed, in his songs he sometimes expressed with poignancy the feelings of a community facing the threat of being swamped by a foreign culture, like the following lines:

Nanan desher nanan bhasha
Bina swadeshio bhasha purey ki asha?
Kato nodi sarobar
Kiba phal chatokir
Dharajal biney kobhu ghuchey ki trisha?[7]

(Different countries have different languages. But can we be happy without our own language? There are numerous rivers and tanks. But can the swallow slake its thirst without the running waters from the rains?)

We should hasten to add, however, that Nidhu-Babu's songs remained confined to the parlours of the rich Bengali households, as evident from the term used for his songs—'Baithaki-gan' (songs meant for gatherings in the sitting rooms of the respectable, rich people). His uncle, Kului Chandra Sen, who was a protégé of Maharaja Nabakrishna Deb of Shobhabazar, introduced a variety of musical instruments and classical tunes in the akhdai—a style of song popular among the rich gentry. Nidhu-Babu enriched the style further, and in 1804 set up two amateur akhdai groups with the sons of the rich—one in the Baghbazar–Shobhabazar area, and the other in Pathuriaghata. This encouraged the rich Bengali families of the Black Town to cultivate the akhdai and set up their respective groups, leading among whom were the Tagores of Pathuriaghata, the Sinhas of Jorasanko, the Basaks of Garanhata, the sons of Kalishankar Ghosh of Shobhabazar (who served American Captains). Competitions used to take place among these groups, and we hear that the Baghbazar group, led by Nidhu-Babu, usually emerged victorious.[8]

But the akhdai, because of its elaborate and ornamental musical acrobatics, never became popular with the masses and remained a sort of parlour musical genre. By 1823–24 it had almost ceased to be a style even among the rich households. Nidhu-Babu's pupil, Mohanchand Basu, encouraged by the popularity of the verbal duels in the kobi performances, introduced a similar style of exchanges of repartees in the akhdai, simplified the musical scales, and came up with the innovation known as the half-akhdai at about this time.[9] It seems that the impact of the urban culture of the lower orders on the upper strata of society was strong enough to make the latter adopt the former's style to some extent. In 1868, describing a half-akhdai troupe in the Black Town, Kaliprasanna Sinha said that most of the singers were 'blacksmiths, peasants, washermen, petty oilmen'.[10]

Another contemporary of Nidhu-Babu's—Rupchand Das (1814–?), popularly known as Rupchand Pakshi—was a favourite of the fashionable members of the Calcutta gentry. Associated with the famous hemp smoking club at Baghbazar, Rupchand indulged in a flamboyant lifestyle, more in tune with the foppish dandies of the idle-rich community than the serious-minded connoisseurs of classical music of the houses of the Debs, Tagores and Sinhas. As a leading member of the Baghbazar hemp smoking club, where members were allotted the names of birds (see Chapter 3, Section I), Rupchand went around the town in a carriage designed as a bird's cage. But Rupchand's songs, composed in a light satirical vein, reflected more directly the social reality around him than Nidhu-Babu's *tappas*. One such song deals humorously with the traditional theme of Krishna's infidelity and Radha's complaints, in a jargon of Bengali mixed with English words which was fashionable among sections of the educated Bengalis in the early nineteenth century:

Amarey fraud korey
Kalia damn tui kothae geli?
I am for you very sorry,
Golden body bolo kali . . .
Shuno rey Shyam
Torey boli
Poor kiriture milk-girl
Tader breastey marili shel
Nonsense, tor naiko liel,
Breach of contract korli.[11]

(Where have you disappeared, damned Kalia, after having deceived me? My golden-hued body has turned black . . .

Listen to me, Shyam. You've hurt deeply the poor creatures, the milk-girls. Nonsense! Don't you have any sense?
You're guilty of a breach of contract.)

Rupchand also wrote songs on the dowry system, on the evils
of female education, on the municipal innovations in Calcutta, and
other topical subjects.

The nautches, Nidhu-Babu's *tappas* and Rupchand Pakshi's
humorous songs, which marked the elite culture of Calcutta in the
early nineteenth century, were contemporaneous with the kobi
songs of Ram Basu, Horu Thakur and Bhola Moira, who were the
city's folk poets. While the latter could, with ease, move to and fro
between the courtyards of the palatial buildings of the Black Town
on the one hand and the streets and marketplaces of the poor folks
on the other, the former led a sheltered existence in the parlours
of the rich, their occasional attempts to borrow the style of the
urban folk culture notwithstanding. Even their flippancies (like
Rupchand's songs) catered to the half-baked English-knowing
parvenu, and never became a part of the cultural heritage of the
city's lower orders.

By the middle of the nineteenth century, both the *akhdai–tappa*
culture of the rich and the kobi songs of the poor had retreated
from the scene. A new generation of English-educated, thorough-
bred bhadraloks had emerged, who were determined to do away
with the eclecticism and cultural anarchy of the past and mould a
distinct elite culture of their own.

II

The development of Bengali bhadralok culture went hand in hand
with the marginalization of Calcutta folk culture. Both the processes were fostered by the British colonial powers. They operated
at several levels—missionary, educational and administrative.

The emergence of distinct cultural forms that could be representative of the newly acquired economic status and educational
position of the bhadralok could be possible only by eliminating the

various forms of popular culture which used to be a part of the common literary and musical heritage of the Bengalis. The urge to demarcate themselves from the lower orders prompted the new bhadralok converts to Western education to dissociate themselves from the urban folk culture.

In making them shed the habit of sharing certain traditional common cultural tastes with the lower orders (like listening to the kobi performances, or panchalis, or watching khemta dances, or participating in community festivities like the kheud contests), the Christian missionaries played an important role. They were the first, in the early nineteenth century, to start a systematic attack on the popular art forms which were still being patronized by the Bengali aristocracy. The Rev. James Ward, chaplain of St John's in Calcutta (who, incidentally, baptized William Makepeace Thackeray in this church in 1811), expressed his reactions to the cultural entertainments of the respectable Bengali classes when, in 1806, he was invited to attend the Durga puja festivities in the house of Raja Rajkrishna Deb (Nabakrishna Deb's son) at Shobhabazar. During the early hours of the programme, the Rev. James Ward appeared to be impressed with 'groups of Hindoo dancing women, finely dressed, singing and dancing with sleepy steps, surrounded with Europeans, who were sitting on chairs and couches . . . ' These were apparently the north Indian baijis whose nautches were the rage of the town in those days. But the clergyman was soon to get what he thought was the shock of his life! Another type of entertainment in an entirely different atmosphere soon followed the nautches.

> Before two o'clock the place was cleared of the dancing girls and of all the Europeans except ourselves, and almost all the lights were extinguished except in front of the goddess,—when the doors of the area were thrown open, and a vast crowd of natives rushed in, almost treading one upon another, among whom were the vocal singers, having on long caps like sugar loaves. The area might be about fifty cubits long and thirty wide. When the crowd had sat down, they were so wedged together as to present

the appearance of a solid pavement of heads, a small space only being left immediately before the image for the motions of the singers, who all stood up. Four sets of singers were present on this occasion, the first consisting of Brahman [Horu Thakur], the next of bankers [Bhavanando], the next of Vaishnavas [Netai] and the last of weavers [Lakshmikanta Biswas], who entertained their guests with filthy songs and danced in indecent attitudes before the goddess, holding up their hands, turning round, putting forward their heads towards the image, every now and then bending their bodies and almost tearing their throats with their vociferations.

Having listened to the famous kobi-walas of those days—Horu Thakur, Bhabani Bene, Netai Bairagi and Lakshmi the weaver—the English clergyman was thoroughly scandalized:

The whole scene produced on my mind sensations of the greatest horror. The dress of the singers, their indecent gestures, the abominable nature of the songs, especially (khayur), the horrid din of their miserable drum, the lateness of the hour, the darkness of the place, with the reflection that I was standing in an idol temple . . . All those actions which a sense of decency keeps out of the most in decent English songs, are here detailed, sung and laughed at, without the least sense of shame.

The Rev. Mr Ward then suggested the punishment: 'A poor ballad singer in England would be sent to the house of correction, and flogged, for performing the meritorious [sic] actions of these wretched idolators.'[12]

The Mr Ward and his English contemporaries in India, who shared his contempt for Bengali folk culture, did not remain content with expressing their disapproval, but set their hands to the task of creating a new Bengali language, just as Macaulay sought to create a new 'class of persons, Indian in blood and colour, but English in taste, in opinions, in morals and in intellect'.

Already, William Carey (1761–1834), who learnt Bengali and became its teacher in the newly established Fort William College, had translated the New Testament into Bengali, and had compiled a collection of dialogues in colloquial Bengali. Carey's contention was that the Bengali language was entirely derived from Sanskrit and hence, the language and its literature should develop along the Sanskritic tradition. Referring to the Sanskrit terms and words in use among the learned Bengali upper class, Carey envisaged a future 'when literature and science become objects of pursuit in Bengal, and works on various subjects are published . . . many of these terms which are now only known to the learned will become more common, and perhaps the language will be enriched by many words borrowed from other tongues.'[13]

Carey and his missionary colleagues in Serampore, who brought out a newspaper in Bengali, *Samachar Darpan*, introduced a style which came to be ridiculed as 'missionary Bengali' because of its artificial and stilted manner. Nevertheless, the attempt to give an unsettled dialect a regular and permanent form provided a model to the educated Bengalis who over the next several generations, through a series of experiments, succeeded in fashioning a language for modern written literature. They stuck to Carey's original aim of stressing the Sanskritized words and eliminating the raw, earthy *tadbhaba* terms that dominated spoken Bengali among the masses. The intention of popularizing the Bible through 'missionary Bengali' was explained some years later by an English writer: 'while the ideas of the Bible elevate the notions of the readers, the language of it accustoms them to the disuse of a vulgar patois'.[14]

The campaign against the 'vulgar patois', and the popular Bengali literature composed in it, had to be a long drawn out one. The hold of the latter was strong enough to influence the first generation of Bengali printers and publishers to bring out from the newly established printing presses in Battala in Calcutta a large number of popular versions of both religious and secular books written in simple Bengali. The attitude of the English educationists comes out clearly in the following comments by E. S. Montagu,

Secretary of the Calcutta School Book Society, in a memorandum he prepared in 1820 on the indigenous works which had appeared from the native presses since 1805: 'the greater part [of the publications] as might be anticipated are principally connected with the prevalent system of idolatry, and not a few . . . are distinguished only by their flagrant violation of common decency; and are too gross to admit of their contents being disclosed before the public eye.' The works in question were popular versions of *Vidya-Sundar* and similar romantic stories as well as mythological tales 'extracted from the Pooranus (which are far below the Vedas and Durshuns, or philosophical portion of Hindoo writings)'.[15]

Mr Montagu succeeded in converting 'one Pundit' to his viewpoint. 'Subsequently he in conjunction with some other natives, concurred among themselves to express their dissatisfaction with such works'.[16]

The above incident shows how the indigenous elite (including the traditionalist pundits) were gradually being 'reformed' and taught to denounce the popular cultural forms. The Sanskrit-knowing Bengali pundits had always looked down upon the popular arts.[17] The joint efforts of the Christian missionaries and the Sanskrit pundits now helped to reinforce the contemptuous attitude among the newly educated Bengali elite. One can well imagine the effect on these sections of the Bengali community of the following disparaging comments on the *Ramayana* of Krittibas (the Bengali version which was popular among the masses) which appeared in an English journal:

It is written . . . in a jingling word-catching metre, that is far inferior, even in harmony, to the sonorous march of the Sanskrit couplets [of the original] . . . If we could imagine Milton's *Paradise Lost* translated into rhyme by a half-educated cobbler, with some of 'Watt's Divine Songs' stuck in various places, and the whole recited to a jury of critical tailors, we should gain some idea of the Bengali *Ramayana*. Its stories are more offensive, its language more indecent, than in the original; and the whole is tainted with an air of downright vulgarity, which would have made Valmiki turn aside in disgust . . . [18]

It did not escape the notice of these Englishmen that folk culture appeared in audiovisual forms of songs and dances. Referring to the themes of the kobi songs, the panchalis and jatra performances, one contemporary English journal commented:

> They must utterly pollute the imagination of those by whom they are read, or to whom they are recited by strolling singers . . . they are frequently both sung and acted by the companies of singers or dancers, who travel through the length and breadth of the land, and who reap a rich harvest at melas, and on the occasion of heathen festivals . . . [19]

It was not only the contents of the songs of Bengali folk culture that shocked the sentiments of the Victorian Englishman, but it was the gay abandon, the playful musical laughter, the uninhibited prancing and rhythmic surprises which were a part of folk singing and dancing that disturbed him most. Even patient efforts by the Christian missionaries could not curb these elemental instincts of the converts from the Bengali lower orders. An early English missionary gives an amusing account of a service at a chapel near Calcutta where the new Bengali converts were singing a hymn (in Bengali):

> They have not the least idea either of harmony or melody; noise is what they best understand, and he that sings the loudest is considered to sing the best . . . 'Sing softly, brother,' I said to one of the principal members. 'Sing softly,' he replied, '[. . .] Did you ever hear us sing the praises of our Hindoo gods, how we threw our heads backward and with all our might shouted out the praises'. [20]

To their chagrin the English found that even the establishment of the printing press had failed to turn public attention away from the themes of folk culture, as evident from the bitter complaint

made by the missionary newspaper *Friend of India* when it found
from the list of about 500 Bengali printed books compiled by Rev.
James Long in 1855 that 'many of the works contained in the list
are wretched trash intended to suit the depraved taste of the country and accumulate the libidinous passions'.[21]

The persistent popularity of the romance of Vidya–Sundar and
the mythological stories narrated in the down-to-earth style (found
to be 'wretched trash' by the missionaries) led to a twofold
approach on the part of the English. First, they took recourse to
the law to stop the publication of such works on the ground of
'obscenity'. Following the recommendation made by the Rev. James
Long, an Act was passed in January 1856 to prevent the public sale
or exposure of obscene books and pictures.[22] The official concept
of obscenity, it should be remembered, was fashioned by the norms
prevailing in contemporary English society, where Shakespeare's
complete works were edited for family use ('bowdlerized', after the
name of Dr Thomas Bowdler, who in 1818 carried out the task of
purging Shakespeare's plays of obscenities), where Evangelism as
a rising religious thought was providing a ripe breeding ground
for bigotry, where the so-called 'polite society' avoided the theatre,
where the word 'legs' when describing a table could not be uttered
in the presence of ladies—and all these social norms maintained
as a facade behind which Victorian high society indulged in all
the proclivities censured by the official code as long as it did not
break the eleventh commandment: 'Thou shalt not be found out.'[23]
Following the establishment of a Society for the Suppression of
Vice in 1809 in England, one observer, Sydney Smith, dubbed it a
society for suppressing the vices of persons whose incomes did not
exceed £500 a year.[24] In Calcutta also the provisions of the anti-
obscenity legislation were directed primarily against expressions
of popular culture, like the cheap chapbooks of Battala. According
to the Rev. James Long, the police arrested three Battala publishers
for having brought out a similar chapbook (probably Dasharathi
Ray's panchali) which was priced at four annas. The Supreme
Court imposed a fine of Rs 1,300 on them.[25] Again in 1873, the

Bengali periodical *Madhyastha* (Falgun, 1280 Bengali era) reported the arrest of several booksellers from Battala for selling editions of Bharatchandra's *Vidya-Sundar*. They were released on bail and raised subscriptions to fight their case.

Incidentally, the English authorities in Calcutta appeared to set the lead for their bosses in London. The latter followed them in 1857 by passing an Obscene Publications Act.

The second part of the English policy was marked by putting pressure on the educated Bengalis to turn their attention to their own native tongue and purge it of all 'impurities' and 'obscenities'. By the mid-nineteenth century, the English educationists and administrators had realized that Macaulay's dream of creating a new class of Bengalis completely denuded of their linguistic and cultural roots was not possible, given the strong hold of tradition and culture. The second-best course for the educated Bengalis therefore was to shape and write in a Bengali that would be in tune with their new tastes and requirements. The course was charted by John Drinkwater Bethune (who was the Chairman of the Education Council and played a leading role in the spread of English education among women in Bengal) in an address delivered to Bengali students in 1849 at a prize-giving ceremony at Krishnagar College:

> It is impossible that the English language can ever become familiar to the millions of inhabitants of Bengal; but, if you do your duty, the English language will become to Bengal what, long ago, Greek and Latin were to England; and the ideas which you gain through English learning will, by your help, gradually be diffused by a vernacular literature through the masses of your countrymen.[26]

At about the same time, in a letter written to a young Bengali he recommended what role the educated Bengalis should play in improving their literature: 'By all that I can learn of your vernacular literature, its best specimens are defiled by grossness and indecency. An ambitious young poet could not desire a finer field for exertion than in taking the lead in giving his countrymen in their own language a taste for something higher and better. He might even do good service by translation.'[27]

Instructed thus to look down upon their existing literature as 'defiled by grossness and indecency', the new generation of educated Bengalis began to dissociate themselves from the folk cultural heritage and its popular urban expressions. Public displays like jatra performances became targets of attack. Writing in 1853, one bhadralok described deridingly how 'hundreds may be seen keeping up whole nights to see and listen' to jatras which treat of the 'amours of the lascivious Krishna and of the beautiful shepherdess Radha, or of the liaison of Bidya [Vidya] and Sundar.' He then warns: 'It is needless to say that topics like these exercise a baneful influence on the moral character of the auditors. They harden the heart and sear the conscience . . . The gesticulations with which many of the characters in these yatras [jatras] recite their several parts are vulgar and laughable.'[28] Another bhadralok, writing in 1855, complains that almost all the plots of jatras are taken from the 'amours of Krishna and of Radhika', and asks: 'Who that has any pretension to a polite taste will not be disgusted with the vulgar mode of dancing with which our play commences; and who that has any moral tendency will not censure the immorality of the pieces that are performed?'[29]

We should remember that this was the period of the popularity of the jatras of Gopal Udey (see Section III of Chapter 3), who had simplified the language of the songs and introduced a spirit of topicality in the staging of the jatras, extending its appeal to the populace. Watching them the educated bhadralok felt that the Hindu divinities were being defiled and looked degraded in the eyes of the English. The typical bhadralok attitude towards these jatras was expressed by Michael Madhusudan Dutta (1824–73) in a short poem introducing his first play *Sharmishtha* (written in 1858), where, describing the contemporary Bengali theatre scene, he regretted the absence of such great poets as Valmiki, Vyasa, Kalidasa and Bhavabhuti, and complained:

Aleek kunatya rangey
Maje lok radhé bangey
Nirokhia prane nahi soy.

(People are obsessed with the false, bad theatre in West
Bengal. Watching this my soul cannot bear it anymore.)

A product of Hindu College, Madhusudan became a Christian,
and started his poetical career by composing poems in English.
But at Bethune's advice (quoted above) he turned to Bengali. It is
significant that Madhusudan chose the highly Sanskritized Bengali
and the ancient Sanskrit classics and their heroes and heroines
for his poems and plays. His treatment of these stories and characters (even when he sought to reverse the conventional pattern
by counterposing Ravana as a hero against Rama in his epic
poem *Meghnadbadha-kavya*) tended to elevate and deify them in
grandiose narrative form—in opposition to the trend of domestication and deglamorization found in the contemporary folk literature around these same events and characters.

The bhadralok's need to go back to the ancient Sanskrit classics
and the heroic stories of past history sprang from a newborn sense
of shame about contemporary Bengali folk culture that was fostered by persistent English denigration of the songs of the jatras,
the panchalis and other popular forms. While the minority among
the educated tried to cope with the inferiority complex by deserting
traditional Hinduism and embracing Christianity or forming the
Brahmo Sabha, the majority (who were shaping from the mid-
nineteenth century their own distinct socio-religious norms—see
Section XII of Chapter 2) sought an alternative counterculture in
accordance with the compromise which they had worked out in
their religious and social behaviour between the traditional norms
of Hindu society and the requirements of a modern society. Thus,
a literature developed which had the 'sophistication of Sanskrit and
secularity of English to suit the growing new social class'.

III

Among the new forms which were introduced under Western influence in bhadralok literature, the most important was Bengali prose, particularly the novel and drama.

Serious prose in Bengali had traversed a tortuous path, starting from the cumbrous style of Rammohan Roy's religious pamphlets (which he wrote to counter the Hindu conservatives), through the ponderous and heavily Sanskritized Bengali articles and translations of Ishwar Chandra Vidyasagar (1820–91) and Akshay Kumar Dutta (1820–86), to the elegant and smooth style of Bankim Chandra Chattopadhyay (1838–93), the leading novelist in nineteenth-century Bengal.

The chaste Bengali of Bankim became a flexible vehicle in his hands for communicating a wide range of ideas—pride in the past Hindu traditions in his historical novels; views and attitudes of the bhadralok on contemporary issues like love in marriage, the Kulin system and position of widows in his social novels; opinions on Hinduism and Utilitarianism in his theoretical articles; and raillery at the expense of the Anglicized babus in his satirical pieces. As for his opinions, although Bankim sometimes showed an awareness of the plight of the rural poor and the need for some sort of egalitarianism, he never challenged the supremacy of British rule in India and expressed his firm belief in the country's prosperity under the British. The code of love as found in English romantic novels of the period, marked by a display of male gallantry and heroism, female subservience and the ultimate triumph of fidelity and domestic bliss, was presented in Bankim's novels in the framework of the traditional Brahmanical value system. In his social novels, however, the characters were delineated in a realistic vein, which made them authentic representatives of the contemporary Bengali society.

Bankim had an intimate knowledge of Bengali folk culture, and his apprenticeship in literary writing began under the guidance of Ishwar Chandra Gupta, the Bengali poet who had preserved for us the old kobi songs and who himself was also at one time a kobi-wala (see Sections II and III—Chapter 3). But the education he received at Hugli College prevailed over his earlier fascination for the poetic style of the kobi-walas and Ishwar Gupta (known as 'Gupta-kobi'). Although he retained a regard for the preceptor of his youthful days and recognized him as a 'genuine Bengali poet', his education in the English system of moral values made him read 'obscenity' in Ishwar Gupta's poems.[30]

The educated bhadralok's contempt for the popular jatras of the period came out clearly in an article on the jatra in *Bangadarshan*, the magazine edited by Bankim Chandra Chattopadhyay. The desecration of the Hindu deities by the lower orders was the main objection:

> Anyone from among the illiterate fishermen, boatmen, potters, blacksmiths, who can rhyme thinks that he has composed a song; singing it, the jatra performer thinks that he has sung a song; listening to it the audience think that they have heard a song. But there is nothing in these songs except rhyming . . . Thanks to the present type of jatras, Krishna and Radha look like 'goalas' [milkmen]; in the past, the qualities of a good poet made them appear as divinities.[31]

The bhadralok's cultural alternative to the folk jatra was the modern theatre. We have already noticed how students of Hindu College were encouraged to stage the plays of Shakespeare and other dramatists. Later in 1831, Prasanna Kumar Tagore established the 'Hindoo Theatre' in his garden house near Calcutta, where an English version of the Sanskrit play *Uttararamacharita* was staged. The first Bengali play to be staged in the style of the European theatre was most probably the ever-popular *Vidya-Sundar* in 1835 by a rich Bengali, Nabin Chandra Basu, at his palatial building in north Calcutta. He employed women for the roles of Vidya, Malini and other female characters, and shifted the scenes from one spot to another—with the audience also moving along with the scenes—in the vast complex of the building. Another sprawling mansion in north Calcutta—the ancestral house of the Tagores at

Jorasanko—also became the centre of theatrical activities in the 1860s. By then, Bengali theatrical performances had become a fairly regular affair. A play on polygamy, *Kulin-kulasarbaswa* by Ramnarayan Tarkaratna, a Sanskrit scholar, was staged in March 1857. This was followed by the staging of Bengali translations of Sanskrit plays like *Shakuntala* and *Benisamhar*—the former in the house of Ashutosh Dey (the son of Ramdulal Dey), and the latter in the house of Kaliprasanna Sinha (who got the *Mahabharata* translated into Bengali and wrote *Hutom Penchar Naksha*), grandson of Shantiram Sinha who was a rich dewan in Calcutta in the late eighteenth century.

A permanent stage was built by the brothers Raja Pratapchandra and Raja Ishwar Chandra Sinha of Paikpara, at their garden house in Belgachhia in the northern suburbs of Calcutta, where in 1858 was staged *Ratnabali*—a Bengali adaptation of a Sanskrit play of Sriharsha Dev's by Ramnarayan Tarkaratna. The Belgachhia Natya-shala, as it came to be known, helped turn the attention of the poet Michael Madhusudan Dutta to the theatre, and he wrote his first play *Sharmishtha*, which, with a theme from the Sanskrit classics and written in Sanskritized Bengali, did away with some of the conventions of the old Sanskrit plays, and introduced the formalities of the European stage.

It will be observed that the bulk of the Bengali plays staged from the 1850s to the 1870s in Calcutta were adaptations of Sanskrit plays or about events and characters from the ancient classics.[32] As one modern critic has said: 'The plays themselves were Sanskrit originals translated into Bengali but theatrically they had to be clothed in robes borrowed second-hand from the English theatre.'[33]

The bhadralok attempts to delve into the ancient classics for churning out Bengali plays in the English theatrical style was encouraged by the contemporary English authorities who by then had given up Macaulay's plan of Anglicizing the educated Bengalis, and were trying instead to 'modernize' them. The Rev. James Long, in a letter to the Government of Bengal in 1859, wrote appreciatively about the theatrical experiments going on in Calcutta then: 'A taste for Dramatic Exhibitions has lately revived among the educated Hindus, who find that translations of the Ancient Hindu Dramas are better suited to Oriental taste than translations from the English plays'.³⁴ For Long and his colleagues in his profession as well as in the administration, the heroic spectacles of the Sanskrit classics and the sonorous movements of the high-flown chaste Bengali dialogues appeared safer than the jatras of Gopal Udey where the songs and gestures often cut too close to the bones in their down-to-earth approach.

It will also be noticed that these Bengali plays were invariably staged in the mansions of the rich dewans, banians and landlords, like the garden house of the Paikpara rajas, the house of Ashutosh Dey, the palatial premises of the Tagores of Pathuriaghata and Jorasanko. The audience of these plays came from the respectable gentry of the city, who were either given invitation cards, or bought tickets to see the performances. Sometimes the host-organizers made a careful distinction between the ranks of the invitees, as evident from the following description of a performance in the house of Ashutosh Dey: 'When the invited gentlemen were entering the courtyard of the theatre after showing their tickets, one person kept a watch on their dresses, and directed them accordingly, shouting: "Sir, Front Seat! Sir, Side Seat!" '³⁵

Quite clearly, both the style of the performances and the character of the audience were different from the milieu of the jatras. A contemporary account of the performance of *Vikramorbashi* at the Bidyotsahini Theatre in the mansion of Kaliprasanna Sinha in November 1857 is quite revealing:

The native gentry of Calcutta and the Suburbs, representing the intelligence, taste, good sense, fashion and respectability of Hindu society, were all present in gorgeous winter garments . . . The stage was most beautifully decorated and the theatre room was as nobly adorned as cultivated taste could dictate or enlightened fashion could lead to. No delicate consideration of economy was ever thought of, and the result was most magnificent and gratifying. The marble painting on the frontispiece of the stage was as neat as elegant, and the stone pictures of Bharata and Kalidas, though mostly imaginary, were executed with so much nicety and taste that one was involuntarily reminded of the classic days of Grecian sculpture and painting, casting into form gods and goddesses of heavenly birth . . .[36]

Another contemporary critic describes the period costume of the actors in *Sharmishtha* as staged in the Belgachhia villa on 3 September 1859:

The period of the drama transports us back to Indian society as it was two thousand years ago, and we are glad to state that the scenic arrangements and the accoutrements of the Corps dramatique pictured forth with a marvellous accuracy the Indian life, habitudes and usages of that distant age . . . The court was splendidly represented, the courtiers observing a fidelity of manner and bearing which those who accuse our countrymen of deficiency in either ought to have witnessed to disabuse themselves of their erroneous ideas . . .[37]

Contrast this with the description of a jatra on *Sitar Banabas* (Sita's days of exile in the forests), as observed by a bhadralok critic: 'Some men, with Mughal turbans around their heads, Albert watch chains [after the fashion set by Prince Albert] hanging down their necks, and specs over their noses, were talking like High Court lawyers . . . Whether the queen, or the female sweeper—they wore the same dress'.[38] It is quite obvious that for the performers as well as the audience of such jatras, what was important was not the 'marvellous accuracy' in delineating a past age, but a simplistic interpretation of the mythological story in familiar terms. Suggestions of a distant past or heavenly grandeur were conveyed through 'marble painting' and 'stone pictures' and 'fidelity of manner and bearing' in the bhadralok theatre, in accordance with the tastes of the respectable Bengali society where 'no delicate consideration of economy was ever thought of'. But the poor jatra-walas, who did not have such resources, sought to project the impression of the past and grandeur through symbols which for them had associations of a distant world of affluence—the Mughal turbans, Albert chains and specs.

What Michael Madhusudan Dutta said about his own plays expressed the impulses working among the bhadraloks behind their theatrical experiments: 'remember that I am writing for that portion of my countrymen who think as I think, whose minds have been more or less imbued with Western ideas and modes of thinking.'[39]

By the end of the nineteenth century, 'that portion' of his countrymen for whom Madhusudan wrote had succeeded in shaking off the influence of the jatras and in living up to the expectations of their English mentors. Writing in 1883, a bhadralok appreciatively described the changed habits of his community:

> The amusements of a Bengali Babu are more or less anglicized. Instead of the traditional Jattras . . . he has gradually imbibed a taste for theatrical performances; and native musical instruments are superseded by European flutes, concertinas and harmoniums, organs and piano-fortes. This is a decided improvement on the old antiquated system, demonstrating the gradual growth of a refined taste.[40]

IV

The novel and the theatre were new cultural forms introduced in mid-nineteenth-century Bengali literature. The traditional form of lyrical verses also underwent a transformation in the hands of the educated bhadralok, both in style and content. Here again, the impact of English education and the tendency to draw upon the reservoir of Sanskrit classics and heroic tales of past history combined to create a new Bengali poetry.

All through the first half of the nineteenth century, the poet who captured the imagination of the respectable Bengali literati was Ishwar Chandra Gupta (1812–59). Known as a *swabhab-kobi* (one born with poetic gifts), Ishwar Gupta could be considered the last representative of the eclectic culture that marked the late-eighteenth–early-nineteenth-century period in Calcutta. Sort of a child prodigy, he was reputed to have composed his first verses when he was three years old and was confined to bed as a sick child in his uncle's house in Calcutta. Tired of being stung by mosquitoes and pestered by flies in his bed, he wrote:

Retey masha, dine machhi
Ei niye Kolkame achhi.
(Mosquitos at night, and flies in the daytime.
With these I live in Calcutta.)

Born in a middle-class landed family of the Vaidya caste (traditional medical practitioners), Ishwar Gupta during his youth in Calcutta used to compose poems for kobi-walas who were still around in the city in those early decades of the nineteenth-century. He inherited the tradition of impromptu compositions and the sarcastic vein which marked the kobi songs. His verses on the surrounding Calcutta society and life were noted for their satirical wit. They ranged from cracks at the habits of the Anglicized babus to merry rhymes in praise of his favourite dishes, from digs at Queen Victoria and her loyal Bengali subjects to waggish glee at the expense of the leaders of the 1857 Sepoy rebellion. He shared the conservative distrust of reforms, the misogynist's suspicion of educated women, and the moral insensitivity to distant rebellions which so often marked the street songs of nineteenth-century Calcutta (see Chapter 3, Section IV). The following lines addressed to Queen Victoria mock at the subservience of the Indians:

You are a generous mother,
And we are your tame cattle.
We haven't even learnt to raise our horns,
We'll only eat oil-cake, straw and grass.
We only hope the white boss
Doesn't file a suit
And break our pots and pans.
We'll be quite happy only with the husk,
A blow will make us give up the ghost![41]

In his use of the colloquial Bengali of Calcutta and in his preference for contemporary urban topics in his compositions, he
came closer to the moods and sentiments of Calcutta's lower
orders. Thus, in one of his poems he looks at the rising market
prices through the eyes of the man in the street:

Shudhu chal boley noy   drobyo samuday
Bikatechhey shab agnimoolyey.
Dar bedechhey char gun   bidhata bigun,
Khabar drobye diley agun jeley.
. . .

Shuney jinisher dar   gaye ashey jawr
Chhutey jai ghar badi pheley.

(Why speak of rice? Everything's selling dear. Prices have
gone up fourfold. The merciless God has set fire to all
food . . . I get allergic whenever I hear the prices. Feel like
leaving my home and everything.)[42]

Ishwar Gupta was the last link between the vibrant, raw, earthy
tradition of Bengali folk poetry and the sedate, chaste mood
of the new poetry that came to be shaped by the English-educated
bhadraloks. One of the first among the latter was Rangalal
Bandyopadhyay (1827–87), who in his early days was inspired by
Ishwar Gupta, but later broke away to compose his *Padmini-
Upakhyan*—a verse-narrative in the grand, heroic style about a
Rajput queen who died on the funeral pyre of her husband when
he fell fighting a Muslim king. This again reflected the newborn
ambition among the educated literati to dig up characters from
ancient Indian history and myths and portray them in the style of
the Greek epics, to which these new converts to Western culture
had just been introduced by their English teachers.

This heroic verse in Bengali received a stimulus in the hands
of Madhusudan Dutta. To quote his biographer: 'no one in Bengal
was as well-versed as he [Madhusudan] in various languages and
was able to project in his mother tongue the ideals of the poetry of
Homer, Virgil, Dante, Ovid and others'.[43]

Madhusudan's major contribution was the introduction of blank verse in Bengali poetry. Till then, the Bengali folk versions of the *Mahabharata* and the *Ramayana* and the various types of poetry prevalent in the literary scene, as well as the verses which were being composed by Rangalal and other newly educated Bengalis, were primarily written in the 'payar', 'tripadi' or 'choupadi' metres. The first consisted of a pair of rhyming lines, each containing 14 letters, while the last two were three-footed and four-footed metres respectively. The blank verse freed the poet from the obligation to confine his thoughts or imagery within the bounds of a fixed measure.

Tilottamasambhab-kavya—the verse narrative where Madhusudan introduced blank verse (he had used it earlier in the dialogues of his play *Padmavati*)—was published in 1860. It was about the mythological story of the creation of Tilottama, a paragon of beauty, by the gods, to seduce and ultimately destroy the demon brothers, Sunda and Upasunda, who had taken over their heavenly abode. Contemporary critics discovered the influence of a variety of poets, ranging from the Greek epic poets and Kalidasa to the English Romantic poets, in the style of its composition. Echoes of Keats' *Hyperion* were found in the following lines with which the poem begins (as translated into English by Madhusudan himself):

Dhabala by name, a peak
On Himalaya's kingly brow
Swelling high into the heavens,
Ever robed in virgin snow;
And endued with soul divine.
Vast and moveless like the Lord
Siva, mightiest of the gods. [44]

In some parts, images and metaphors were reminiscent of Kalidasa's *Kumarsambhava,* while Tilottama sometimes reminded the readers of Eve in Milton's *Paradise Lost.*

Members of the Calcutta Bengali elite hailed *Tilottamasambhab-kavya* immediately on its publication. A contemporary Bengali intellectual, Rajendralal Mitra, who was to earn fame later as an archaeologist, admitted that 'the ideas are no doubt borrowed, and Keats and Shelley and Kalidasa and Milton have been largely, very largely, put in requisition', but welcomed the poem as 'the first and a most successful attempt to break through the jingling monotony of the "payar", and as a poem the best we have in the language'.[45]

Among the city's old-time aristocrats, Jatindramohan Tagore of the Pathuriaghata raj family (who was one of the patrons of the poet), on receiving the manuscript of the poem autographed by Madhusudan, wrote to him:

> I feel sure that my descendants . . . will . . . be proud to think that the manuscript in the author's autograph of the first blank-verse Epic in the language is in their posses-sion, and they will honour their ancestor the more, that he was fortunate enough to be considered worthy of such an invaluable present by the poet himself.[46]

The need for blank verse to express the new thoughts and feelings was recognized even by the traditionalist Sanskrit scholars. One such 'pundit', Dwarkanath Vidyabhushan, who was a teacher in Sanskrit College, wrote in his journal *Somaprakash*:

> Payar, Tripadi, Choupadi and verses of these types are all rhymed. They are not fit for treating any profound subject. Because of the morals in the country, or the habits of the people, our people are fond of the erotic. Payar and similar metres are fit for such erotic verses. For serious profound compositions, compound words and well-articulated let-ters are necessary. . . Now is the time for profound com-positions . . . Michael Madhusudan Dutta's efforts are therefore timely . . . [47]

The switchover from the rhyming couplets or quadruplets with simple, *tadbhaba* words, to blank verse with compound, sonorous Sanskrit words, was a reflection of the change in the readership of Bengali poetry. The 'payar' or 'choupadi' was suitable for reading out verses from the epics like the *Mahabharata* and the *Ramayana*,

as in the folk form of kathakata or in reciting verses as in the panchali. This was necessary for the vast audience of the unlettered
poor, among whom these traditional folk forms were popular. Such
recitations, by their very nature, were public performances.

But the educated readership could dispense with such public
display. The reading habit was becoming a private norm, to be pursued in seclusion in one's home, or among close acquaintances
(as the first generation of educated Bengali bhadraloks did by
reading out Madhusudan's poems or Bankim's novels to their still-
unlettered wives to educate them in the new ideas).

Heroic tales, mythological stories, romances of classical heroes
and heroines could thus be treated in blank verse in an unrestricted
flow of gorgeous images and ornamental metaphors in a vein of
sublimity. The appeal of such epic poems was directed at those who
had been trained in Hindu College, Hugli College and other such
institutions, who had read Shakespeare, Milton, Shelley and Keats
on the one hand, and inherited the love for Sanskrit classics from
their forefathers on the other.

The superiority of the written word over the oral, of printed literature over verbal folklore, was sought to be established by
the educated bhadraloks through the widespread publicity they
gave to the publications of poets like Madhusudan, Rangalal
Bandyopadhyay, Nabinchandra Sen, Hemchandra Bandyopadhyay
and the poets who followed them towards the end of the nineteenth century. It was simultaneously accompanied by a campaign
against the oral literature of urban folk culture. The public recitations of kathakata used to provide the unlettered populace with a
chance to listen to the epics explained in popular language. This is
how an English journal describes a typical kathakata performance
in mid-nineteenth-century Calcutta:

> like the Hellenes in the time of Homer, these rhapsodists,
> or kothaks [talkers], as they are popularly styled, take their
> stand upon any vacant space, and erect a small awning,
> under which they ensconce themselves, and there, for
> hours together, they pour forth or rather scream, the

Ramayun, Mahabharat, and other popular poems. The multitudes, who crowd to these exhibitions, instead of crushing round the speaker, as the boors do in England, sit down in a circle, and give themselves wholly up to the inspiration of the rhapsodist. The latter never attempts anything like mannerism, . . . but allows his words, as it were, to pour out of his mouth, without attention to anything save the obvious meaning . . . [48]

But the bhadralok society of Calcutta appeared to be increasingly intolerant of such public performances. Their objection was again directed at the mode of presentation of mythological subjects in these kathakatas. The frank description of the erotic, or the note of facetiousness in narrating the exploits of the divinities in colloquial Bengali which marked kathakata (as well as jatra and panchali performances), stood in sharp contrast to the sombre tone and etherealization of the romantic love affairs of the gods and goddesses in the heroic verses of Madhusudan or Hemchandra. A bhadralok commentator in a contemporary Bengali journal complained: 'During the narration of Krishna's carousals [known as Krishna-Leela], it is not possible for an uneducated young woman to remain unexcited when listening to episodes like Raas [Krishna's dance with the milkmaids] or Krishna's escape with the clothes of the milkmaids.' He then proposed: 'since it [kathakata] has become a source of so much evil, it is not advisable for bhadraloks to encourage it. Those who allow their ladies to go to kathakata performances should be careful'. He then recommended the course to be followed by the bhadraloks with regard to their womenfolk:

If, during kathakata performances, women stay home and are provided with opportunities to listen to good instructions, discussions on good books and to train themselves in artistic occupations, their religious sense will improve and their souls will become pure and they will be suited to domestic work.[49]

Just as the theatre was held up by the bhadraloks as superior to jatra, the Bengali novels and poems written by the respectable and educated members of the gentry were projected as morally preferable to the kathakatas and panchalis. Ever since 1855, when the Rev. James Long in his 'Descriptive Catalogue' described the panchalis as 'filthy and polluting', the educated Bengali bhadralok sought to dissociate himself from these songs. Having ousted it from male society in his milieu, he sought to eliminate it from his 'andarmahal' (the women's quarters) where it still lingered in the last quarter of the nineteenth century. Writing in 1883, a bhadralok complained: 'The Panchali (with female actresses only) which is given for the amusement of the females . . . is sometimes much too obscene and immoral to be tolerated in a zenana having any pretension to gentility . . . Much is yet to be done to develop among the females a taste for purer amusements, better adapted to a healthy state of society.'⁵⁰ Mahendranath Dutta informs us that by the end of the century, 'meye-panchali', or panchali performances by women only as described above, had disappeared since 'educated people began to denounce them'.⁵¹

With the staging of Bengali plays in the style of European theatre and the publication of the novels of Bankim and the poetry of Madhusudan, the Bengali bhadralok society appeared to have come up with its distinct cultural forms fit for the contemporary era and its own class, which could be projected as an alternative to the folk culture of Calcutta's lower orders. Critics who all these years had been inveighing against the 'obscenities' in popular Bengali culture and urging the educated Bengalis to banish them from their society now found reasons for rejoicing in the fruits their patient and persistent efforts had borne. Reviewing Bankim's *Bishabriksha* (1873), an English journal commented:

It is indeed a pleasure to see a healthy tone of morals, fast winning its way into Bengali fiction. Time was when the Vidyasundara or Jivantara or some other equally indecent tale in verse would have been thought good reading by many grown up natives . . . In these happily-stern days, everything savouring of indecency or childishness, anything that does not either afford innocent amusement

or add a little to our stock of knowledge, is sure to be
put down with a high hand, consigned by the unanimous
verdict of critics to the dead store of the pastry cook
or the boxmaker; while works of real merit, like the
Durgeshanandini [a historical novel by Bankim]. . . are read
and re-read until there are others to supply their place . . [52]

The 'high hand' of the authorities came down even on the
bhadraloks whenever anyone among them dared to depart from
the 'healthy tone of morals' as fixed by the Victorian elders and
wrote anything that could be interpreted as 'savouring of indecency
or childishness'. This was the fate of a particular literary genre that
flourished in the latter half of the nineteenth century for a brief
period—the Bengali farces and belles-lettres—which, unlike the
historical and social novels and heroic verses, took up contemporary social topics, and treated them in a satirical vein in colloquial
urban Bengali which brought them nearer the urban folk culture
to some extent.

V

The nimble-witted drollery and gusto and the colloquial simple
Bengali of the masses, which the eighteenth-century Bengali gentry shared with the kobi-walas and jatra-walas, was banished from
the serious literature of the respectable and educated classes by the
end of the nineteenth century. The collective gaiety of a panchali
session was cut down to individual compositions to be printed in
magazines and books for the consumption of the educated few. As
literary pursuits acquired a private chamber character, the language
itself of the new compositions created a private, defensive world
insulated from the general stream of life in the streets.

But the surrounding reality of the streets and the marketplace,
their sounds and colours, the carnival and the billingsgate of the
lower orders occasionally did intrude into the literary works of the
bhadraloks. While the chastened moral sense of the educated
bhadraloks rebelled against the language and the cultural forms of
the marketplace, the latter also fascinated the bhadralok's primal

instincts. It offered him a glimpse of the spontaneous gaiety which his own class had lost. The ad-khemta measure of Gopal Udey's songs which could aptly express a certain mood, the turn of a phrase in Bhola Moira's couplet which could sting a target to the quick, were artistic simplicities which shone in contrast with the Madhusudans and Rangalals perspiring with their far-fetched metaphors and conceits.

Many among the first generation of English-educated Bengali intellectuals who had heard in their childhood the kobi-gans, pan- chalis and jatras could not quite erase these memories, and almost all through their lives suffered from a sort of dichotomy, torn between a fascination for the old street culture of the lower orders and an obligation to write in accordance with the fixed norms of the new respectable society. A typical example is Bankim Chandra Chattopadhyay, who fulminated against the use of facetious rustic terms and the vulgar tongue in jatras, and yet took time off to make use of them in the dialogues he introduced in his belles-lettres like *Kamalakanter Daptar* or satirical pieces like *Muchiram Guder Jee- bancharit* (a take-off on the habits and lifestyle of an upstart babu) or essays in a lighter vein collected in his *Loka-Rahasya*. The con- tradiction, the struggle between the two inclinations, comes out clearly in Bankim's essay on Ishwar Chandra Gupta, where he says: 'observing the aesthetically new Bengali literature of the modern times ascendant on the path of progress, I sometimes wonder it may be beautiful, but perhaps it is alien, not ours. Why don't I find the pure Bengali feelings in the pure Bengali style?' He then picks up Ishwar Gupta as the representative of the latter and adds: 'Madhusudan, Hemchandra, Nabinchandra, Rabindranath are the poets of the educated Bengalis—Ishwar Gupta is the poet of Bengal.' He then hastens to add, as if to assure himself as well as members of his elite community:

Pure Bengali poets are not born nowadays—there's no chance of their birth—there's no need of their birth . . . We do not want to leave *Britra-samhar* [by Hemchandra Bandyopadhyay] and opt for *Poush-parban* [by Ishwar

Gupta]. Yet, for a Bengali, the delight we find in *Poush-Parban* [festivities towards the close of the Bengali month of Poush] cannot be found in *Britra-samhar* [the story of the Hindu god Indra's destruction of the demon, Britra]. The pleasure in [eating] the cakes [made during *Poush-parban* festivities] is missing in the nectar of Sachi's [Indra's wife] red lips . . . [53]

The blank verse, the heroic measures, the Sanskritized words were ill-equipped to express the thoughts and feelings roused by the stark reality of daily experiences. Many among the nineteenth-century Bengali poets, novelists and playwrights therefore sought to let their hair down and relax in farces and belles-lettres. The extravagant wit of Calcutta's street Rabelaises and the beefy paint strokes of the Kalighat Daumiers influenced their literary forays into the contemporary social reality.

The fact that the same individuals who were fond of the bombast and tinsel when writing in the Bengali–Sanskrit style about classical subjects and Aryan heroes and heroines in their plays, poems and novels could switch over to the easy, colloquial style when treating contemporary social themes in a satirical vein, indicated their creative versatility as well as a certain cultural ambivalence. The sinewy vigour of the language of the plebeians fascinated them, and yet there was the constant fear of being stigmatized by their social peers and the English mentors for adopting such a language.

The new Bengali stage offered these versatile talents an outlet for their adventures in the language of the populace. Plays and farces on contemporary social topics afforded them a chance to make use of colloquial speech in the dialogues put in the mouths of certain type characters. Michael Madhusudan Dutta, who institutionalized the heroic style of poetic compositions and became a model for the succeeding generations (till Rabindranath appeared on the scene to change the style), wrote two farces—*Ekei ki Baley Sabhyata?* (Is This Called Civility?) and *Budo Shalikher Ghadey Ron* (The Dotard Sports a Plume)—between 1859 and 1860.

The typical earthy expressions in the racy dialogues of the characters, and the downright portrayal of reality, made both the plays
powerful pieces of satire. The first caricatured the ways of the
Anglicized young Bengalis of Calcutta, who in the name of rebellion against orthodoxy, indulged in orgies of drunkenness and
whoremongering. The second lampooned the Hindu orthodox
leaders who, under cover of religious piety, exploited the rural poor
and seduced their women.

Farce composition in the hands of the bhadraloks often
became substitutes for the verbal duels of folk culture. The primal
need for excitement, best found in slanging matches between
rivals, was something the bhadralok society could not escape, reformation and education notwithstanding. The witty exchanges in
tarjas, kheuds, songs of the kobi-walas and other folk forms kept
the unlettered masses agog. The bhadralok writers borrowed this
spirit from the culture of the lower orders and gave it a new form.
Farces became the modernized versions of such folk contests
among the bhadraloks. They rolled out, all through the last half of
the nineteenth century, one in reply to another. Jatindramohan
Tagore of Pathuriaghata wrote a piece called *Bujhley Kina* (Do You
Understand?), in retaliation to which Bholanath Mukhopadhyay
came up with another farce—*Kichhu Kichhu Bujhi* (I Understand
a Little), attacking Tagore. The playwright-actor Amritalal Basu tells
us in his memoirs that the Calcutta bhadralok society in those days
waited for one farce to follow another, curious to know which
prominent citizen was being attacked in one farce, and whose turn
was the next in another farce.[54]

But these farces were of a short-term value. The best farces
in the 1860s, after Madhusudan, were produced by a friend and
contemporary of Madhusudan's—Dinabandhu Mitra (1830–73). A
student of Hindu College, Dinabandhu had his apprenticeship in
literature under Ishwar Gupta—an experience which stood him in
good stead later when he chose the weapon of satire to attack the
habits of the rich babus of nineteenth-century Calcutta, the
hypocrisy of the orthodox Hindus, the manners of persons from

different strata of society in plays like *Sadhabar Ekadashi, Biye Pagla Budo* and *Jamai Barik* where, both in dialogues and in the characterization of the heroes and heroines, Dinabandhu resorted to the colloquial Bengali and the humour of the marketplace. One could find echoes of the doggerels and proverbs that were current in the Calcutta streets in the dialogues; of the panchalis of Dashu Ray in the songs that interspersed the dialogues; of the gossips and intrigues that were the staple of Calcutta bhadralok society in the stories of his plays.

Dinabandhu's farces were written in the 1860s. By the beginning of the next decade, the Bengali theatre saw a proliferation of farces. They became a convenient vehicle in the hands of the bhadralok playwrights to take up contemporary events. One such event was the sensational case involving the head priest of the Tarakeshwar temple in 1873, which inspired the Kalighat Patuas to paint innumerable *pats* (see Chapter 3, Section VI). At least nineteen contemporary farces on the incidents have been traced till now.[55] Thus, the farce form became a cultural outlet for the bhadraloks to share certain common concerns with the populace, often in the language of the latter. On some occasions, these farces harked back to the urban folk forms like street doggerels or sawngs. Ardhendu Sekhar Mustafi (1851–1908), a versatile actor of those days, introduced around 1873 pantomime shows on the stage ridiculing the English. These were repartees against similar pantomimes ridiculing the Bengalis which were put up by an Englishman, Dave Carson, on the boards of the Opera House in Calcutta. Ardhendu's take-off on a typical English sahib was accompanied by a funny song in the Hindi–English jargon spoken by the English in India in those days:

Hum barah sahb haey duniamey
None can be compared hamara saht—
. . .
Coat pini pantaloon pini pini more trousers.
Every two years new suits pini
Direct from Chandny Bazar—
Rom-ti-tom-ti-tom . . .[56]

Such comic retorts in the shape of pantomimes, or short farces, we must note, were in the tradition of the early contests between the kobi-walas. Verbal ridicule, or visual denigrations (in street pantomimes like sawngs) were the only weapons which the lower orders had with them to defy adversity. These were borrowed from them, often lock, stock and barrel, with their pungent barbs and bawdy expressions, by the bhadraloks whenever they felt the need to attack their adversaries, or deride a new fashion.

The tendency to fall back on the culture of the marketplace was not confined to the theatre. There was a flow of belles-lettres, picaresque novels, satirical sketches of everyday life in Calcutta with a farcical streak running through them, generally using the language and idiom of the streets. A little over 500 publications of these types, which came out between 1854 and 1899, have been traced by a modern researcher.[57] Printed by the cheap presses at Battala in north Calcutta, many have disappeared without leaving any trace. The social topics which they dealt with were polygamy, widow remarriage, the dowry system, alcoholism, lechery, whore-mongering, religious hypocrisy, Hindu orthodoxy, women's education, and the habits of the babu—the issues that dominated the Kalighat *pats,* the street songs and the sawngs of the latter half of the nineteenth century. Battala books often betrayed the same sentiments, which, however, produce mixed responses today. While we can still laugh with them when they ridicule the aping habits of the Anglicized babu, or the self-conceit of the impostor priest, we feel rather uncomfortable when they use the same barbs against widow remarriage or women's education.

We have to acknowledge at the same time that this particular literary genre of nineteenth-century Calcutta—farces, belles-lettres, picaresque novels, satirical sketches—was the only cultural output of the bhadraloks that came closest to the culture of the city's lower orders.

But curiously enough, the pacesetter in this genre was the scion of a typical Bengali aristocratic family—Kaliprasanna Sinha (1840–70), grandson of the eighteenth-century dewan Shantiram

Sinha. While on the one hand he patronized the translation of the Sanskrit *Mahabharata* into chaste and refined Bengali, on the other hand it was he again who wrote a series of sketches of life and manners in nineteenth-century Calcutta under the pseudonym 'Hutom', in' a Bengali which could be described as peculiar to the Calcutta streets of those days, with its distinctive accent and mode of expression. Described in graphic details, a host of typical characters and events, feasts and festivities pass before the readers' eyes in a rollicking procession. The metaphors are turned upside down, which create a special kind of irony full of shocks and surprises. Here, for instance, is the description of approaching night:

> Prankish boys in the villages sneak behind old temples, dilapidated houses and bushes to catch a glimpse of women at the bathing *ghats* in the early morning. Like them, darkness all this time was waiting inside locked rooms, wells and water jars. Now, at the sounds of bells and conch-shells announcing the approach of evening, he is coming out. The sight of his terrible appearance made the lotus bend her head and close her eyes out of fear and womanly shame. But who's going to hold in leash the flippant flirts? Look at the moon—how she's smiling shamelessly![58]

Or, take this picture of early dawn breaking over Calcutta streets:

> The church clock chimed-tung-tang-dhong, tung-tang-dhong. It's four a.m. The rakes are returning home. The Oriya Brahman sweetmeat makers have started kneading mounds of wheat in their shops. The street lights are no longer that bright. There's a light breeze. The cuckoos have begun to sing from the balconies of the whore-houses . . . One or two groups of women have just come out for a dip in the Ganga. The butchers of Chitpur are carrying bags of mutton. The police sergeants, inspectors and constables and other such enemies of the poor are squeaking back to their posts after having finished their

rounds; everyone has his pocket jingling with coins and packed with rupees . . .⁵⁹

Kaliprasanna's daring innovation seemed to bring a fresh, healthy breeze into the Calcutta bhadralok literary world, suffocating beneath the heavy burden of the stylized theatrical performances of adaptations from Sanskrit plays and the heroic verses of Rangalal and Madhusudan. A contemporary observer who read *Hutom Penchar Naksha* when he was a student describes his feelings: 'We were then very young. His [Kaliprasanna's] language, the fun of his style, bowled us over. We felt that our Bengali language can light fireworks, play with crackers, let loose a spring. We felt that our mother tongue was sportive in every respect.'⁶⁰

No wonder that Kaliprasanna inspired innumerable followers— some imaginative and original, but most mere imitators—who fell back on the colloquial Bengali which they spoke and on the Calcutta street slang to write satires on contemporary events and characters. Kaliprasanna, in the introduction to the second edition of his *Hutom Penchar Naksha* in 1868, informs us that 'the Battala presses have come out with about 200 cheap books in imitation of "Hutom's" sketches'.⁶¹ A modern research scholar lists a number of such farces and satirical sketches covering a variety of contemporary topics ranging from spicy tales of the Calcutta red-light areas to events like a cyclone in 1867, the building of a bridge (Howrah Bridge) over the Hugli river connecting Calcutta with the rest of West Bengal in 1873–74, the scandal over the head priest of the Tarakeshwar temple in 1873–74, and a rumour in Calcutta in 1875 about a fish epidemic.⁶²

The most ubiquitous figure who prances about in the pages of *Hutom* and other such satirical sketches is the babu. He is now carousing with his cronies in bordellos, now holding forth in broken English over drinks, now worshipping before the image of Durga and the next moment sneaking off to taste a dish of beef roast.

The babu in fact had been a perennial butt of ridicule in the farces written by the bhadraloks all through the nineteenth century. The class composition of the babu had changed through the years, but certain characteristics had remained common.

The term babu also had been used liberally—sometimes in a sense of respect (when attached as a prefix to the names of the rich banians, as distinct from the term 'raja' or 'maharaja' used for the richer aristocratic landowners), sometimes in a pejorative sense to describe the parvenu. With the rise of the professional middle class, consisting of government officers, lawyers, school and college teachers, doctors and followers of similar occupations, the term babu came to be used as a Bengali version of the English 'mister' (like Babu Bankim Chandra Chattopadhyay).

In the early nineteenth century, the babu as he appeared in the farces and sketches was the pampered son of a parvenu dewan or banian, who having inherited his father's wealth dissipates it on drinking, whoring and other amusements with a host of syco-phants. The writers make fun of his cowardice, his ignorance and his final downfall. One of the earliest farcical accounts describes the babu's nine habits:

Ghudi, tudi, jash, dan, akhda, bulbuli, munia, gan,
Ashtahe bano bhojan ei nabodha babur lakshan.[63]

(Kite-flying, snapping his fingers to show disregard for everyone, fame, charity, attending musical rehearsals, watching contests of 'bulbuli' birds, looking after pet 'munia' birds, listening to songs, and picnics over eight days—these nine are the signs of a babu.)

The caricature of the early nineteenth-century babu and his habits, as well as that of his wife and mistress, became highly enter-taining satire in the hands of Bhabanicharan Bandyopadhyay (1787–1848) whose three books—*Kolikata Kamalalaya* (1823), *Naba Babu Bilas* (1825) and *Naba Bibi Bilas* (1832)—are a faithful record of the lives and activities of the Calcutta nouveau riche, the intrigues in their homes, the secret rendezvous of their wives and daughters, the customs current in bordellos, the different types of mistresses and sycophants of the babus, etc. Starting his career as

a clerk in the office of an English merchant, Bhabanicharan rose
to be a banian and was therefore well acquainted with the habits
of the social climbers of his class. But unlike most of his colleagues
in the profession, Bhabanicharan had an intellectual bent. He
collaborated with Rammohan Roy in founding and editing the
newspaper *Samvad Kaumudi* in 1821, but left it soon, following
differences with Rammohan on religious and social issues, to start
his own paper *Samachar Chandrika* in 1822. A conservative in his
views, Bhabanicharan led the organization of the orthodox Hindus,
the Dharma Sabha, to campaign against the reforms launched by
Rammohan and his followers. His satires were in fact the humorous counterparts of his serious broadsides against the reformists
in the columns of his newspaper. The sarcastic motive which
necessitated the graphic depiction of the contemporary society
made his books both entertaining and authentic.

When three decades later, Pyarichand Mitra (1814–83), a
Hindu College-educated bhadralok reformer (who played a leading
role in educating Bengali women through his writings), decided
in 1858 to bring out a satirical piece, he again chose the model
set by Bhabanicharan—the Bengali babu, the pampered son of a
parvenu—as the hero of his tale *Alaler Gharer Dulal* (The Spoilt
Child of a Rich Parent).

Pyarichand wrote under a pseudonym—Tekchand Thakur.
While the hero, Motilal, has the same habits as his predecessors
in Bhahanicharan's books, Pyarichand adds new characters who
had emerged in Calcutta during the intervening period—teachers
of English, lawyers and the different categories of touts involved
in any legal proceeding, and the Anglicized sycophants. While
the babu in Bhabanicharan's works reminded readers of decadent
feudal dandies, here we find the babu as a typical representative of
the new era, when the English administration with its paraphernalia is fully entrenched and English education had created new
tastes and habits among the city elite.[64] The language of *Alaler
Gharer Dulal* was the chaste *sadhubhasha* but it was simpler than
Bhabanicharan's or the Bengali that was being written at about the

same time by Ishwar Chandra Vidyasagar and Akshay Kumar Dutta in the magazine *Tattwabodhini Patrika,* which used to be highly Sanskritized. The need for putting dialogues in the mouths of the various characters made Pyarichand use the colloquial style in certain parts of his novel. We are thus given a chance of listening to the dobhashi sort of dialect spoken by a Muslim character— Thak Chacha.

But these attempts by a section of the nineteenth-century Calcutta bhadraloks to write in the language of the populace soon received a setback. There were various pressures from their own community as well as from the colonial authorities. It is significant that though Madhusudan's two farces were written for the Belgachhia Theatre, and were printed at the expenses of the Paikpara rajas who owned the Theatre, they were never staged there. Their fate throws light on the adverse social pressures that operated on Bengali bhadralok writers who dared to depart from the established conventions. After Madhusudan's death, one of his friends gave out the story behind the Belgachhia Theatre's refusal to stage the plays.

> A few of the Young Bengal class, getting scent of the farce *Ekei ki Baley Sabhyata* and feeling that the caricature made in it touched them too closely, raised a hue and cry; and choosing for their leader a gentleman of position and afflu-ence who, they knew, had some influence with the Rajahs [of Paikpara], deputed him to dissuade them from produc-ing the farce on the boards of their Theatre . . . Rajah Issur Chunder Singh was so disgusted at this affair that he resolved not only to give up the other farce [Budo Shalikher Ghadey Ron] too, but to have no more Bengali plays acted at the Belgachia Theatre . . . [When] Michael . . . pestered me with repeated enquiries why the farces were not taken up in earnest by the Belgachia dramatic corps . . . I could only give him an evasive reply saying, that as one farce exposes the faults and failings of Young Bengal and the other those of the old Hindus, and as the Rajahs were

popular with both the classes, they did not wish to offend either class by having them acted in their Theatre.[65]

The frequent tendency on the part of the authors of these farces to hide their real identity under a pseudonym (e.g. Tekchand Thakur for Pyarichand Mitra; 'Hutom' for Kaliprasanna Sinha; 'Bholanath Sharma' for Bholanath Mukhopadhyay who wrote a farce entitled *Aponar Mukh Apuni Dekho;* 'Bhand' for Kedarnath Dutta who wrote *Sachitra Guljar-nagar*—to quote only a few of the authors who were published between 1860 and the late 1870s) indicates the cultural ambivalence of these authors. Fond of writing in the patois of the lower orders, and yet scared of adverse criticism by their social peers, they chose anonymity.

Although Kaliprasanna's *Hutom Penchar Naksha* became highly popular among the Bengali readers of his age, its raw humour, often bordering on the risqué, offended the conservative intellectuals. Bankim, while praising its 'racy vigorous language', complained that it was 'not seldom disfigured by obscenity'.[66] Later essayists and playwrights who sought to follow Kaliprasanna's style often drew Bankim's criticism. Reviewing Sisir Kumar Ghosh's farce on dowry, *Naesho Rupeya,* in 1873, he accused the playwright of 'rustic vulgarity' and of putting 'obscene' words in the mouth of a female character. One of the words which he objected to was 'bhatar'—a term used by Bengali women of villages and the lower orders for 'husband'.[67]

Bankim was not alone in nursing misgivings about the flow of farces, satirical sketches and poems on contemporary society from the Battala presses. Referring to the publication of 'obscene litera-ture and prints', the Christian missionary-edited *Friend of India* urged on the bhadraloks: 'The duty is one especially to be under-taken by educated natives of character, that they may wipe out the reproach so often cast with good reason on their community'.[68]

Soon after, on 20 September 1873, the 'educated natives' gathered at a meeting in the Calcutta Town Hall and established a Society for the Suppression of Public Obscenity. The object of the Society was to 'aid the Government in putting in force the sections of the Penal Code and the Printing Act which were meant to preserve public purity'. Among those who spoke at the meeting were Keshub Chandra Sen, the Brahmo reformer; Kali Charan Banerjee, a Christian professor in Dr Duff's College. Raja Kali Krishna Deb of the Shobhabazar Raj family, who represented the Hindu orthodox group of the city, became president of the new Society, while Keshub Chandra Sen and the Rev. Soorya Coomar (Surya Kumar) Ghose became its secretary. Welcoming its formation as 'an important step in the history of Native progress', the *Friend of India* commented: 'Christians and Brahmos, Mahomedans and Hindoos, united on the ground of a common moral principle to declare that the nascent literature of the country should no longer be allowed to run the risk of becoming polluted and polluting'.[69]

The campaign by the Society and the enactment of the Dramatic Performances Control Act of 1876 (whose provisions were directed not only against political plays, but also against 'obscenity') made many among the bhadralok writers shy away from writing in colloquial Bengali about social topics. The transposition of familiar speech patterns and street patois in printed literature was regarded as obscene not only by the English administrators, but by the leading English-educated bhadraloks. Bankim, offering support and cooperation to the Society for the Suppression of Public Obscenity, wrote:

It would not be an exaggeration to say that obscenity is the national vice of the Bengalis. Those who may consider this to be an exaggeration, should merely think of Bengali jokes, Bengali abuses, the wranglings among Bengali women of the lower orders, and Bengali jatra, kobi contests, panchalis. Listen for a moment to the conversation among the Bengali peasants . . .[70]

Colloquial Bengali therefore crawled back into the semi-basement printing presses in the poor quarters of Battala in north Calcutta, from where it continued to appear in cheap chapbooks (printed on thin paper and priced between six paisa and one anna each) which were either reprints of old mythological stories, popular versions of the Vidya–Sundar romance, or farces by obscure authors which were often sold surreptitiously to escape the law. In respectable circles, the 'Battala books', as they came to be known, were associated with dirty stories, spicy accounts of local scandals and poor print.

By the beginning of the twentieth century, satires and farces had almost disappeared from the market. Amritalal Basu, a nineteenth-century doyen of the Bengali stage, was to regret in the early 1920s that he had been trying for 30 years to procure copies of old Battala chapbooks written in a mixture of prose and poetry, or often composed in verses which were available for a pice or two when he was young. 'They were not like Byron, Browning, Shelley, Swift, Hem [Chandra Bandyopadhyay], Nabin [Chandra Sen], Rabindra [Nath Tagore] or Satyendra [Nath Dutta]. But those books had a language, a flavour, a rhythm of their own'.[71]

Pressures from the conservative bhadraloks and the colonial administration put a halt to the Bengali literati's attempts to take up explosive contemporary topics for treatment in familiar terms. The tendency to reinforce the elite-oriented cultural and social norms prevailed over the fledgling tendency to move nearer the popular literature of the lower orders.

Farces drew the ire of the authorities not only for their exposure of social aberrations in the down-to-earth idiom of the populace, but for their growing propensity towards another explosive direction. From the last quarter of the nineteenth century, there was a growing trend in the Bengali stage for taking up political issues in the form of dramatic farces.

We should mention in this connection that Dinabandhu Mitra, whose farces have been discussed earlier, was also the author of one of the earliest plays of protest in modern Bengali dramatic literature. The play *Nildarpan* (1860) was about the exploitation of Bengali peasants by British indigo planters who forced them to cultivate indigo. A two-year revolt from 1859 to 1860 by the peasants against forced cultivation in the Bengal countryside compelled the government to appoint an Indigo Commission in 1860, which came out with its report the same year denouncing the system of forced cultivation as 'vicious in theory, injurious in practice and radically unsound'.[72] Soon after the publication of the report, Dinabandhu wrote *Nildarpan,* the incidents described there being based on actual events. Dinabandhu was working as an officer in the postal services where among the senior English administrators there were many who were counted as friends by the English indigo planters. Dinabandhu therefore published his play under a pseudonym ('kasyachit pathikasya'—of a certain traveller), got it printed in Dhaka in east Bengal (where it was also staged for the first time), and in his introduction appealed to Lord Canning, then Governor-General (who had earlier suppressed the 1857 Sepoy rebellion), to stop the atrocities of the indigo planters. Its publication stirred a hornets' nest. The Rev. James Long, as a representative of the Christian missionary interests in Bengal, felt that the rural lower orders (regarded as potential converts to Christianity) were being alienated from the English by the oppressive acts of the indigo planters. He got the play translated by Madhusudan Dutta in 1861, printed it with the help of the local English administrators (including W. S. Seton-Karr, the then Secretary to the Government of Bengal), and sent copies to the authorities in London. The local indigo planters filed a suit against Long; the English magistrate sentenced Long to imprisonment for a month and imposed a fine of Rs 1000 (immediately paid in the courtroom by Kaliprasanna Sinha). But the government soon after passed legislation forbidding the planters to force cultivators to sow indigo, thus acceding to the demands of the rebels, but more under pressure from a section of its own administrators and the Christian missionaries.[73]

By the time *Nildarpan* was staged in Calcutta (in 1872), the excitement over the rebellion had died down. Amritalal Basu, who was a famous actor and playwright, and acted in the role of a female character (Sairindhri) in the first production in the city, narrates an amusing incident:

Once when *Nildarpan* was being staged, we heard that the
deputy commissioner of police . . . had arrived and many
of us thought that he would arrest some [among the
actors]. None of us got dispirited; we got more merry
instead . . . When the police boss heard this, he laughed
and sent us the message: 'I knew well Dinabandhu-Babu.
So, I've come to see this excellent play of his. Why are you
thinking otherwise?'[74]

It seems that the only example of the nineteenth-century
bhadralok's literary response to a contemporary peasant rebellion
was after all a hothouse rebellion—performed under the protection
of a section of the colonial administrators, and to be accepted by
the latter within a decade as a harmless piece of protest in Bengal.
But although *Nildarpan* did not portray the rebellion of the peasants (it confined itself to a depiction primarily of the atrocities of
the English planters, the sufferings of the victims and an isolated
example of an individual protest by a peasant), it cropped up occasionally as a symbol of protest and was recognized by the British
as a potential weapon of rebellion. Thus, in 1875, when the Great
National Theatre of Calcutta went with its troupe to Lucknow and
staged *Nildarpan* there, it created a stir among the local English
administrators. A famous Bengali actress, Binodini, who acted in
the play, describes vividly the uproar among the European audience
during a scene where an English planter who tried to rape a peasant woman was humbled by a Muslim peasant: 'As soon as that
happened, there was a commotion among the European spectators.
They became agitated and crowded near the footlights. A few
red-faced soldiers took out their swords and climbed on the stage.
Others tried to hold them back . . . ' The English magistrate later
cancelled the show and asked the troupe to leave Lucknow.[75] The
English administration, which could afford to ignore the performance of *Nildarpan* in Calcutta in 1872, took a hostile stance in
Lucknow, which, having been the centre of the 1857 rebellion, was
still regarded by the British as a potential source of explosion of
anti-colonial sentiments. The colonial administration was quite

sensitive to the mood of the local people as evident from its decision to ban the performance of *Nildarpan* in Bengal in 1908, when armed revolutionary bands of Bengali nationalists were planning insurrection against the British regime. In the later stages of the national movement also, copies of the play were seized by the police.

It needs to be added that by the 1870s when *Nildarpan* was first staged, the social base of Bengali-theatre patronage had undergone a change, paralleling the change in the political attitude of the Bengali bhadralok society which was increasingly articulating its demands through the formation of pressure groups like the India League and later the Indian Association (see Chapter 2, Section xv). The Bengali stage was no longer dependent on wealthy patrons like the Paikpara Rajas or the Tagores of Pathuriaghata and Jorasanko as in the 1850s and 1860s. Middle-class professionals had begun to form their own theatrical groups, leading among which were the Bengal Theatre and the Great National Theatre. Among the actor-playwright producers who earned fame were Girish Ghosh, who was a clerk in a commercial office in Calcutta; Amritalal Basu, son of a schoolteacher; Ardhendu Sekhar Mustafi, who, born in a declining aristocratic family, earned his living by acting. Plays were no longer being written at the request of wealthy aristocrats (as happened with Ramnarayan Tarkaratna or Madhusudan Dutta), but were becoming independent expressions of the feelings and aspirations of the rising middle-class Bengalis.

In 1875 two political plays drew the wrath of the administrators leading them to bring in a legislation called the Dramatic Performances Act to prohibit the production of plays that were 'likely to excite feelings of disaffection to the Government established by law in British India, or likely to deprave and corrupt persons present at such performance'.[76] The two plays in question were *Cha-kar Darpan* (about the brutal treatment of the Assam tea-plantation workers by the English planters) and *Gaekwad Darpan* (about the victimization of the Maharaja of Baroda by the English Resident there). In 1876 again, the Great National Theatre staged a farce called *Gajadananda and the Prince*, lampooning a local lawyer, Jagadananda Mukherjee, who had entertained the Prince of Wales at his Bhowanipore residence, women from his andarmahal welcoming the Prince—a departure from the convention of Hindu households where ladies of the andarmahal were not allowed to be seen by any outsider. The Government clamped down an ordinance prohibiting dramatic performances which were 'scandalous, defamatory, seditious, obscene or otherwise prejudicial to the public interest'. The Great National Theatre responded by producing another farce, *The Police of Pig and Sheep* (referring to the then police superintendent Mr Lamb and the police commissioner Sir Stuart Hogg). The playwright-actor, Amritalal Basu, and the director, Upendranath Das, were arrested and sentenced to a month's imprisonment. Soon after this the Great National Theatre 'came to terms with the new situation and from then on put up safe, mythological plays'.[77]

The enactment of the Dramatic Performances Control Act in 1876 put an end to the production of political satires or farces aimed at the English on the Bengali stage.

Along with repressive laws to subdue the mavericks and rebels among the bhadralok playwrights, administrative pressures, backed by the bhadralok elite organization, the Society for the Suppression of Public Obscenity, were being used at the same time against the culture of the lower orders. The popular sawng performances (see Chapter 3, Section VI) became special targets of bhadralok attacks during this period. These pantomime shows held up the respectable classes of Calcutta as objects of ridicule, and the exposure of their hypocrisy, aping habits and hollowness in public naturally roused the ire of the Bengali elite. The term 'obscenity' became handy enough as it could be stretched as far as they wanted to, to cover any act of protest and prohibit it on grounds of morality. During the 1874 Chadak festivities, the city's leading bhadralok personalities persuaded the then police commissioner Sir Stuart Hogg to ban the sawng performances. But in spite of these pressures, the sawngs of Kansaripada (the braziers' colony) did manage to bring out a procession lampooning the bhadraloks, and their newly discovered concept of 'obscenity'. Moving round the streets of Calcutta, they sang:

Shahorey ak nutan hujuk
Uthechey re bhai,
Ashleelata shabdo mora agey shuni nai,
Er Vidyasagar janmadata
Bangadarshan er neta . . .[78]

(A new frenzy has appeared in the city. We've never heard before the word 'obscenity'. It has been spawned by Vidyasagar. *Bangadarshan* [the journal edited by Bankim Chandra Chattopadhyay] is its leader . . .)

The sawng song then continued to describe how once every year the braziers sang and danced in sawng processions, and how the rest of the poor people enjoyed them. Addressing the bhadraloks, it then said: 'If you think these are bad for society, and for your culture, why don't you keep your wives locked up in your houses [so that they may not watch our performances]?'[79] In the early 1880s the Kansaripada sawng went up to the house of Krishnadas Pal (1838–84), a leading political personality among the city's bhadraloks, who was known for his sycophancy towards the British, and sang a song deriding his habit of dining with the English top brass. At about the same time, in another performance they ridiculed the hypocrisy of the Brahmo reformer Keshub Chandra Sen (1838–84), who for all his championship of women's emancipation married off his 14-year-old daughter to the minor Maharaja of Cooch Behar (an event which led the young Brahmo radicals to break away from Keshub and set up their own separate Sadharan Brahmo Samaj). Describing these two performances as 'going beyond their limits', Mahendranath Dutta (Swami Vivekananda's brother) tells us in his reminiscences: 'On account of these two [performances], the bhadraloks became extremely annoyed [with the sawngs], and sawngs went out of fashion . . . '[80]

VI

Along with new literary forms, the nineteenth-century Calcutta elite sought distinct expressive forms in the visual arts too. Here also their tastes and attitudes were shaped by the English educationists and art connoisseurs. Prevailing English attitudes towards Indian art ranged from admiration of classical Indian sculpture and architecture as sublime expressions of philosophical ideas (by men like James Forber and James Ferguson) to a denunciation of all forms of Indian art by historians like James Mill of the 1817 *History of British India* fame, who held that Indian art was 'unnatural, offensive and not infrequently disgusting'.[81] When the English educationists and administrators decided to educate Bengalis in art, they more often subscribed to Mill's views and introduced a training system which was Eurocentric in its approach with its stress on the academic style of painting which was current in the schools in England in those days. Writing in 1855, an English observer found that 'a Bengalee is peculiarly deficient in the power' of realistic depiction. He added: 'He has naturally as little knowledge of perspective as a Chinese, while he is embarrassed by that inability to copy shadows which seems peculiar to Orientals.'[82] That there could be different styles of paintings, and other criteria for their appreciation, completely escaped the ken of these English critics who were brought up for generations on the standards influenced by the naturalistic tradition of Graeco-Roman sculpture and Renaissance paintings with their attempts at accurate representation of the human body.

In 1854 a number of citizens got together to set up a Society for the Promotion of Industrial Art and established the Calcutta School of Industrial Arts, with the blessings of Mr Hodgson Pratt, who was an under-secretary in the government. Monsieur Rigaud, a French plaster-coat maker, was its first teacher. The aim was to train Bengalis in architectural drawings, modelling, etching, pottery, etc. 'The objective was not at all to impart a training in the higher forms of art, the main attempt being to provide means of livelihood to some people of the country'.[83] The students used to receive a stipend of 16 to 17 rupees per month. They were employed to prepare plaster work in the premises of the Legislative Council, and the houses of Raja Pratapchandra Sinha of Paikpara, and Kaliprasanna Sinha of Jorasanko. It seems therefore that the requirements of the English administrators and the rich Bengali gentry of the city primarily motivated them to train up the local people.

In the course of the training, however, the students came to learn the European style of painting and modelling. Reviewing the first annual exhibition of the School, an English critic appreciatively noted the figures 'executed in the coarsest of materials by boys' like the 'Greek Woman Crouching', 'Samuel' and 'Lion and Deer', which were 'all of course copies' of European models.[84]

The Western style in sculpture and paintings was coming to be accepted by the educated Bengali bhadraloks as the highest model to be followed. The mouthpiece of the Bengali intelligentsia, the *Hindoo Patriot*, welcoming the establishment of the School of Industrial Arts, said: 'It was in subservience to idolatrous purposes that the noblest productions of great artistic genuines [*sic*] were created, just as the masterpieces of modern Europe owe their existence to a similar impulse given by the spirit of Roman Catholicism.' It then turned to indigenous art, and added: 'The idols we worship, on the contrary, outrage taste as the worship itself outrages all reason. Let our readers now consider what would be the effect of a body of artists [trained in the School] with high conceptions and a refined taste modelling the idol-forms we worship.'[85] A year later, the same paper was to complain again:

> We still mould our gods and goddesses after forms devoid
> at once of imaginative richness and chastity of conception
> and our pictures are to this day daubed with the hideous-
> ness of savage imagery—undignified by the striking rude-
> ness which the untutored fancy of savages not infrequently
> infuses into their works . . . [86]

The high respect in which the bhadralok held Western fine arts is expressed in the following outpourings of a contemporary educated Bengali:

Oh! for the pencil of a Guido [Reni] or a Raphael to paint on the canvas the beauties of a fair face or the grandeur of nature with the glorious Orb of day careering in the high-ways of the heavens, or for the pencil of a Phidias or a Michael Angelo, to mould into stone the fairest of human shape or the divinest of human form . . . Are not the arts of these genial men of genius worth hearty pursuit?

He then advised his countrymen: 'Go then, ye sons of India, and reap laurels in these fields', adding the materially enticing assurance: 'They will give you an honourable and independent livelihood which in these days of tight markets and bankruptcy is much to be valued'.[87]

Soon the Bengali gentry were commissioning students of the School to do portraits or paint copies of European masterpieces which were to adorn their parlours. After the school was taken over by the Government in 1864 and Henry Hover Locke of the South Kensington School of Design (which later became the Royal College of Art, London) was appointed its principal, the students who became proficient in the European academic style of painting got lucrative appointments. Locke employed these students for interior decoration and painting of frescos for St Peter's Church within the precincts of Fort William.[88] European zoologists who visited India also employed Locke's students for preparing repro-ductions of the indigenous fauna.[89]

Among the products of the school, the leading painters were Annada Bagchi, Shyamacharan Srimani, Harish Chandra Khan, Nityananda Dey and Biharilal Das. Annada Bagchi set up in 1878 the Calcutta Art Studio in Bowbazar, where with the help of other European-trained Bengali painters he began to produce coloured lithographs of Hindu gods and goddesses. Along with the newly imported German oleographs, these lithographs of the Bowbazar studio were to oust the Kalighat *pats* from the market within a few years.

The cultivation of the Western style of fine arts among the indigenous elite went hand in hand with an ideological campaign

against the local Bengali folk art. We have already noted how journals like the *Hindoo Patriot* had earlier inveighed against the
Kumortuli images which were 'devoid at once of imaginative rich-
ness and chastity of conception' and against the Kalighat *pats* which
were 'daubed with the hideousness of savage imagery'. When
Locke's pupils arrived on the scene, they were even more vocifer-
ous against the Kalighat *pats,* thoroughly educated as they had been
in the European tradition. Shyamacharan Srimani found in the
contemporary *pats* signs of decadence which he linked to the
character of the jatras, sharing the same views as expressed by
Bankim Chandra Chattopadhyay and other educated intellectuals
about Calcutta folk culture. Srimani wrote:

> The *pats* which are in vogue in these days stand in the
> same relation to the ancient paintings as the modern jatras
> and dramatic performances are in comparison with the
> plays of Kalidasa and others. Having ousted plays like
> *Shakuntala, Malatimadhava* from our country, common
> operas like jatras are now ruling over the scene with ease.
> It is no wonder therefore that the lifeless and grotesque
> paintings of the modern days would dare to step in to
> replace the poetic paintings of the ancient times in our
> country.[90]

The phase of copying Western masterpieces soon gave way to
a period of painting Hindu divinities and characters and events
from classical Sanskrit plays in the style learnt from the English
teachers. In 1885 Annada Bagchi and Sarachchandra Deb founded
the journal *Shilpapushpanjali*—said to be the first art journal in
Bengali. It used to carry litho-illustrations of stories from the
Mahabharata and Kalidasa's *Shakuntala*. The stylized characterization, the attempts at shading to indicate the play of light and
shadows, the efforts to portray emotions of varying degrees—all
these bore the traces of the new schooling.

It is interesting to note the parallels in contemporary literature.
The portrayal of Hindu classical characters and mythological
heroes and heroines in Madhusudan Dutta's poetry and verse

dramas, or of historical events and personalities in Bankim Chandra Chattopadhyay's novels, in the heroic and romantic style of European literature, synchronized with the depiction of similar characters in the new types of paintings in a style borrowed from the Western academic school. The best Indian representative of this style was, however, not a Bengali from Calcutta, but a prince from Kerala in the south—Raja Ravi Varma. His illustrations in oil of events from the *Ramayana* and the *Mahabharata* became highly popular with the Bengali gentry, who used to frame copies of his paintings in their houses. Describing the different levels of art appreciation in Calcutta at the end of the nineteenth and the beginning of the twentieth century, the well-known Bengali artist, Jamini Roy, said: 'For the common people, there were the Kalighat *pats* and lithographs of Battala. For the educated middle class there were the Bowbazar Art Studio reproductions of *pats* and oil paintings; and for the rich, the landlords and the "rajas" and "maharajas", there were the paintings of Ravi Varma.'[91]

The introduction of oil painting through the European art education system affected the patrons of the Kalighat *pats* also. A latter-day art critic tells us:

In the nineteenth century owing to a perverse preference for Western art, the hereditary painters, chiefly in the larger cities, were induced by their patrons to produce pictures of mythological subjects on canvas in oil colours—a medium quite foreign to their art. These pictures are still to be found in old homes, especially in Calcutta . . . they are almost without exception devoid of all artistic merit . . . [92]

What developed as indigenous Bengali painting as patronized by the bhadraloks was therefore a depiction of Hindu mythological characters in the image of the Greek gods and goddesses, but dressed in Indian clothes—the heroes in semi-Mughal attire, and the heroines draped in the Bengali saree. In Bankim Chandra Chattopadhyay's novel *Bishabriksha*, we find the bhadralok couple—Nagendra and his wife Suryamukhi—commissioning 'an Indian painter who was a pupil of the English' to prepare paintings on selected topics from Kalidasa's *Kumarasamhhava* and the epics *Ramayana* and *Mahabharata*.[93] Towards the end of the nineteenth century when some Bengali intellectuals turned to Positivism, they asked a Calcutta painter, Hari Charan Mazumdar, to do in oil on canvas a painting of 'The *Dhyana* of Humanity' (The Meditation of Humanity). We are told that the 'source of his [Mazumdar's] inspiration was in the main one of Raphael's paintings as accessible here in prints or photos'. We are assured the next moment: 'But the picture is that of the Hindu Mother in the simple dress of a matronly Brahman woman.'[94] Even at the Hindu Mela, which was organized by the Bengali intellectuals to turn the attention of the educated among their community to indigenous culture, the specimen of Indian painting chosen by its founder, Nabagopal Mitra, was a portrait of Britannia with Indians sitting at her feet with folded hands.[95]

When at the end of the nineteenth century, inspired by a sense of nationalism (which in the political arena found expression in the formation of the Indian National Congress in 1885), the English-educated Bengali painters sought alternative styles from indigenous sources, they turned not to the folk tradition, but to the court paintings of the Mughal and Rajput days. The search in this direction was reinforced by E. B. Havell, who became the Principal of the Calcutta Government Art School in 1896. From the early years of the twentieth century, the Bengal School of Art flourished, its products being wash paintings in watercolours done in the style of the old miniatures, with subjects ranging from contemporary life like village vignettes and landscapes to nationalistic themes like Abanindranath Tagore's 'Bharat Mata' (Mother India). Instead of the clear bold outlines and heavy brush strokes of the Kalighat *pats*, we find in these paintings delicate figures done in faint, thin lines, the background enveloped in hazy colours.

A similar trend was discernible in the experiments in music that were taking place in the Bengali elite society of Calcutta at that time. Bengali folk music, in spite of its long and rich cultural tradition, was looked down upon by the English and their Bengali pupils. This is how an early nineteenth-century English observer describes the music of the lower orders:

It is principally at marriages, during religious processions and such great solemnities, that the full din of music is heard proceeding from eight different sorts of drums, gongs, kinds of hautboys, the horns of buffaloes, and brass trumpets performed by the lowest dregs of the people. From these formidable implements of sound, each man extorts as much noise as he can, paying little or no atten-tion to what his comrades are about.[96]

The educated Bengalis were also initiated into this way of judging folk music. Thus, a mid-nineteenth-century Bengali bhadralok writes: 'Of Bengali songs I cannot speak very highly. Though I must confess that some of them are harmonious, and abound with beautiful coruscations of fancy, yet there are none that can be compared to "Allan Water", Campbell's "Ye Mariners of England", or Burns' "Mary Morison" '.[97]

In its search for a distinct musical identity, as in literature, the Calcutta Bengali elite fell back on the ancient classical Hindu cul-ture of the feudal courts and the temples. Early nineteenth-century English Orientalists like William Jones and Augustus Willard had certified that classical Indian music possessed 'intrinsic claim to beauty in melody'.[98]

Cultivation of classical Indian music was common among the Calcutta aristocratic families like the Tagores of Pathuriaghata and Jorasanko, and the sons of Ramdulal Dey. *Ustads* from north India were patronized by these families in their ancestral houses, and they taught the Bengali music lovers of the city. The arrival of Nawab Wazed Ali Shah (of Oudh, whose state was annexed by the British in 1856) as an exile in Metiabruz in the southern extremity of Calcutta further encouraged the flourishing of north Indian classical music in the city. The Nawab, who himself was a lover of music and composed songs in the light classical *thumri* style, brought along with him his entourage of musicians. Descendants of the pupils and proteges of the Nawab's Metiabruz court are names well known in Calcutta even today. The famous tabla player Keramatullah was the son of Masit Khan, whose father Nanne Khan was the court musician at the Metiabruz court. Another pupil was Raichand Baral, who became well known as a composer of songs in the Calcutta film world in the 1930s and '40s.

But it was a Bengali grandee who was responsible for training the rising educated middle-class bhadraloks in north Indian classical music in nineteenth-century Calcutta. Shourindramohan Tagore, brother of Jatindramohan Tagore of the Pathuriaghata Raj family (who was one of the first to recognize the talents of Michael Madhusudan Dutta), founded in 1871 the Bengal Music School, which attracted the bhadraloks aspiring to cultivate classical Indian music. Shourindramohan, who himself was proficient in the genre, delved into ancient Sanskrit treatises on music and wrote books in English and Bengali, explaining the complicated nuances of Indian music.

Shourindramohan Tagore's efforts drew praises from contemporary English newspapers—not so much for the intrinsic merits of the music which he patronized as for his scrupulous attention to the requirements of the city's English top officials. The *Friend of India* was impressed by the 'Fifty Stanzas in Sanskrita in Honour of H.R.H. the Prince of Wales', composed and set to music by Shourindramohan Tagore, in which the English commentator found that 'the generous exaggeration of a loyal poet, especially when the poet is an Oriental, must not be counted a fault.'[99] Describing a function at Shourindramohan Tagore's palace where 'a large number of European ladies and gentlemen, as well as natives assembled', *The Englishman* complimented Tagore for 'introducing an entirely new description of native performance which is certainly preferable to the unchanging nautch, as well as for the genial hospitality that he displayed to his guests'. The 'native performance' referred to consisted of a 'series of Tableaux Vivants representing various Eastern nations paying their homage to the Imperial Crown'.[100]

The journals of the Bengali intellectuals were also full of praise for Shourindramohan for improving the tastes of the bhadraloks. The journal of the Brahmos, the *Indian Mirror*, thanked him for having 'introduced a spirit of enlightenment into the whole subject which has taken away much of the voluptuousness and animalism characterizing the pleasures of music in this country for a long time'.[101]

While Shourindramohan's efforts did create a generation of Bengali artistes proficient in north Indian court music of the past, they indirectly led to their alienation from the roots of Bengali folk music. As a modern music critic has pointed out: 'Those who came forward to compose music at the end of the nineteenth century were enlightened and educated people. Common people had to make efforts to understand their music. In this respect, one will have to admit that their music was somewhat artificial. The human appeal of their songs did not percolate down to the common masses; they expressed primarily the emotional dalliance of the upper classes'.[102]

The development of the elite cultural forms of the Bengali bhadralok society in nineteenth-century Calcutta thus appeared to be moving along a course which was increasingly drifting away from that particular aspect of the common heritage which was rooted in folk culture (and which acquired a distinct shape in the urban popular cultural forms in nineteenth-century Calcutta). It was moving instead towards the other source—the traditional elite culture consisting of classical Sanskrit literature, court painting and music. The nineteenth-century elite culture that emerged was shaped by two prevailing attitudes—one, the tendency to despise the folk tradition and the popular literary forms under the influence of English education; and two, the desire to discover a cultural identity with the upper-class literature, music and fine arts of the past based on Sanskrit classics and Mughal court culture. Western education and training introduced new ideas like the need for social reforms (issues taken up in the novels of Bankim and others) or provoked the concept of nationalism (expressed under the thin veneer of historical romances in contemporary plays and poetry).

But the form of expression harked back to the elitist style of the past, modified by the new education that the bhadralok had received. This was in keeping with the Bengali bhadralok's reluctance to be completely Anglicized (under the pressure of the strong hold of traditional social norms) and yet, his desire to demarcate himself from the lower orders (from which society, ironically, many among his ancestors had arisen). The compromise worked out in the cultural arena was an echo of the social adjustment—the 'combination of Mill and Manu, the latter largely expurgated of its priestly and patriarchal excesses' and the former affording 'a tool for intellectual analysis'.[103]

CONCLUSION

I

From a rather uncomfortable and uncertain coexistence in the eclectic atmosphere of the cultural chaos of the early nineteenth century, the two sets of cultural beliefs and patterns—the entertainments of the lower orders and the literature and art of the Bengali elite—had travelled in two opposite directions by the end of the century.

By the 1870s the cultural forms of expression of the Bengali bhadraloks had developed a stylistic unity which resulted from the patronage of a social group that had become economically, culturally and politically unified. The urban middle class, which the elite culture represented, reconstituted the lines of deference, patronage and moral authority in Calcutta society by distancing itself from, and suppressing later on, the old popular culture of the lower orders. In its efforts to create a distinct culture of its own based on some commonly affirmed array of values and morals, it tried to exalt a mythical past and increasingly identified itself with it while dealing in a sedate vein with the social and religious problems that concerned exclusively the educated gentry.

The city's lower orders, whose beliefs and behaviour were considered by the elite as annoying, wasteful, immoral and even dangerous at times, on the other hand, remained by and large fragmented, bound as they were to their respective caste occupations. The social ties which used to bind them together in their old villages and, later, in early nineteenth-century Calcutta snapped as the years passed and the first generation of the urban nouveau riche disappeared. But in their cultural output the lower orders also appeared to be moving towards a stylistic unity, perhaps unconsciously. From the mid-nineteenth century onwards, they were becoming more and more irreverent of the religious myths of the past (which were being glamorized by the bhadralok intellectuals) and sarcastic towards the events of the surrounding present, their most outspoken expression or social satire being the sawng performances. We can observe the stylistic unity in their choice of the same plump, foppish figures in the satirical portraits of the babus and their mistresses in the Kalighat *pats,* as in the dress and manners adopted by the sawng performers to ridicule the hypocrisy of the Anglicized gentry and the religious prigs, or in the verbal descriptions of the habits of the parvenu in the city's street songs or Dashu Ray's panchalis.

We must add here that these cultural products and performances of the city's lower orders were often involuntary, defensive responses to the encroachments of the new market forces of a colonial economy and social structure—the entry of the newly educated Bengali babus who replaced their old patrons and had no use for their panchalis, jatras and *pats.* From this perception, the lower orders tended to identify Western education as a threat to their survival, since it was this that had turned out a new generation of consumers who not only rejected the traditional products—whether functional items like handloom garments, or forms of entertainment like jatras or panchalis—but tried to suppress them. As a result, education, the new propertied classes, their habits, their social reforms, were looked upon with resentment and suspicion by the lower orders. This was reflected in the contemporary street songs and Kalighat *pats* which lampooned these developments. 'Working class culture has been built around the task of making fundamentally punishing conditions more inhabitable.'¹ Their rejection by the upper classes could be handled by them only by laughter which cut their superiors down to size.

We should also recognize the gender-specific elements in this culture of Calcutta's lower orders. Women were often chosen as butts of ridicule in the popular songs, Kalighat *pats* and jatras. They were depicted as upstarts and shrews. This tendency—seemingly similar to that expressed by the orthodox Hindus among the contemporary Bengali elite—might have reflected the sexist bias of a male-dominated society (which was prevalent among large sections of the Bengali lower orders too) through which the subordination of women was secured in their communities. Topics like women's education and widow remarriage were objects of derision, and held up as warnings (probably against their own womenfolk) about the arrival of the apocalyptic 'Kali-yuga' where everything was upside down, as predicted in the scriptures.

The thoughts of the lower orders of nineteenth-century Bengal were still structured more by perceptions of traditional orders than of classes. The well-knit village society where the local elite—dominated by the brahmanical code of behaviour—was required to demonstrate and conform to the code was still very much a part of the psyche of the migrants who came to Calcutta. Although they themselves—the lower-caste artisans and peasants—followed their own customs like *sanga* marriage of widows, or cohabitation, they usually expected their superiors to stick to their respective traditional roles which, in the perception of the lower orders, helped to bind together the old society. Social reforms like women's education or widow remarriage, or social evils like the greed and hypocrisy of the priestly class among the city's elite were therefore regarded as dangerous departures from the traditional mores. These tensions between the traditional mores and the emerging new modes of behaviour in nineteenth-century Calcutta society could possibly explain the position of social ambiguity, or often of downright conservatism, found in the folk culture of the period. The portrayal of women in the Kalighat pats or Dasharathi Ray's diatribes against educated women were examples of the orthodox, patriarchal values of the Brahmanical tradition often internalized by the subordinate classes.

The popular opinion expressed in nineteenth-century Calcutta folk culture, therefore, was rebellious but traditional at the same time. The folk artistes recognized the central issues of the time, like inequities following from the division between the propertied classes and the underprivileged, between the colonial rulers and the indigenous people. But these issues were never couched in a terminology that could imply the overthrowing of the oppressive order—a terminology that characterized the contemporary songs of the rebellion of Santal peasants (1855–57), or the revolt of the Mundas under Birsa in 1895.[2] A unilinear interpretation that would hold nineteenth-century Calcutta folk culture as totally feudal and conservative, or take the other extreme position of hailing it as the radical voice of the proletariat, would miss the complex, multi-layered fabric that was made up by the thoughts and perceptions of the city's lower orders at that time.

As mentioned earlier, the main components of the stylistic unity that was emerging in nineteenth-century Calcutta folk culture were the satirical stereotypes (the Anglicized Bengali, the parvenu babu, the crafty priest, the educated woman, etc.) and the earthy Bengali language enriched by the Calcutta slang. These stylistic elements were powerful enough to fascinate and tantalize the adventurous impulses of some among the literati of the Bengali elite. People like Kaliprasanna Sinha, and a host of farce-writers who followed him, tried to incorporate the satirical images and the colloquial language of urban folk culture in their belles-lettres, farces and plays. But such experiments were discouraged and were even suppressed later by elite leaders and the authorities. This starved the Bengali language and literature of a vivacious, indigenous literary source. The literature of the elite developed along a course which was marked heavily by the use of Sanskrit words and borrowings from the Sanskrit classics, thus departing from the original path of innovating *tadbhaba* (Bengali simplified from Sanskrit) words and incorporating Arabic and Persian terms, which characterized the folk literature.

While elite culture survived to develop further and attain maturity in the twentieth century in the hands of Rabindranath Tagore (whose poetry, music, plays, novels and experiments in other areas of Bengali culture were regarded as the summit of the creative genius of 'bhadralok society'), Calcutta's popular culture became increasingly marginalized and faced virtual extinction by the turn of the twentieth century.

As 'enlightenment' closed in around it, blotting out its familiar world and its old patrons, with education, industrialization and new cultural tastes and activities, the folk culture of Calcutta had to beat a steady retreat, starting with the gradual fading away of the kobi-walas from the mid-nineteenth century. Later on, the jatra-walas lost a chunk of their middle-class patrons to the new spectacle of the theatre mounted by the bhadraloks. Along with panchalis, kathakatas and tarjas, the jatras somehow managed to linger on among the lower orders till the educated gentry launched a concerted campaign against their public performances on grounds of 'obscenity'. They then sought refuge in the Bengal countryside, where they hoped to rediscover the ties that led to their birth. As one modern perceptive Bengali critic observes:

> Faced by the powerful onslaught of English education, prudery camouflaged by Brahmo Samaj fastidiousness, and the mid-Victorian morals of the Bankim group . . . the *kobi* songs with their tumult, jugglery of tunes and rustic slanging matches had to wind up from Calcutta. Quitting the gas-lit urban atmosphere, the *kobi* songs, *tarjas* and *panchalis* descended on the dimly-lit village stage in evenings ringing with the chirp of crickets . . . [3]

It was not only the new social values cultivated by the bhadraloks under English education that drove to the wall popular cultural forms like the jatras, and later on the sawngs. Better technological innovations (like the oleograph and lithograph) succeeded in ousting the Kalighat pats from the market.

Towards the end of the century, describing the plight of the various forms of urban popular culture, a Bengali journal observed: 'All the entertainments and festivities of the common people are disappearing one by one. The jatras, the panchalis are no longer there, let alone the kobi [songs]. What will the common people live on? Only country liquor?'[4]

A combination of different social factors and policies—change in the conditions of existence of the patron groups, new desires and tastes among the economically and socially dominating sections, technological innovations, and hostile interventions— ousted popular culture from the streets and marketplaces of Calcutta. Latter-day academic and elitist indifference to and depreciation of its various forms of expression reduced it to a 'culture of silence'. This was again related to the different levels of dominance–dependence relationship that shaped the growth and development of Calcutta in the nineteenth century. According to Paulo Freire,

> the culture of silence is born in the relationship between the Third World and the metropolis . . . understanding the 'culture of silence' presupposes an analysis of dependence as a relational phenomenon which gives rise to different forms of being, of thinking, of expression, those of the 'culture of silence' and those of the culture which 'has a voice' . . . The dependent society is by definition a silent society. Its voice is not an authentic voice, but merely an echo of the voice of the metropolis—in every way, the metropolis speaks, the dependent society listens. The silence of the object society in relation to the director society is repeated in the relationship within the object society itself. Its power elites, silent in the face of the metropolis, silence their own people in turn.[5]

The voice of the indigenous elite of the dependent society of Calcutta was primarily an echo of the voice of the metropolis, England. The 'voice', or the culture that was shaped by the Calcutta elite, was, as we have seen, based on what the metropolis 'spoke'—

the concepts of morality, the ideas of Utilitarianism, the political principles, the poetry of Homer, Byron and Shelley. The same relationship of silence was repeated within the 'dependent society' of Calcutta—the cultural world of the Black Town. The Bengali 'power elites', silent in the face of the metropolis, silenced their own people in turn—the culture of the lower orders.

It is interesting to note that a similar silencing of the culture of the lower orders was taking place in the metropolis too at the same time. Speaking of the gradual decline of the art of mumming (acting in dumb shows—an English version of the Indian sawng) in nineteenth-century England, one modern critic observes: 'In the past, mumming had been used to reaffirm the solidarity of local communities, a function which became less and less viable in the nineteenth century . . . it could be used like many other similar rituals, either to reaffirm, or to attack the social order'. Explaining the reasons for the withering away of 'specific popular cultural items' in nineteenth-century England, the critic refers to 'the withdrawal of social elements which had once played significant roles in their organization or presentation; pressure by the state and its new, nineteenth-century agencies of discipline, regulation and repression; pressure on the uses of urban spaces'.[6] Thus, as in the creation of upper-class culture in Calcutta, in the suppression of popular culture also it was the metropolis which 'spoke', and the dependent society which 'listened'.

II

The gradual dissociation of the culture of the Calcutta bhadralok from folk culture, accompanied by a cultivated tendency to condemn all forms of entertainment of the city's lower orders, had lasting implications for the future of Bengali elite culture—the literature, music and fine arts of the educated class.

Divorced from the vibrant buoyancy and robust sense of humour manifested in the dialect and idiom of the lower orders, and from the lusty and sinewy mode of expression of their cultural output, the literature and paintings of the bhadralok assumed the character of a private, defensive world insulated from the general stream of life in the streets. The language itself, instead of becoming a mode of free and easy communication among all segments of society, was turned into an agent of excommunication shaped in such a way as to deny the lower orders any access to it. The observations made by a perceptive bhadralok in the last quarter of the nineteenth century throw an interesting light on this basic linguistic disjunction in Bengali society that was assiduously cultivated by the educated. In a rare moment of honest introspection, the writer blamed the Sanskrit-knowing pundits for distorting the elementary character of original Bengali, and commented: 'If indeed the object were to confine knowledge to a cast [sic], there could not be a cleverer contrivance than to make the written language diverge widely from the spoken.' Referring to the role of the colonial administration in bolstering up this artificial Bengali, he continued: '[the State] has . . . interfered in disseminating a knowledge of book Bengali by the establishment of schools and the institution of competition tests, by the award of scholarships and so forth. Things have not been allowed to work themselves out spontaneously'.

Turning towards the masses, he said: 'The dumb millions cannot judge, or speak for themselves. If they could they would with one voice denounce the pedantic jargon that now presses so heavily on them as a dead weight'.[7]

All through the nineteenth century, both the language and the style, as well as the contents taken up for treatment in Bengali literature of the elite, remained far removed from the thought pattern and framework of references of the lower orders.

The heroic verse pastoral poetry, and historical romances of the nineteenth-century Bengali writers paved the way to the evolution of what is known as modern Bengali literature in the twentieth century. Literary language and style reached their present form in the hands of Tagore, in whose poems the world of the individual soul with all its nuances ranging from personal emotions to spiritual contemplation, from romantic love to communion with nature, was endowed with suggestions and overtones of infinite power. His social novels continued to deal with the problems taken up earlier by his predecessor Bankim Chattopadhyay—the man–woman relationship, the conflict between generations, the collision between tradition and modernity, the middle-class response to Western values. The heroes and heroines glide through their pages in solemn dignity, slow movement and monumental isolation. Although some of his short stories and poems occasionally introduced characters from the lower stratum of society—the poor peasant, the migrant from the village working as a servant in the city—they rarely speak in their own language about their basic needs and aspirations. Their poverty is sometimes romanticized, their loyalty to their masters often glamorized. A powerful creative genius in his own right, Tagore experimented with folk tunes among other styles in his songs. But while these songs, based on the melodic forms of Baul, bhatiali and *sari* songs, are popular in Bengali middle-class homes, they are hardly sung by the peas-ants of the Bengal countryside among whom the roving Baul or the boatman's songs still remain popular. Even when discarding the heavily Sanskritized *sadhubhasha* (the conventional bookish Bengali of the nineteenth century) and using a simple Bengali in his novels and short stories in the 1930s—the period when he also switched over to prose-poems—his language never somehow acquired the vigorous force and the picturesque vividness of the colloquial Bengali as spoken by the man in the street. Being a sensitive soul, he was honest enough to recognize his limitations in this direction. In one of his poems composed towards the end of his life, he regretted: 'My poems, I know, though they have traversed diverse roads, have not reached everywhere.' Describing them as having been composed in the 'narrow portico of the upper stage of society', he expressed the hope that one day he would be able to listen to the works of that poet who was 'close to the soil', who was a 'partner in the life of the peasant, who had sincerely achieved the kinship between words and work'.[8]

That sums up the dilemma of the socially conscious Bengali intellectual who, having been trained for generations in a style of communication that is far removed from that of the masses, still suffers from the dichotomy that plagued his predecessors like Kaliprasanna Sinha, Madhusudan Dutta, Bankim Chandra Chattopadhyay, who veered occasionally towards the language of the masses in an effort to make their works accessible to them, but drifted back the next moment to the sophisticated forms of expression learnt from the Sanskrit classics and the modern West.

In the visual arts also, Western training and the European painting style with its stress on shade and perspective led first to imitations produced by such painters as members of the Bowbazar studio, and later, in the early twentieth century, gave rise to the Bengal School, largely moulded by the personal style of Abanindranath Tagore, nephew of Rabindranath. The 'wash' technique which he used for his watercolours was eminently suitable for the subjects which he chose—romantic tales from the Hindu epics or Indian history, everyday scenes with suggestions of a dream world. The elegance and finish with which Abanindranath and his pupils created the delicate, fragile figures removed them from the real world to a fairyland of loveliness—an echo of the same desire to distance oneself from one's surroundings which we find in the literature. [9]

Even when Jamini Roy sought to experiment with the traditional Bengali folk art style in general and Kalighat *pat* style in particular, his creations, like Tagore's similar experiments with the style of folk songs, remained distant from the stark reality of the living present. As his critics pointed out: 'His purity has been personal, his clearing-ground too large an area of human life. There is not one violent man, not one shrewish woman in the whole of Jamini Roy's world, with its calm of mind and subdued passion.'[10]

Throughout the nineteenth century, the bhadralok's attitude towards folk culture was marked by an oscillation between revulsion and attraction, and his behaviour by that between rejection and adoption. The bhadralok was intrigued by a way of thinking prevalent among the lower orders which he could not fathom, by their way of living which was strange to him, and perhaps, above

all, by a kind of spontaneous gaiety found in their forms of entertainment which his own class had hardly ever experienced. This
explains the occasional forays by nineteenth-century mavericks like
Kaliprasanna Sinha and the farce-writers into the vast reservoir of
Calcutta folk dialect where various speech patterns excluded from
respectable society lay accumulated.

While this was a recognition of the principle that culture
should find room for conversational commonplaces as well as for
profound utterances, for light, unguarded confessions as well as
for long-pondered truths, it was all the same tinged by the
bhadralok's supercilious posture towards the culture of the lower
orders. Folk forms were held as capable of dealing with light
trivialities only, while for deep reflection the educated gentry's
'high art' alone was regarded as the proper medium. As the
nineteenth-century Bengali scholar Dwarkanath Vidyabhushan,
referring to traditional folk literary forms, wrote: 'They are not
fit for treating any profound subject . . . For serious profound
compositions, compound words and well-articulated letters are
necessary . . . ' (see Chapter 4, Section IV).

This tendency to identify folk cultural forms with an inferior
level of sensibility had grave implications for the future interaction
between elite and folk culture in Bengal. In the later phase in the
history of the dominating Bengali elite, folk forms began to be used
as raw material to be wrung dry by the elite for its entertainment
only. Following the boom in the mass entertainment industry in
the post-Independence period, the bhadralok suddenly rediscov-
ered folk culture in a new light. Hard pressed for new ideas and
styles, the commercial film industry and the theatre of the
bhadralok society turned to Bengali folk culture in search of fresh
pastures.

The result has been a sudden spurt in so-called folk music, folk
dances, folk theatre, etc.—all produced and performed by the
bhadraloks. In Calcutta in particular, the jatra has been revived, its
form and content transformed almost beyond recognition in the
commercial environment of the modern metropolis.

These typical 'folk' forms of the mass media today are not a continuation from but a corruption of the popular culture of nineteenth-century Calcutta. Whereas in the popular art forms of the past the conventions of folk culture provided an agreed base from which innovations began, in the mass entertainments of the commercial media today the formula is predominant. 'The popular artist may use the conventions to select, emphasize and stress (or alter the emphasis and stress) so as to delight the audience with a kind of creative surprise. Mass art uses the stereotypes and formulae to simplify the experience, to mobilize stock feelings and to get them going.[11]

A typical example of this is the jatra in its revived form as staged by the commercial jatra troupes of Calcutta today. Completely abandoning the open-stage convention of the old jatras, the modern jatra has moved closer to the theatre by adopting the stage with drop-scenes, lighting systems, orchestral music, and sometimes even cabaret dances to provide titillation to the city's gentry who flock to these performances. Characteristic features of the old jatras—the hero, the villain, the chorus—which were given new forms by innovators like Gopal Udey, have now become stereotypes in the modern jatra. Modes of expression which would have been left behind by innovative forms in the course of the jatra's normal development have been frozen into ridiculous anachronisms. The old folk music at the same time has been vulgarized, its surface characteristics heavily stressed while the subtle humour and suggestiveness slip through the bhadralok imitator's fingers.

Such appropriation of folk forms by the elite can be described as a manifestation of cultural imperialism in the modern phase of dominance–dependence relationship. The tradition of colonial exploitation of indigenous resources has been extended by the indigenous elite to the country's folk culture. The cultural products manufactured by the elite-dominated commercial entertainment industry from the ingredients of folk culture are sold to a captive audience in the form of escapist fantasies.

In the country's economy, the workers have no say in the pattern of production in which they are made to participate. This estrangement that lies between the worker's labour and the finished product he produces is carried a step further in the mass entertainment industry where the lower orders have no role whatsoever to play in the production of what is sold as 'folk' culture. What is masquerading as folk culture in the commercial network is sans the participation of its original artistes—common folks. Produced and performed by the bhadralok, folk culture in Calcutta expresses the fantasies of the city elite.

With the increasing appropriation of folk forms by the elite-dominated commercial media, the lower orders find themselves threatened with alienation from their own cultural forms of entertainment. In economy, the ruling elite appropriates the workers' means of production and puts them to use to manufacture commodities necessary for itself. In culture, the ruling elite appropriates the means of expression of the lower orders and distorts them to manufacture entertainment for itself.

NOTES

Introduction

1 Stuart Hall and Paddy Whannel, *The Popular Arts* (London: Hutchinson, 1964).

2 Hall and Whannel, *The Popular Arts.*

3 Robert Redfield and Milton B. Singer, 'The Cultural Role of Cities', *Economic Development and Cultural Change* 3(1) (1954): 53–73.

4 See Raymond Williams, 'Communications of Cultural Science' in C. W. E. Bigsby (ed.), *Approaches to Popular Culture* (London: Edward Arnold, 1976), pp. 27–38.

5 See E. B. Havell, *Ideals of Indian Art* (London: J. Murray, 1911).

6 Rabindranath Tagore, in a lecture delivered at Dhaka in 1926, translated and reproduced in Prithwish Neogy (ed.), *Rabindranath Tagore on Art and Aesthetics* (New Delhi: Orient Longman, 1961), pp. 60–4.

7 Quoted in *Friend of India* (25 September 1873).

8 Hiren Mukherjee, 'The Crisis in Culture', speech delivered at the All-India Progressive Writers' Conference, Calcutta, 1938.

9 Leon Trotsky, *Literature and Revolution* (Ann Arbor: University of Michigan Press, 1960).

10 Frantz Fanon, 'On National Culture' in *The Wretched of the Earth* (Richard Philcox trans.) (New York: Grove, 2004[1965]), pp. 145–80.

11 Paulo Freire, *Cultural Action for Freedom* (London: Penguin, 1972).

12 Janet Wolff, 'The Interpretation of Literature in Society: The Hermeneutic Approach' in Jane Routh and Janet Wolff (eds), *Sociology of Literature: Theoretical Approaches* (Newcastle: University of Keele, 1977), pp. 18–31.

Economy and Society in Nineteenth-Century Calcutta

1 Bholanath Chunder, 'Calcutta: Its Origin and Growth' in Alok Ray (ed.), *Calcutta Keepsake* (Calcutta: Riddhi, 1978), pp. 8–35; here, p. 39. See also Prankrishna Dutta, *Kalikatar Itibritta* (Calcutta: Pustak Bipani, 1981), p. 39.

2 Pradip Sinha, *Calcutta in Urban History* (Calcutta: Firma KLM, 1978), pp. 16–17.

3 Bholanath Chunder, 'The System of Banyanship' in Alok Ray (ed.), *Nineteenth Century Studies, 8* (Calcutta: Bibliographical Research Centre, 1975), pp. 462–3.

4 Clive's letter, dated 30 September 1765, in Romesh Dutt, *The Economic History of India under Early British Rule: From the Rise of the British Power in 1757 to the Accession of Queen Victoria in 1837* (London: Kegan Paul, Trench, Trubner, 1908), pp. 323–37.

5 Dutt, *The Economic History of India*, p. 45.

6 Chunder, 'The System of Banyanship', p. 463.

7 P. J. Marshall, 'Indian Officials under the East India Company in Eighteenth Century Bengal', *Bengal, Past and Present* 84 (July–December 1965): 95–120. Quoted in Sinha, *Calcutta in Urban History*, p. 83.

8 Similar were the beginnings of many other affluent Bengali families. Lakshmikanta (Noku) Dhar, founder of the Raj family of Posta in north Calcutta, was said to have saved an English sailor in distress, and through him, found his way to success. Piritram Marh, who was born in a low-caste poor family and traded in bamboo logs, made a fortune when the price of bamboos went up in 1780, and he set up his palatial mansion in Janbazar in that area. See Pramathanath Mullick, *Sachitra Kolikatar Itihas* (Calcutta: Sri Prabodh Krishna Bandyopadhyay, 1935), pp. 27, 125.

9 Comment by Price, in Chunder, 'Calcutta', p. 42.

10 'In order to preserve the Esplanade, lying West of the Road, leading from the Government House to Kidderpore Bridge, Peons will be stationed after the 5th instant at different places, where hitherto Native foot passengers have crossed the plain, to prevent such practice in future . . . ' (By order, H. Seymour Montague, Captain, Fort William, 1 June 1818). Also:

> It having been represented to the Most Noble the Governor of Fort William that considerable inconvenience is experienced by the European part of the community who resort to the respondetia from the crowds of Native workmen and Coolies who make a thoroughfare of the Walk. His Lordship is pleased to direct that Natives shall not in future be allowed to pass the Sluice Bridge . . . between the hours of 5 and 8 in the morning and 5 and 8 in the evening' (By Order of the Most Noble the Governor of Fort William. C. T. Higgins, Offg. Town Major, 7 July 1821).

11 James Ranald Martin, *Notes on the Medical Topography of Calcutta* (Calcutta: G. H. Huttmann, Military Orphan Press, 1837), pp. 19–21.

12 'For some years in the past . . . during "nautches" extremely indecent happenings had been taking place. Englishmen who gathered there were unable to control their senses because of drinking' (Translated from news report in *Samachar Darpan*, 22 November 1823; quoted in Brajendranath Bandyopadhyay (ed.), *Sambadpatrey Sekaler Katha*, VOL. 1 [Calcutta: Bangiya Sahitya Parishat, 1949), p. 137]. Also:

> The native entertainers have superadded to the Nautch, temptations which we presume they consider it impossible for an European to withstand—viz. suppers and wines— and bands of music. These, no doubt, have their effect, judging from the uproarious—and we regret to add disreputable scenes—which have been known to occur at them, and which were calculated to give anything but respectable or exalted impressions of the European character to our Native friends.' (*Calcutta Gazette* (5 October 1829) in Anil Chandra Dasgupta (ed.), *The Days of John Company: Selections from Calcutta Gazette 1824–32* [Calcutta: West Bengal Government Press, 1959], p. 419).

13 Mullick, *Sachitra Kolikatar Itihas*, pp. 134–5; Dutta, *Kolikatar Itibritta*, p. 20.

14 Quoted in Raja Binaya Krishna Deb, *The Early History and Growth of Calcutta* (Calcutta: Riddhi, 1977), p. 199.

15 Ananda Krishna Bose, 'A Short Account of the Residents of Calcutta in the Year 1822' in Ray, *Calcutta Keepsake*, p. 307.

16 Wakil Ahmed, *Unish Shatokey Bangali Musalmaner Chinta Chetanar Dhara*, VOL. 1 (Dhaka: Bangla Academy, 1983), p. 34.

17 A. K. Ray, *A Short History of Calcutta: Town and Suburbs* (Calcutta: Riddhi, 1982), p. 94.

18 Ahmed, *Unish Shatokey Bangali*, pp. 32–6.

19 Clive's letter to Hastings dated 28 November 1768; quoted in 'Warren Hastings in Lower Bengal', *Calcutta Review* (October 1877): 220.

20 *Memoirs of William Hickey*, VOL. 4, quoted in Mullick, *Sachitra Kolikatar Itihas*, Appendix, pp. 4–5.

21 S. N. Mukherjee, *Calcutta: Myths and History* (Calcutta: Subarnarekha 1977), p. 20.

22 Sinha, *Calcutta in Urban History*, p. 37.

23 Sinha, *Calcutta in Urban History*, pp. 16–17.

24 Sinha, *Calcutta in Urban History*, p. 30.

25 Martin, *Notes on the Medical Topography of Calcutta*, p. 21.

26 Sinha, *Calcutta in Urban History*, p. 59.

27 A report in the twenties of the nineteenth century describes their plight: 'In the visits which the Magistrates are constantly making to various parts of the town, they are perpetually struck with the appearance of ruinous and decayed premises either vacant or occupied by the remnants of wealthy families' (*John Bull*, reprinted in Ray (ed.), *Nineteenth Century Studies*, 5, p. 6).

28 Rama Deb Roy, *Glimpses on the History of Calcutta, 1600–1800* (Calcutta: Socio-Economic Research Institute, 1985) (cyclostyled copy), pp. 24–5.

29 Ray (ed.), *Nineteenth Century Studies*, 5, p. 5.

30 Bireshwar Bandyopadhyay, 'Kolkatar Kumortuli'. *Purashree* (23 October 1978).

31 Dutta, *Kolikatar Itibritta*, p. 83.

32 The Reverend James Long, *Calcutta in the Olden Times* in Ray (ed.),

31 Dutta, *Kolikatar Itibritta*, p. 83.

32 The Reverend James Long, *Calcutta in the Olden Times* in Ray (ed.), *Nineteenth Century Studies*, 5, p. 46; Ranajit Kumar Samaddar, *Bangla Sahitya O Samskrititey Sthaniya Bidroher Prabhab: Sannyasi thekey Sipahi Bidroha Parjyanta* (Calcutta: n.p., 1982), p. 25.

33 Quoted in Mullick, *Sachitra Kolikatar Itihas*, p. 36.

34 Sinha, *Calcutta in Urban History*, pp. 220, 223.

35 Mullick, *Sachitra Kolikatar Itihas*, Appendix, p. 28.

36 *Report on the Census of the Town of Calcutta, 1876*, p. 40.

37 Deb Roy, *Glimpses on the History of Calcutta*, p. 24.

38 'Last Week, a deputation from the Government went in procession to Kalighat and made a thank-offering to this goddess of the Hindus, in the name of the Company, for the success which the English have lately obtained in this country' (John Clerk Marshman, *Life and Times of Carey, Marshman and Ward: Embracing the History of the Serampore Mission*, VOL. 1 (London: Longman, Brown, Green, Longmans & Roberts, 1859), quoted in Deb, *The Early History and Growth of Calcutta*, p. 64) .

39 Quoted in Frederick Charles Danvers et al., *Memorials of Old Haileybury College* (London: A. Constable, 1894), pp. 244–5.

40 W. S. Seton-Karr's speech at a Haileybury Dinner in the Town Hall, Calcutta, on 23 January 1864, quoted in Danvers et al., *Memorials of Old Haileybury College*, p. 93.

41 Eric Stokes, *The English Utilitarians and India* (New Delhi: Oxford University Press, 1982).

42 Stokes, *The English Utilitarians and India*, pp. 30–1.

43 Quoted in Stokes, *The English Utilitarians and India*, pp. 31–4.

44 Stokes, *The English Utilitarians and India*.

45 See *Calcutta Review* 1(2) (1844): 116–17. Concern for the rapid increase in the number of children born out of wedlock among the European population is expressed in the following comments by a Christian missionary in the early nineteenth century: 'The number of children born to Europeans by native women is every year increasing, and to provide employment for them has already become a matter of serious consideration; by the present regulations of the East India Company this class of young men is excluded from the service of Government in every capacity whether

civil or military' William Tennant, *Indian Recreations; Consisting of Thoughts on the Effects of the British Government on the State of India: Accompanied with Hints Concerning the Means of Improving the Condition of the Natives of That Country*, VOL. 3 [Edinburgh: University Press, 1808], p. 283).

46 Chunder, 'The System of Banyanship', p. 468.

47 Kissen Mohun Mullick, 'A Brief History of Bengal Commerce' in Ray (ed.), *Nineteenth Century Studies*, 8, pp. 413–14.

48 W. Lester, *The Happy Era of One Hundred Millions of the Human Race, or the Merchant, Manufacturer and Englishman's Recognized Right to an Unlimited Trade with India* (London, 1813), pp. 39–40, quoted in Stokes, *The English Utilitarians and India*, pp. 38–9.

49 Deb, *The Early History and Growth of Calcutta*, p. 104.

50 Kylas Chunder Dutt, 'Scenes in Calcutta', *The Hindu Pioneer* 1(7) (March 1836), reprinted in Ray, *Calcutta Keepsake*, pp. 156–66, here, p. 161.

51 M. G. Ranade, 'Present State of Indian Manufactures', reprinted in Ray (ed.), *Nineteenth Century Studies*, 8, p. 489.

52 H. R. Panckridge, *A Short History of the Bengal Club*, quoted in Benoy Ghose (ed.), *Selections from English Periodicals of 19th Century Bengal*, VOL. 3 (Calcutta: Papyrus, 1980), p. 257.

53 *Hindoo Patriot* (24 May 1855), quoted in Ghose, *Selections from English Periodicals*, pp. 171–2.

54 Ghose, *Selections from English Periodicals*, pp. 171–2.

55 Ray, *A Short History of Calcutta*, p. 264.

56 *Jnyananweshan* (13 October 1832), quoted in Bandyopadhyay, *Sambadpatrey Sekaler Katha*, VOL. 2, p. 286.

57 *Jnyananweshan* (26 October 1839), quoted in Bandyopadhyay, *Sambadpatrey Sekaler Katha*, VOL. 2.

58 *Calcutta Review* 1(2) (1844): 329–31.

59 George Gogerly, *The Pioneers* (London: John Snow, 1871), pp. 133–4; D. Kopf, *British Orientalism and the Bengal Renaissance* (Calcutta: Firma KLM, 1969), pp. 159–60.

60 Deb, *The Early History and Growth of Calcutta*, pp. 76–7.

61 Sir E. H. East's letter to the Earl of Buckinghamshire dated 17 May 1816, reproduced in Ray (ed.), *Nineteenth Century Studies*, 9, p. 148.

62 *Calcutta Gazette* (17 January 1828), reproduced in Dasgupta, *The Days of John Company*, p. 276.

63 Quoted in *Calcutta Review* 9(17) (1848): 245.

64 *Report on the Colleges and Schools for Native Education under the Superintendence of the General Committee of Public Instruction in Bengal, 1831* (Calcutta: G. H. Huttmann, Military Orphan Press, 1832).

65 C. E. Trevelyan, *On the Education of the People of India* (London: Longman, Orme, Brown, Green & Longmans, 1838).

66 *Bengal Past and Present* 1 (July–December) (1907): 214.

67 Government despatch of July 1823, quoted in D. P. Sinha, *The Educational Policy of the East India Company in Bengal to 1854* (Calcutta: Punthi Pustak, 1964), p. 85.

68 Henry Woodrow, 'Macaulay's Educational Minutes', reprinted in Ray (ed.), *Nineteenth Century Studies*, 9, p. 79.

69 Ray, quoted in *Nineteenth Century Studies*, 11, p. 387.

70 Gautam Chattopadhyay (ed.), *Bengal: Early Nineteenth Century (Selected Documents)* (Calcutta: Progressive Publishers, 1978[1965]), p. 32. For an excellent analysis of the movement initiated by Derozio and his pupils, see Sumit Sarkar, 'The Complexities of Young Bengal' in *A Critique of Colonial India* (Calcutta: Papyrus, 1985), pp. 18–36.

71 Dasgupta, *The Days of John Company*, pp. 288–93.

72 Quoted in Ray (ed.), *Nineteenth Century Studies*, 9, pp. 42–3.

73 Quoted in Sarkar, 'The Complexities of Young Bengal', p. 20.

74 Stokes, *The English Utilitarians and India*, pp. 45–7.

75 Benoy Ghose (ed.), *Samayik Patrey Banglar Samajchitra* (henceforth *SPBS*), VOL. 4 (Calcutta: Papyrus, 1980), p. *ix*.

76 *SPBS*, p. *ix*.

77 *SPBS*, p. 187.

78 *Hindoo Patriot* (11 October 1855), reprinted in Ghose, *Selections from English Periodicals*, pp. 196–7.

79 Noting the connection between small landholders and English education, one scholar explains:

> The landed middle class were gradually finding it difficult, particularly with the growth of their families, to sustain

their standard of living solely on the rents they received from land. They found an opening for supplementing their family income from land. It was no wonder that the demand for English education came mainly from this landed middle class who aspired to a career in the newly opened service sector or as a professional. In fact, English education became a craze among them (Paromesh Acharya, 'Reforms of Language Textbooks at the Primary Level of Education in West Bengal', Working Paper no. 78 [Calcutta: Indian Institute of Management, 1984, cyclostyled copy], p. 13).

It is significant that although the directors of Hindu College were members of the *abhijata* or old aristocratic families of Calcutta, like Chandra Coomar Tagore, Gopi-mohan Deb and Joykissen Singh, very few from among their families studied in the college. Following the old tra-dition, these families had arrangements within their households for the education of their children. When Gour Mohan Auddy, a member of the city's old gold-merchant family, opened the Oriental Seminary in 1823, it attracted the 'sons of the opulent Mullicks and other members of the Sonar-bunniah [gold-merchant] caste, who looked upon the Hindu College as the terror of Hinduism (Kissory Chand Mitra, 'On the Progress of Education in Bengal' [1867], reprinted in Ray [ed.], *Nineteenth Century Studies*, 9, p. 120).

The fear of conversion to Christianity and the devel-opment of Anglicized habits among the Hindu College stu-dents could have posed a threat to the sense of religious and social security of these traditional families who would not allow their own sons to be exposed to such influences, while permitting those born in humble circumstances to attend the college and seek opportunities in professions. The landed aristocracy could still fatten on the income from land and did not feel the need for procuring degrees from colleges for their sons to make them eligible for jobs. From an analysis made in 1871 of the annual report of the Director of Public Instruction of Bengal that year, we find that sons from upper and middle classes formed 50.74 per cent of the total number of pupils in schools. Of these, those belonging to the titled aristocracy formed only 0.97 per cent while 12.26 per cent came from the landholders and 7.6 per cent from the higher professions, like barristers, surgeons, engineers. Sons of *muktears, amlas* and similar lower professionals in the administrative and judicial services formed 17 per cent (*Hindoo Patriot* [16 January 1871]).

Most of the serious-minded students of the Hindu College, who were later to take a prominent part in the social reform movement, came from middle-class backgrounds, and could continue their studies mainly because of the free studentships provided by David Hare. See Sarkar, 'The Complexities of Young Bengal'.

80 *Samachar Darpan* (1830), quoted in Bandyopadhyay, *Sambadpatrey Sekaler Katha,* VOL. 2, p. 171. See also Sivanath Shastri, *Ramtonu Lahiri O Tatkalin Banga Samaj* (Calcutta: S. K. Lahiri, 1909) for amusing accounts of similar acts of defiance by Hindu College students.

81 *Bengal Spectator* (1 September 1842), reprinted in *SPBS,* VOL. 6, p. 35.

82 Mukherjee, *Calcutta,* p. 56. Radhakanta Deb was one of the first among the traditional *abhijata* families of Calcutta to start a school in his ancestral house for girls to study English.

83 Mukherjee, *Calcutta,* pp. 46–7.

84 Pradip Sinha, *Nineteenth Century Bengal: Aspects of Social History* (Calcutta: Firma KLM, 1965), p. 109.

85 Sushil Kumar Dey, *Bangla Prabad* (Calcutta: A. Mukherjee, 1986), p. 73.

86 Indian Factory Commission, 1890 Report.

87 Usha Chakraborty, *Condition of Bengali Women around the Second Half of the 19th Century* (Calcutta: Bardhan Press, 1963), p. 3.

88 *Tattwabodhini Patrika* (1880), quoted in Ghose, *SPBS,* VOL. 5, pp. 71–2.

89 'According to [W.] Ward, three-quarters of the total number of Brahmins in Calcutta and the Twenty-Four Parganas were domestics' (Mukherjee, *Calcutta,* pp. 31–2).

90 'Although the "Bhadralok" was almost exclusively a Hindu group, caste had no part in the selection; men who held a similar economic position, enjoyed a similar style of living and received a similar education were considered as "bhadralok" ' (Mukherjee, *Calcutta*, p. 31).

91 Jogesh Chandra Bagal, *Sahitya Sadhak Charitmala*, 72 (Calcutta: Bangiya Sahitya Parishad, 1943–44), quoted in Sarkar, 'The Complexities of Young Bengal', p. 25. An idea of the city's lower orders' attitude to Christianity and the missionaries can be had from the following account of a missionary who describes the interruption of a prayer meeting in Calcutta in the 1820s:

> [W]e had just commenced the service, two of these men [Boiragis with their bodies covered with the dried mud of the Ganges and almost in a state of nudity] . . . entered the bungalow and in loud threatening tones commanded us to be silent. Then, turning to the people, they declared that we were the paid agents of the Government, who not only had robbed them of their country, but who were determined by force to put down both Hindooism and Mohammedanism. Pointing to us then they exclaimed, 'These men come to you with honeyed words, but there is poison in their hearts; they intend only to deceive that they may destroy.' The people listened to this furious address with alarm, and believing every word, rose in a body and rushed upon us, striking our persons, tearing our clothes and threatening our lives (Gogerly, *The Pioneers*, pp. 54–5).

The lower-class identification of Christian missionaries as the cultural counterparts of the economic and political aggressors of a colonial regime and as the common enemies of both Hindus and Muslims appears to be closer to the objective reality than the perception of the Bengali upper and middle classes.

92 Chattopadhyay, *Bengal: Early Nineteenth Century*, p. 235.

93 Dasgupta, *The Days of John Company*, p. 214.

94 *Calcutta Municipal Gazette* (Special Issue 1977): 67.

95 *Samvad Prabhakar* (17 February 1851): 2–3.

96 *SPBS*, VOL. 2, p. 195.

97 *Samvad Bhaskar* (11 December 1849): 408.

98 Martin, *Notes on the Medical Topography of Calcutta*, pp. 19–21; Bishop Heber, *Heber's Indian Journal: A Selection, with an Introduction by P. R. Krishnaswami* (Calcutta: Oxford University Press, 1923), p. 9.

99 *Census of Calcutta*, 1876.

100 *Census of Calcutta*, 1876.

101 *Census of Calcutta*, 1876.

102 Captain Steel, 'General Abstract of Census of Population and Houses in Calcutta in 1831', quoted in F. W. Simms, *Report on the Survey of Calcutta* (Calcutta: Military Orphan Press, 1850).

103 *Census of Calcutta*, 1876.

104 *Census of Calcutta*, 1876. Amritalal Basu, the famous Bengali playwright and actor of the late nineteenth century, gives a delightful description of scavengers, 'bhisties' who used to keep the roads clean by sprinkling water from their leather bags, and 'bharis' who supplied households with drinking water (Amritalal Basu, 'Calcutta as I Knew It Once', *Calcutta Municipal Gazette* [Silver Jubilee Number 1949]).

105 *Census of Calcutta*, 1876.

106 Gogerly, *The Pioneers*, pp. 84–6. A Bengali observer towards the end of the century notes: 'About one-fifth of the Hindoo population of Calcutta consists of people that are coming from contiguous villages and parganas of the Presidency Division . . . They do not care for David Wilson biscuits and sponge-cakes, or a glass of raspberry ice-cream or Roman punch on a summer day; their bill of fare is as short and simple as their taste is primitive' (Shib Chunder Bose, *The Hindoos as They Are* [Calcutta: Edward Standford, 1883], pp. 129–30).

107 *Report on Condition of the Lower Classes of the Population in Bengal* (Calcutta, 1888), p. 12.

108 *Census of Calcutta*, 1876.

109 *SPBS*, VOL. I, p. 59.

110 *Sulabh Samachar* (1 Agrahayan 1277 B. S. [1870]).

111 Mary Carpenter, *Six Months in India*, VOL. I (London: Longmans Green, 1868), p. 183.

112 Kanailal Chattopadhyay (ed.), *Bharat Sramajibi* (Calcutta: National Book Agency, 1975), p. 5.

113 *Sulabh Samachar* (22 Agrahayan 1277 B. S. [1870]).

114 *Sulabh Samachar* (24 Sraban 1278 B. S. [1871]); (1 Agrahayan 1277 B. S. [1870]).

115 Babu Chunder Nath Bose, 'Thoughts on the Present Social and Economic Condition of Bengal and Its Probable Future' (1869), reprinted in Bela Dutta Gupta (ed.), *Sociology in India* (Calcutta: Centre for Sociological Research, 1972).

116 *Sulabh Samachar* (3 Falgun 1277 B. S. [1870]).

117 *SPBS*, VOL. 2, p. 195.

118 For an exhaustive account of the growth of trade unionism among the first-generation industrial working class in Calcutta, see Ranajit Dasgupta, 'Material Conditions and Behavioural Aspects of Calcutta Working Class, 1875–1899' (Calcutta: Centre for Studies in Social Sciences, 1979) (cyclostyled copy).

119 For a comprehensive history of peasant rebellions in the eighteenth and nineteenth centuries in Bengal, see Suprakash Ray, *Bharater Krishak Bidroha O Ganatantrik Sangram*, 2nd EDN (Calcutta: DNBA Brothers, 1972).

120 *Sulabh Samachar* (26 Magh 1277 B. S. [1870]).

121 Some of the popular sects were the Karta-bhaja sect founded by Aulchand; the Spashtadayaka sect founded by Roopram Kabiraj; the Balarami sect founded by Balaram Hari.

122 Rabindranath Tagore's novel, *Gora*, set in Calcutta towards the end of the nineteenth century, begins with a Baul singing some plaintive notes in the streets.

123 Lalan was a colourful character who was born in a village in Kushthia (now in Bangladesh) in 1772. He is variously described as a Hindu or a Muslim. But till the end of his life (he died at the age of 117 years), Lalan remained a true Baul and refused to imprison himself or his followers in the institution of any particular religious or caste rituals.

124 *Somprakash* (20 Chaitra 1270 B. S. [1863]).

125 *Samvad Prabhakar* (18 Chaitra 1254 B. S. [1847]), quoted in *SPBS*, VOL. I, pp. 136–8.

126 Sudhir Chakravarty, 'Gabhir Nirjan Pathey' in *Ekshan* (Autumn) (1392 B. S. [1985]): 6.

127 Mullick, *Sachitra Kolikatar Itihas*, p. 211.

128 *Somprakash* (20 Chaitra 1270 B. S. [1863]).

129 Chakravarty, 'Gabhir Nirjan Pathey'.

130 As among the Bengali Hindus, class divisions were sharp among the Bengali Muslims also in the nineteenth century. See 'The distance between the Urdu-speaking elite and their Bengali Urdu-speaking rural counterparts, the mofussil landholders . . . on the one hand, and the Bengali-speaking Muslim peasantry, on the other, was often wider than the gulf separating the latter from their Hindu neighbours' (Rafiuddin Ahmed, *The Bengal Muslims* [Delhi: Oxford University Press 1981], p. 6). The author also mentions heterodox Sufi sects like the 'pagla-panthis' of Mymensingh, and 'neda-fakirs' of Rajshahi—both in East Bengal.

131 *Samvad Prabhakar* (18 Chaitra 1254 B. S. [1847]), quoted in *SPBS*, VOL. I, pp. 136–8.

132 Rajnarayan Basu, *Rajnarayan Bosur Amarcharit* (Calcutta: P. C. Dass, 1912) , p. 63.

133 From Rajnarayan Basu's letter to Baboo Shib Chunder Deb, 15 June 1878, quoted in *SPBS*, VOL. 4, pp. 351–2.

134 The consistent campaign against the Bengali race and Bengali culture was conducted through the columns of newspapers like *Friend of India*, books on history like James Mill's *History of British India*, and sermons by Christian missionaries and speeches by British administrators.

135 The need for the educated Bengali middle class to articulate their demands and pressurize the administration to concede them was intensified by their experience following the suppression of the 1857 Sepoy rebellion. The bhadraloks found that in spite of their professed and steadfast loyalty to the British during the rebellion, they were being treated with suspicion and hostility by the colonial power. Once having tasted security and progressive benefits, they now suddenly found themselves being threatened by a possible loss of these advantages. The famous playwright Amritalal Basu in his reminiscences describes the plight of the Bengali middle class in Calcutta after the suppression of the rebellion:

When the white [soldiers] arrived in Calcutta after having liquidated the sepoys, many householders dared not keep their main gates open . . . The administrators at the time could not keep cool heads. Who were to control the white [soldiers] who had come back after vanquishing the sepoys? . . . Not to speak of the streets, even the houses of the bhadraloks were not safe, as the whites entered them and created trouble . . . (Arun Kumar Mitra, *Amritalal Bosur Smriti O Atmasmriti* [Calcutta: Sahityalok, 1982], pp. 171–2).

The main mouthpiece of the educated, politically conscious Bengali middle class, *Hindoo Patriot*, regretted the possible loss of opportunities for better prospects and further benefits for the bhadraloks as a result of the suspicions generated among the British by the rebellion: 'The mutinies have made coalition for a time impossible, and reconciliation a thing of distant hope.' But it correctly pointed out at the same time that the politics learnt would not allow them to rest. Expressing the newborn feelings of assertion of the educated bhadraloks, it warned: 'The rights of the Bengalee as a citizen cannot and shall not be ignored . . . The Bengalee will not remain a slave. He is strong enough, if not in body, still in mind and knowledge to assert his right of citizenship among the confused nationalities of India'. The author of this editorial simultaneously assured the administrators: 'It is as much his [the Bengalee's] duty to support the State in which he seeks protection for his person and property as it is his right to enjoy the protection without disturbance' (31 December 1857). It was this realization that rights would have to be teased out from a suspicious colonial regime by blowing hot and cold, sometimes by threatening agitations, sometimes by professing loyalty and sometimes by reminding their rulers of their duties, that led the educated Bengalis to combine into organizations, and marked their politics during this phase.

136 'Chheley ghumolo, pada judolo, bargi elo deshey, / Bulbulitey dhan kheyechhey, khajna debo kishey?' (My baby sleeps; the neighbourhood is at peace. Suddenly, the bargis appear! The birds have eaten up all our crops. How are we to pay our revenue?)

137 Rangalal Bandyopadhyay's long poem *Padmini Upakhyan* and Romesh Chandra Dutt's *Rajput Jeeban Sandhya* are two typical

literary products inspired by Tod. Other books of a similar nature written by European historians which roused the educated Bengalis to a rediscovery of the past history of India were *History of the Marhattas* (1836) by James Cunningham Grant Duff, and *Historical Sketches of the South of India in an Attempt to Trace the History of Mysoor* (1868) by Mark Wilks. It was thus the Orientalists among the Europeans who indirectly paved the way for the rise of nationalism among the bhadraloks by giving them a new self-esteem.

138 See Ahmed, *Unish Shatokey Bangali*, VOL. 2, p. 28.

139 Quoted in Bagal, *Jatiyatar Nabamantra* (Calcutta: Maitri, 1968[1945])

140 *Madhyastha* (Falgun 1280 B. S. [1873]).

141 Quoted in Bagal, *Jatiyatar Nabamantra*, Appendix 3.

142 Quoted in Bipin Behari Gupta, *Puratan Prasanga* (Calcutta: Vidya-bharati Sanskaran, 1966), p. 298.

143 Mukherjee, *Calcutta*, p. 58.

Nineteenth-Century Calcutta Folk Culture

1 Hitesh Ranjan Sanyal, 'Chaitanyadev ebong Bangali Samaj O Samskriti', *Baromash* (April 1986): 38.

2 The old popular version of Mahabharata in Bengali was by Kashiram Das.

3 The story of Vidya and Sundar had been treated by many Bengali poets, the earliest being a composition by the sixteenth-century poet Govinda Das of Chittagong (now a part of Bangladesh). But Bharatchandra's composition earned both fame and notoriety. Much of his poem is taken up by rather uninhibited descriptions of the various stages of love-making, couched in beautiful lyrical imagery. As for the story, Sundar is finally caught after Vidya is found to be pregnant. As he is about to be executed, he prays to Kali who saves him. When his identity is revealed, the king of Bardhaman welcomes him as his son-in-law and everything ends happily.

4 Commenting on these ballads, Dineshchandra Sen, the well-known Bengali critic who collected them, said:

The folk poets [who composed them] . . . could not or did
not want to moralize. They were not propagandists. They
knew love was pure gold; before it, the sacred incantations
of priests, social norms and public scandal were of no
consequence . . . Their heroines, who are involved in
extra-marital relations, who are the so-called fallen, stand
encircled by a divine halo . . . when reading these folk
ballads, the reader will breathe the air of an unknown
world, which is completely different from the polluted air
of the closed world of the Brahman-dominated Hindu
society . . . We find in them the ancient music of the
Bengali village; the unmistakable smell of the mother's
milk that clings to the baby (Dineshchandra Sen, *Brihat
Banga*, VOL. I [Calcutta: University of Calcutta, 1934–35],
pp. 398–404).

5 Shantikumar Dasgupta and Haribandhu Mukhoti (eds), *Ishwar
Gupta Rachanbali*, VOL. I (Calcutta: Sanskrita Pustak Bandar, 1954),
pp. 3–11.

6 Dasgupta and Mukhoti, *Ishwar Gupta Rachanbali*, VOL. I, p. 11.

7 *Bharatchandrer Granthabali* (Calcutta: Basumati Sahitya Mandir,
n.d.), pp. 66, 78.

8 Durgadas Lahiri, *Bangalir Gan* (Calcutta: Paschimbanga Academy,
2001[1905]).

9 Lahiri, *Bangalir Gan*, p. 29.

10 Dasgupta and Mukhoti, *Ishwar Gupta Rachanabali*, VOL. I, p. 13.

11 Harihar Seth, *Pracheen Kolikata* (Calcutta, 1341[1934]), p. 314.

12 Kaliprasanna Sinha, *Hutom Penchar Naksha* (Calcutta, 1862), p.
46. [Reprinted as Arun Kumar (ed.), *Satik Hutom Pyanchar Naksha*
(Calcutta: Subarnarekha, 1997)]

13 Chandrasekhar Bandyopadhyay, *Jatadharir Rojnamcha: Orphe
Gangadhar Sharma* (Calcutta: Pragyabharati, 1982[1883]), p. 5.

14 Seth, *Pracheen Kolikata Parichay*, p. 323. Similar sayings about
eighteenth–nineteenth-century Bengali personalities of Calcutta
have become proverbs in current usage, like 'Hari Ghosher Goal'
or the cow-pen of Hari Ghosh, who was a dewan of the Company
and amassed a fortune, a large part of which was spent on providing shelter in his house to his indigent friends and relations.

The proverb therefore applies to such establishments where everyone has access. Another proverb, still in vogue, is 'Lagey taka debey
Gouri Sen' (if you need money, go to Gouri Sen), after Gouri
Sen who lived in Barabazar and was famous for his open-handed
liberality. He spent large sums in liberating prisoners confined for
debts. The proverb is still used for rich people who are willing to
be milch-cows. Some other sayings about contemporary rich
citizens have however failed to overcome the limits of time and
space and to be accepted as current proverbs. One such saying
popular in eighteenth–nineteenth-century Calcutta was: 'Dhonir
modhye agrogonya Ramdulal Sarkar/Babur modhye agrogonya
Prankrishna Haldar' (The first among the rich is Ramdulal Dey-
Sarkar; the first among the Babus is Prankrishna Haldar)—a
socially significant, popular saying which makes a subtle distinction between the first generation of banian millionaires like
Ramdulal Dey and the next generation of rich Bengalis who had
made money through dubious means and were famous for their
extravagant habits. Prankrishna Haldar was a typical example. His
name crops up in contemporary newspapers in the twenties of
the nineteenth century as a rich babu throwing gala parties for
Europeans and 'respectable' Bengalis (see *Calcutta Gazette* (6
September 1827); and *Samachar Chandrika* (20 October 1827). His
prodigality went to the extent of making cigars from currency
notes and smoking them away! (Mullick, *Sachitra Kolikatar Itihas*,
p. 167). In 1830, however, Haldar was convicted on a charge of
forging Company securities—the possible source of his earlier
wealth—after which his name disappeared from the newspaper
columns (see Mullick, *Sachitra Kolikatar Itihas*, p. 167).

15 Seth, *Pracheen Kolikata Parichay*, p. 316. The favourite sport of the
Bengali nouveau riche was the 'bulbulir ladai' or fights between a
class of singing birds. A contemporary observer describes such
fights in a north Calcutta lawn of the Black Town:

> A number of tents used to be pitched up. Raja Narasinha
> of Posta [the warehouse area in north Calcutta on the
> banks of the Hugli] used to bring 150 bulbulis. Some food-
> grains were sprinkled in the space between the two
> groups [of bulbulis]. They then started fighting ever the
> foodgrains. Those who lost, flew away. Immediately, the
> supporters [of the victorious birds] began shouting: 'Bo
> Mara!' This contest used to last from 11 a. m. till 4 p. m.

(Reminiscences of Krishnakamal Bhattacharya, as related to Gupta, *Puratan Prasanga*).

16 Purnachandra Dey Udhhatsagar, 'Kolikata Baghbajarer Pracheen Itihas', *Desh* (20 January 1940): 405.

17 Mullick, *Sachitra Kolikatar Itihas*, p. 148.

18 Seth, *Pracheen Kolikata Parichay*, p. 322.

19 Seth, *Pracheen Kolikata Parichay*, p. 315.

20 Soudamini Devi, 'Pitrismriti', *Prabasi* (1912): 232.

21 Seth, *Pracheen Kolikata Parichay*, p. 332.

22 Seth, *Pracheen Kolikata Parichay*, pp. 331–2.

23 Seth, *Pracheen Kolikata Parichay*, pp. 314–315.

24 See Chapter II, NOTE 8.

25 Kumar Dey, *Bangla Prabad*, p. 33.

26 Seth, *Pracheen Kolikata Parichay*, p. 333.

27 Jaynarayan Ghoshal, *Karunanidhan Bilas* (Calcutta, 1820), p. 247.

28 'A woman from the Kin caste [singers] called Jaganmohini . . . became outstanding in the singing of *dhop-kirtan*. People of those days were very fond of Jaganmohini's *dhop*. Her pronunciation was as good as her voice-modulation' (*Vishvakosh*, VOL. 4 [Calcutta, 1893], pp. 434–5.

29 Manomohan Basu, *Manomohan Geetabali* (Calcutta: Gurudas Chattopadhyay, 1886).

30 Dasgupta and Mukhoti, *Ishwar Gupta Rachanabali*, VOL. I, p. 110.

31 Dasgupta and Mukhoti, *Ishwar Gupta Rachanabali*, VOL. I; Lahiri, *Bangalir Gan*, pp. 110–95.

32 Debaprasad Sarbadhikary's reminiscences of his childhood in a Bengali village give us a glimpse into the Bengali feminine psyche which could easily identify the immersion of the goddess Durga with the departure of the newlywed daughter for the home of her husband. He describes a typical scene on the day of the immersion: 'when the village housewife with tears in her eyes, and in a choked voice, bade goodbye to the Mother [Durga], no one seemed to remember the great, omnipotent goddess. It was as if the sad scene of seeing off a village bride on her way to her father-in-law's house had just been re-enacted' (*Smritirekha* [Calcutta: Nikhilchandra Sarbadhikari, 1933], p. 83).

252 SUMANTA BANERJEE

33 D. D. Kosambi, *The Culture and Civilization of Ancient India in Historical Outline* (New Delhi: Vikas Publications, 1977), pp. 22, 48, 117, 179.

34 Harekrishna Mukhopadhyay, *Gaudbanga Samskriti* (Calcutta: Pustak Bipani, 1999[1972]), pp. 117–18. Also see:

> The dark, half-heroic and half-divine Rama and Krishna were incarnated before all to bring salvation to the dark millions who formed the majority of the population, and who had been groaning under poverty and oppresssion for ages beyond mind. It was therefore natural that the marvellous feats and the heroic exploits of such popular gods which form the subjects of the 'Yatras' should be recited in the popular speeches of the land (Nisikanta Chattopadhyay, *The Yatras or the Popular Dramas of Bengal* [London: Trubner, 1882], p. 44).

35 Lahiri, *Bangalir Gan*, p. 186.

36 Lahiri, *Bangalir Gan*, pp. 110–95; Dasgupta and Mukhoti, *Ishwar Gupta Rachanabali*, VOL. I, pp. 106–210.

37 Dasgupta and Mukhoti, *Ishwar Gupta Rachanabali*, VOL. I, pp. 148–9.

38 Sinha, *Hutom Penchar Naksha*, pp. 38, 98.

39 Haripada Chakravarty, *Dasharathi O Tanhar Panchali* (Calcutta: A. Mukherjee, 1960), pp. 13–14.

40 Prafulla Chandra Pal, *Pracheen Kobiwalar Gan* (Calcutta: University of Calcutta, 1958), p. 36.

41 Dasgupta and Mukhoti, *Ishwar Gupta Rachanabali*, VOL. I, p. 104.

42 Dasgupta and Mukhoti, *Ishwar Gupta Rachanabali*, VOL. I, p. 208.

43 Dasgupta and Mukhoti, *Ishwar Gupta Rachanabali*, VOL. I, p. 167.

44 Lahiri, *Bangalir Gan*, p. 194; Pal, *Pracheen Kobiwalar Gan*.

45 Pal, *Pracheen Kobiwalar Gan*. Describing the respective qualities of Antony Firingi and Bhola Moira, Shambhu Chandra Mukhopadhyay (1839–94), editor of well-known English journal *Mookerjee's Magazine*, who watched their performance at a function in Baranagar, near Calcutta, said: 'It was a keen contest between labour and genius' (quoted in Pal, *Pracheen Kobiwalar Gan*).

46 *Vishvakosh*, VOL. 3 (Calcutta, 1892).

47 Sinha, *Kobial Kobigan* (Calcutta, 1977), p. 1.

48 *Samachar Darpan* (27 November 1828), quoted in Bandyopadhyay, *Sambadpatrey Sekaler Katha*, VOL. I, p. 144.

49 Ghose, *Kolikata Shaharer Itibritta* (Calcutta: Prakash, 1975), p. 417; Mullick, *Sachitra Kolikatar Itihas*, p. 83.

50 Ghose, *Kolikata Shaharer Itibritta*, p. 83.

51 Legend has it that Gopal Bhand, the court jester employed by Maharaja Krishnachandra of Nabadwip, could get away with anything. Double entendre on sex was Gopal's speciality. Once the king said to Gopal: 'Your son looks like a prince.' 'No wonder, Your Majesty. Because I'm the father of the prince' (Mullick, *Sachitra Kalikatar Itihas*, p. 13).

52 Dasgupta and Mukhoti, *Ishwar Gupta Rachanabali*, VOL. I, p. 207.

53 Lahiri, *Bangalir Gan*, p. 360.

54 Gaurishankar Bhattacharya, *Bangla Lokanatya Sameeksha* (Calcutta: Rabindra Bharati University, 1972), pp. 66–7.

55 When a Russian, Gerasim Lebedef (1749–1817), staged the first Bengali play in Calcutta in 1795, local Bengali actresses were employed. Long before this, in the fifteenth century, women acted in the jatras of Ray Ramananda, a contemporary of the Vaishnavite preacher Chaitanya. See Subir Ray Chowdhury, *Bilati Jatra thekey Swadeshi Theatre* (Calcutta: Department of Comparative Literature, Jadavpur University, 1972), pp. 2–3.

56 Dineshchandra Sen, *Bangabhasha O Sahitya* (Calcutta: Paschimbanga Rajya Pustak Parshad, 1986[1896]), p. 376.

57 An excellent description of the functions of a procuress is to be found in Bhabanicharan Bandyopadhyay's *Naba Bibi Bilas* (Calcutta: Subarnarekha, 1979[1830]).

58 Lahiri, *Bangalir Gan*, p. 366.

59 Bhattacharya, *Bangla Lokanatya Sameeksha*, pp. 236–7.

60 Baishnabcharan Basak, *Bharatiya Sahasra Sangeet* (Calcutta: Basak, n. d. [early twentieth century]), p. 572.

61 Basak, *Bharatiya Sahasra Sangeet*, p. 553.

62 Bhattacharya, *Bangla Lokanatya Sameeksha*, pp. 236–7.

63 From the reminiscences of Radhamadhav Kar as narrated to Bipin Behari Gupta and recorded in the latter's *Puratan Prasanga*, pp. 254–8.

64 See Rajyeshwar Mitra's comments in *Desh* (10 Chaitra 1362 B. S. [1952]): 574.

65 Jyotirindranath Tagore's letter to Goonendranath Tagore, dated 14 July 1867.

66 Chakravarty, *Dasharathi O Tanhar Panchali*; Gupta, *Puratan Prasanga*, pp. 264–5.

67 Rajyeshwar Mitra, *Banglar Geetikar O Banglaganer Nanadik* (Calcutta: Punashcha, 1973), pp. 40–6; Chakravarty, *Dasharathi O Tanhar Panchali*, p. 73.

68 Mukhopadhyay, *Dashu Rayer Panchali* (Calcutta, n. d).

69 Chakravarty, *Dasharathi O Tanhar Panchali*, p. 375.

70 The list includes mythological heroines like Satyavati, with whom, before her marriage, the sage Parashara fell in love which resulted in the birth of Vedavyasa, the composer of the *Mahabharata;* Ambalika and Ambika, who, on the death of their husband, slept with Vedavyasa and gave birth to Dhritarashtra and Pandu; Kunti, who, before her marriage, slept with the sun-god Surya and became the mother of Karna.

71 Mukhopadhyay, *Dashu Rayer Panchali*, p. 639.

72 Basak, *Bharatiya Sahasra Sangeet*, p. 456.

73 Chakravarty, *Dasharathi O Tanhar Panchali*.

74 Chakravarty, *Dasharathi O Tanhar Panchali*.

75 Chakravarty, *Dasharathi O Tanhar Panchali*, pp. 18–22.

76 Basak, *Bharatiya Sahasra Sangeet*, p. 454.

77 Basak, *Bharatiya Sahasra Sangeet*, p. 457.

78 Dasgupta and Mukhoti, *Ishwar Gupta Rachanabali*. One of his poems lampoons educated women: 'Snapping their fingers, all the girls are picking up books. They'll learn A, B, C, deck themselves up like white women. And start talking English.'

79 Mahendranath Dutta, *Kolikatar Puratan Kahini O Pratha* (Calcutta: Mahendra Publishing Committee, 1983), pp. 29–30.

80 Lahiri, *Bangalir Gan*, p. 1041.

81 Basak, *Bharatiya Sahasra Sangeet*, p. 455.

82 Barun Kumar Chakravarty, *Loka-Samskriti: Nana Prasanga* (Calcutta: Book Trust, 1981), pp. 20–1.

83 Basak, *Bharatiya Sahasra Sangeet*, p. 534.

84 Basak, *Bharatiya Sahasra Sangeet*, p. 582.

85 Basak, *Bharatiya Sahasra Sangeet*, p. 582.

86 Unpublished diary of Kumudbandhu Ray, Arkandi, Faridpur (now in Bangladesh).

87 Martin, *Notes on the Medical Topography of Calcutta*, pp. 49–50.

88 M. K. A. Siddiqui, *Muslims of Calcutta: A Study in Aspects of Their Social Organisation* (Calcutta: Anthropological Survey of India, 1974), pp. 19–20.

89 *Indian Evangelical Review* (January 1883): 287–92.

90 Anisuzzaman, *Muslim Manas O Bangla Sahitya* (Dhaka: Mukto-dhara, 1983), p. 161; Girindranath Das, *Bangla Peer Sahityer Katha* (Calcutta: Subranarekha, 1998[1976]), pp. 315–20.

91 Qazi Abdul Mannan, *The Emergence and Development of Dobhasi Literature in Bengal up to 1855* (Dhaka: University of Dhaka, 1974), pp. 26–30.

92 Dinendra Kumar Ray, *Palli Baichitrya* (Calcutta: Ananda, 1982), pp. 101–102.

93 *Census of Calcutta*, 1876.

94 Mannan, *The Emergence and Development of Dobhasi Literature*, p. 193.

95 Anisuzzaman, *Muslim Manas O Bangla Sahitya*, pp. 114–15.

96 Mannan, *The Emergence and Development of Dobhasi Literature*, pp. 215–16. Also see: '[O]ur modern Bengali writers have imported so many *tatsama* words in and out of season, they have to such an extent searched out, as it were, the whole Sanskrit vocabulary to enrich their own, that the literature which a class of them have produced looks "more like bad Sanskrit than good Bengali" ' (Chattopadhyay, *The Yatras or the Popular Dramas of Bengal*, p. 25).

97 Mannan, *The Emergence and Development of Dobhasi Literature*, p. 85.

98 Anisuzzaman, *Muslim Manas O Bangla Sahitya*, p. 148.

99 Anisuzzaman, *Muslim Manas O Bangla Sahitya*, p. 141.

100 Anisuzzaman, *Muslim Manas O Bangla Sahitya*, p. 141.

101 Anisuzzaman, *Muslim Manas O Bangla Sahitya*, p. 158.

102 Although the first printing press in Bengal brought out a Bengali grammar by an Englishman, N. B. Halhed, in 1778, printing

started in right earnest from 1800 when the Christian missionaries in Serampore brought out religious books in Bengali. By 1816–17, a number of printing establishments had been set up in Calcutta, and soon Battala in the north became the centre of Bengali printing. Cheap books printed in these presses came to be known as Battala books or chapbooks, and were popular among the poor, semi-literate classes.

103 James Long, *A Descriptive Catalogue of Bengali Works* (Calcutta: Sanders, Cones and Co., 1855).

104 *Calcutta Review* 13(26) (1850): 257–83. For the popularity of Battala reprints of Hindu myths and scriptures, see 'There is not a ryot in the country who has learnt to read but who does not seek religious solace in the pages of the Mahabharata. There is generally a reader in the village in the Muffossil who, after the day's work is done, reads in the evening to crowded audiences the sacred verses of Kasiram or Keertibas' (Kristo Das Pal, in *Hindoo Patriot* [13 August 1866]).

105 *Indian Evangelical Review* (January 1883): 280–1.

106 *Hindu Intelligencer* (1 October 1855), reprinted in Benoy Ghose, *Selections from English Periodicals of 19th Century Bengal*, VOL. 2 (Calcutta: Papyrus, 1980), pp. 135–6.

107 Ahmad Rijaluddin, *Hikayat Perintah Nageri Benggala* (C. Skinner trans. and ed.) (The Hague: Martinus Nijhoff, 1982), p. 52.

108 During Chadak the devotees used to pierce themselves with spikes fixed atop poles and swirl. Although it was a form of self-flagellation meant as a penance, over the years it assumed the character of a popular entertainment. The following description of a Chadak hook swinging in Calcutta in the early nineteenth century gives an idea of the entertaining nature of the festival:

> Of the five who ascended [the pole], two performed the task to admiration, the first, with a cool and unimpassioned aspect, and a decorum suited to the solemnity of the occasion; but to the third, it seemed mere pastime. He was dressed in a white linen vest, blue trousers and a hat; and while the crowd with outstretched hands stood ready to receive the proferred plantain, he frequently disappointed them by eating it himself. Gay and facetious, he often pulled off his hat to salute the company, and at

length descended amidst the applause of the multitude
. . . ('Letter by a Traveller' in *Calcutta Gazette* [22 April
1819], reprinted in Hugh David Sandeman [ed.], *Selections
from Calcutta Gazette 1816–23*, VOL. 5 [Calcutta: Government of India, 1869], pp. 302–04).

Bishop Heber in his *Indian Journal* gives a detailed account of
the pageantry in the Calcutta streets during the Chadak festival in
April 1824. See Heber, *Indian Journal*, pp. 201–202.

109 *Samachar Darpan* (5 February 1825), reprinted in Bandyopadhyay,
Sambadpatrey Sekaler Katha, VOL. I, p. 123.

110 Mrs Colin McKenzie, *Life in the Mission, the Camp, and the Zenana;
or Six Years in India* (London, 1853), VOL. I, pp. 62–3, quoted in *Calcutta Review* 21 (1853): 529.

111 *Jnyananweshan* (27 April 1833), reprinted in *SPBS*, VOL. 4, pp.
796–7.

112 *Hindoo Patriot* (13 April 1868).

113 *Hindoo Patriot* (15 April 1872).

114 *Anusandhan* (17 Ashadh 1304 B. S. [1897]).

115 *Madhyastha* (Falgun 1280 B. S. [1873]).

116 Trailokyanath Mukherji, 'Art Manufacturers of India' (compiled
for the Glasgow International Exhibition, 1888), Calcutta.

117 *Samvad Prabhakar* (15 October 1852).

118 Mukherji, 'Art Manufacturers of India'.

119 *Dashi* (July 1895).

120 Sharananda Sharma, 'Durgotsab' (n. p., 1883), reprinted in
Kalikata Purasree (26 September 1980).

121 *Nabajeevan* (Agrahayan 1291 B. S. [1884]).

122 Sinha, *Hutom Penchar Naksha*, p. 27.

123 Sen, *Brihat Banga*, p. 435.

124 W. G. Archer, *Bazaar Paintings of Calcutta* (London: Victoria and
Albert Museum, 1953), pp. 58–9.

125 Archer, *Bazaar Paintings of Calcutta*, p. 49. A couplet popular in
the nineteenth century ridicules the hypocrisy of these Vaishnavites: 'Magur machher jhol, jubotir kole / Hari bole, Hari bole
(They have a curry of magur fish for their meal; they are fond of
the laps of young girls. And they chant: Hari, Hari!).

126 Archer, *Bazaar Paintings of Calcutta.*

127 Archer, *Bazaar Paintings of Calcutta*; W. G. Archer, *Kalighat Drawings from the Basant Kumar Birla Collection* (Bombay: Marg Publications, 1962); *Kalighat Painting: A Catalogue and Introduction* (London: Her Majesty's Stationery Office, 1971; Santiniketan, 1986). Archer's explanations appended to the paintings reproduced in his books are often wide of the mark, as he misses the implications of the proverbs or contemporary events illustrated in the *pats*. Thus, the *pat* on the babu and the musk-rat chorus is described as the Mouse Peepshow in his *Bazaar Paintings of Calcutta*, p. 48.

128 Sen, *Brihat Banga*, pp. 447–8.

129 Sen, *Brihat Banga*, pp. 447–8.

130 Sonargaon Museum, Dhaka, Bangladesh.

131 Prodyot Ghosh, *Kalighat Pats: Annals and Appraisals* (Calcutta: Shilpayan Artists Society, 1973). In the Nandan museum in the Santiniketan Kala Bhavana, there is a Calcutta 'Mohammedan *pat*' which shows a 'hoori' or a fairy, dressed in Middle Eastern robes and playing a musical instrument. The *pat* is painted by Mohem Madan Paul, the name suggesting the peculiar Hindu–Muslim mix which was a typical characteristic of the Patua community.

132 Ghosh, *Kalighat Pats.*

133 Sen, *Brihat Banga*, p. 448.

134 Ghosh, *Kalighat Pats.*

135 Calcutta School Book Society, *Reports*, 1818–19.

136 Calcutta School Book Society, *Reports*, 1818–19.

137 Ashit Paul (ed.), *Woodcut Prints of Nineteenth Century Calcutta* (Calcutta: Seagull Books, 1983); Sukumar Sen, *Battalar Chhapa O Chhobi* (Calcutta: Ananda, 1984).

138 Sen, *Battalar Chhapa O Chhobi.*

139 Mukherji, 'Art Manufacturers of India', pp. 28–30.

140 *Hindoo Patriot* (3 May 1855).

141 Dasgupta and Mukhoti, *Ishwar Gupta Rachanabali*, p. 107.

142 *Bangadarshan* (Paush 1279 B. S. [1872]).

143 *Somprakash* (13 Jaisthya 1292 B. S. [1885]).

144 *Friend of India* (11 September 1873).

145 Kumar Dey, *Bangla Prabad.*

146 Lahiri, *Bangalir Gan,* p. 365.

147 Sen, *Brihat Banga,* p. 435.

148 Mikhail M. Bakhtin, *Rabelais and His World* (Cambridge, MA: MIT Press, 1968), p. 90.

149 *Vishvakosh,* VOL. 3. See also: 'In those days, during Navami, after the sacrifice of a goat or a buffalo, people used to smear themselves with blood and muck and move round the roads carrying the skull. And old grandfathers, with men of their own age, sons and grandsons, used to sing *kada-matir gan* [songs of mud and slime]. They were extremely obscene and indecent songs' (Dutta, *Kolikatar Puratan Kahini O Pratha,* p. 39).

150 William H. Martineau, 'A Model of the Social Function of Humor' in Jeffrey H. Goldstein and Paul E. McGhee (eds), *The Psychology of Humor* (New York: Academic Press, 1972), pp. 101–25.

151 R. M. Stephenson, 'Conflict and Control Function of Humor' *American Journal of Sociology* 56 (1951): 569–74; quoted in Martineau, 'A Model of the Social Function of Humor', p. 107.

152 'Popular Literature in Bengal', *Calcutta Review* 13(26) (1850).

153 Sinha, *Hutom Penchar Naksha,* p. 55. On their way back after suppressing the Sepoy rebellion, these same Highlanders roused fear among the Bengali inhabitants of Calcutta, as evident from the reminiscences of Amritalal Basu (see Chapter II, NOTE 135).

154 For the attitude of the educated Bengali gentry towards the 1857 rebellion, see the series of articles on the Mutiny in *Hindoo Patriot,* in Ghose, *Selections from English Periodicals of 19th Century Bengal,* VOL. 4. It was not only the educated Bengali class which welcomed the British victory over the Sepoy rebels, but the commoner too. Amritalal Basu tells us that the sweetmeat-maker Paraney Moira of his locality, Kombuliatola in north Calcutta, prepared a special sweetmeat in honour of Lady Canning, wife of Lord Canning who was responsible for suppressing the rebellion. Transformed into Bengali patois, the sweetmeat is still popular as 'ledi-keni' in Bengali homes (Mitra, *Amritalal Bosur Smriti O Atmasmriti,* p. 180).

155 Mark Twain, *A Connecticut Yankee at King Arthur's Court* (New York: Scholastic Book Services, 1979[1889]), p. 241.

Elite Culture in Nineteenth-Century Calcutta

1 Descriptions of nautches can be found in *Calcutta Gazette* (excerpted in Dasgupta, *The Days of John Company*) in Maria Graham, *Journal of a Residence in India* (Edinburgh: Archibald Constable, 1812); and a host of diaries left by contemporary European visitors to Calcutta. Among paintings of these nautches, those by Mrs Belnos, wife of a European miniature painter in Calcutta in the 1830s, are the most famous.

2 *Samachar Darpan* (16 October 1819).

3 N. N. Ghosh, *Memoirs of Maharaja Nabkissen*, quoted in Raja Binaya Krishna Deb, *The Early History and Growth of Calcutta* (Calcutta: Riddhi, 1977), p. 192.

4 Basu, *Banger Jatiya Itihas*, p. 321.

5 Bishop Heber, *Narrative of a Journey through the Upper Provinces*, VOL. 2 (London: J. Murray, 1828), pp. 232–52.

6 Mitra, *Banglar Geetikar O Banglaganer Nanadik*, p. 27.

7 Mitra, *Banglar Geetikar O Banglaganer Nanadik*, p. 25.

8 Basu, *Manomohan Geetabali*.

9 Ramakanta Chakravarty (ed.), *Bismrita Darpan* (Calcutta: Sanskrit Pustak Bhandar, 1971), pp. 39–40.

10 Sinha, *Hutom Penchar Naksha*, p. 22.

11 Lahiri, *Bangalir Gan*, p. 403.

12 Quoted in Bose, *The Hindoos as They Are*, pp. 118–19.

13 From William Carey's *Introduction to a Dictionary of the Bengali Language* (1818). Also see 'Halhed in 1778 and later Henry Pitts Forster and William Carey, considering the Bengali language as being the offspring of Sanskrit, forcefully pleaded against the unauthorized Arabic and Persian usages. And in fact, Bengali became Sanskritic in no time by the efforts and labour of these three English pundits' (Sajani Kanta Das, *Bangla Gadya Sahityer Itihas*, p. 32, quoted in Acharya, 'Reforms of Language Textbooks', p. 21).

14 'Early Bengali Literature and Newspapers', *Calcutta Review* 3(25) (1850).

15 *Calcutta School Book Society Reports, Third Report, 1819–20*, Appendix 2.

16 *Calcutta School Book Society Reports, Third Report, 1819–20,* Appendix 2.

17 See Acharya, *Reforms of Language Textbooks,* p. 18, for an account of the biased attitude of Sanskrit-educated Bengali Brahman and upper castes towards colloquial Bengali.

18 *Calcutta Review* 13(25) (1850): 48–9.

19 *Calcutta Review* 13(26) (1850).

20 Gogerly, *The Pioneers,* pp. 133–5. Adopting a purely Eurocentric approach, the nineteenth-century Englishmen found any music not conforming to their own standards distasteful. A typical example is the following comment by J. R. Martin: 'It is impossible to speak of Bengallee music with any feeling short of disgust, or to compare it to anything but the noise made by cows in distress, with an admixture of the caterwaulings of a feline congregation and the occasional scream of an affrighted elephant' (*Notes on the Medical Topography of Calcutta,* pp. 51–2). Unaffected by the bias imparted by English education, the nineteenth-century Bengali poet-critic Ishwar Gupta showed a more objective attitude in the appreciation of music; explaining the difficulties faced by outsiders in understanding Bengali songs, he said: 'one needs aid and advice to understand an unfamiliar subject. Unless one gets acquainted with the manners and techniques of anything, one can never develop any love for it' (Dasgupta and Mukhoti [eds], *Ishwar Gupta Rachanabali,* VOL. I, p. 131).

21 *Friend of India* (7 June 1855), reprinted in Ghose, *Selections from English Periodicals of the 19th Century,* VOL. 3, p. 76.

22 *Samvad Bhaskar* (5 February 1856).

23 The nineteenth-century concept of 'obscenity' in England should also be understood in the context of the rise of puritanic Evangelism (discussed in Section III of Chapter 2), which among other things shaped the views of the Christian missionaries who came to Calcutta. For an idea of Victorian morality, see Michael Brander, *The Victorian Gentlemen* (London: Gordon Cremonesi, 1975); Elizabeth Burton, *The Early Victorians at Home, 1837–1861* (London: Longman, 1972); and G. Kitson Clark, *Churchmen and the Condition of England, 1832–1885: A Study in the Development of Social Ideas and Practice from the Old Regime to the Modern State* (London: Methuen, 1973).

24 *Edinburgh Review* (1809).

25 Sukumar Sen, *Battalar Chhapa O Chhobi* (Calcutta: Ananda, 1984), p. 47.

26 Jogindranath Basu, *Michael Madhusudan Dutter Jeebancharit* (Calcutta: Sanyal and Co., 1925), pp. 160–1.

27 Bethune's letter to Gaurdas Basak dated 20 July 1848, reproduced in Basu, *Michael Madhusudan*, p. 160.

28 Hur Chunder Dutt, *Bengali Life and Society: A Discourse* (Calcutta: Sanders, Cones and Co., 1853), pp. 10–11.

29 Letter in *Morning Chronicle* (January 1855).

30 Dasgupta and Mukhoti (eds), *Ishwar Gupta Rachanabali*, p. 9.

31 *Bangadarshan* (Kartik 1280 [1873]).

32 Subir Ray Chowdhury (ed.), *Bilati Jatra thekey Swadeshi Theatre* (Calcutta: Jadavpur University, 1972), pp. 26–7.

33 Kironmoy Raha, *Bengali Theatre* (New Delhi: National Book Trust, 1978), p. 16.

34 Quoted in Manmathanath Ghosh, *Memoirs of Kali Prussunno Singh* (Calcutta: Barendranath Gupta, 1920), p. 27.

35 From the memoirs of Mahendra Nath Mukhopadhyay, quoted in Bipin Behari Gupta, *Puratan Prasanga*, p. 87.

36 *Hindoo Patriot* (3 December 1857), quoted in Ghosh, *Memoirs of Kali Prussunno Singh*, pp. 33–9.

37 Grish (Girish) Chunder Ghose in *Hindoo Patriot* (10 September 1859), reprinted in Ray (ed.), *Nineteenth Century Studies, 6*.

38 Sanjiv Chandra Chattopadhyay, *Jatra Samalochana*, quoted in Bhattacharya, *Bangla Lokanatya Sameeksha*, pp. 211–12.

39 Basu, *Michael Madhusudan*, p. 231.

40 Bose, *The Hindoos as They Are*, p. 211.

41 Dasgupta and Mukhoti, *Ishwar Gupta Rachanabali*, VOL. I, p. 11.

42 Dasgupta and Mukhoti, *Ishwar Gupta Rachanabali*, VOL. I, p. 3.

43 Basu, *Michael Madhusudan*, pp. 196–7.

44 Basu, *Michael Madhusudan*, p. 283.

45 Basu, *Michael Madhusudan*, p. 294.

46 Basu, *Michael Madhusudan*, pp. 263–4.

47 Basu, *Michael Madhusudan*, p. 297.

48 *Calcutta Review* 13(25) (1850): 48–9.

49 *Somprakash* (23 Chaitra 1270 [1863]).

50 Bose, *The Hindoos as They Are*, pp. 18–19.

51 Dutta, *Kolikatar Puratan Kahini O Pratha*, p. 29.

52 *Calcutta Review* 57(114) (1873).

53 Dasgupta and Mukhoti, *Ishwar Gupta Rachanabali*, VOL. I, pp. 403–404.

54 Mitra, *Bosur Smriti O Atmasmriti*, p. 44.

55 Ray Chowdhury, *Bilati Jatra thekey Swadeshi Theatre*, p. 44.

56 Ray Chowdhury, *Bilati Jatra thekey Swadeshi Theatre*, pp. 40–1.

57 Jayanta Goswami, *Samajchitrey Unobingsha Shatabdir Bangla Prahasan* (Calcutta: Sahityashree, 1974).

58 Sinha, *Hutom Penchar Naksha*, p. 106.

59 Sinha, *Hutom Penchar Naksha*, p. 5.

60 Akshay Sarkar, quoted in Sinha, *Hutom Penchar Naksha*.

61 Quoted in Alok Ray, Introduction to Bholanath Mukhopadhyay, *Aponar Mukh Apuni Dekho* (Calcutta: Pragya Bharati, 1982).

62 Ray, Introduction to Mukhopadhyay, *Aponar Mukh Apuni Dekho*.

63 *Samachar Darpan* (24 February 1821), reprinted in Bandyopadhyay, *Sambadpatrey Sekaler Katha*, VOL. I.

64 The babu appears in a different shape in Bankim Chandra Chattopadhyay's satirical piece 'Babu', where in the list of his characteristics he includes those of clerks, teachers, Brahmos, banians, medical practitioners, lawyers, magistrates, landlords, editors and the audience of plays staged by the National Theatre.

65 Letter of Keshub Chunder Gangooly, reprinted in Basu, *Michael Madhusudan*, pp. 678–9. The views of the orthodox Hindu society are reflected in the comments of Ramgati Nyayaratna in his 'Bangla Bhasha O Sahitya Bishayak Prastab' (1872), where he criticized Madhusudan for having shown the Hindu zamindar Bhaktaprasad trying to entice a Muslim woman. Even Madhusudan's biographer, Jogindranath Basu, found his farces 'blemished by obscenity' (pp. 307–308).

66 From Bankim Chandra Chattopadhyay's article in *Calcutta Review* (1871), quoted in Sinha, *Hutom Penchar Naksa*.

67 *Bangadarshan* (Baishakh 1280 B. S. [1873]).

68 *Friend of India* (11 September 1873).

69 *Friend of India* (25 September 1873).

70 *Bangadarshan* (Paush 1280 B. S. [1873]). Abuse, smutty jokes and wranglings among women, which were considered by Bankim as 'obscene', had been in every society quite often innocent indulgences in ribaldry without any intention to rouse sexual passions as suspected by moralists. As Mikhail Bakhtin says:

> It is characteristic for the familiar speech of the market-place to use abusive language, insulting words or expressions, some of them quite lengthy and complex. The abuse is grammatically and semantically isolated from context and is regarded as a complete unit, something like a proverb. This is why we can speak of abusive language as a special genre of billingsgate (*Rabelais and His World* [Bloomington: Indian University Press, 1984], p. 16).

Kaliprasanna Sinha gives an amusing account of such billingsgate of his times:

> In the Shobhabazar market of the Rajas, which was about to put up the shutters, the fisherwomen with lamps in their hands were selling rotten fish and leftovers, inviting the customer with endearing calls—'Hey, you over there with the towel on your shoulders, want a good piece of fish?'; 'You with your broomstick moustache! Shell out four annas.' (Sinha, *Hutom Penchar Naksha*, p. 4)

71 Mitra, *Amritalal Bosur Smriti O Atmasmriti*, p. 117.

72 Quoted in Ray, *Bharater Krishak Bidroha O Ganatantrik Sangram*, p. 327.

73 Swapan Basu, *Gana Asantosh O Unish Shataker Bangali Samaj* (Calcutta: Pustak Bipani, 1984), pp. 143–5.

74 Mitra (ed.), *Amritalal Bosur Smriti O Atmasmriti*, pp. 61–2.

75 Raha, *Bengali Theatre*, pp. 26–8.

76 Pramila Pandhe (ed.), *Suppression of Drama in Nineteenth Century India* (Calcutta: India Book Exchange, 1978), p. 92.

77 Raha, *Bengali Theatre*, pp. 30–1.

78 *Basantak* 2(10) (1874).

79 *Basantak* 2(10) (1874).

80 Dutta, *Kolikatar Puratan Kahini O Pratha*, p. 37. It would not be quite correct to say that *sawngs* went out of fashion, as Dutta says. They continued in the Calcutta streets till the thirties of the present century.

81 For an excellent account of eighteenth- and nineteenth-century British attitudes towards Indian art, see Partha Mitter, *Much Maligned Monsters* (Oxford: Clarendon, 1977).

82 *Friend of India* (18 October 1855).

83 *Shilpapushpanjali* I (1292 B. S. [1885]), p. 255.

84 *Friend of India* (18 October 1855).

85 *Hindoo Patriot* (4 May 1854).

86 *Hindoo Patriot* (21 June 1855).

87 Paul, *Young Bengal Vindicated*, pp. 21–3.

88 Kamal Sarkar, *Shilpi-saptak* (Calcutta, 1977).

89 For such illustrations, see Joseph Fayrer, *The Thanatophidia of India: Being a Description of the Venomous Snakes of the Indian Peninsula* (London: J. and A. Churchill, 1872). There are 29 illustrations by Annada Bagchi, Harishankar Khan, Biharilal Das and Nityananda Dey.

90 Shyamacharan Srimani, *Sukshma Shilper Utpatti O Aryajatir Shilpachaturi* (Calcutta: Roy Press, 1874), p. 71.

91 Quoted in Asok Mitra, *Bharater Chitrakala* (Calcutta: Ananda, 1995[1966]), p. 249.

92 Ajit Ghosh, 'Old Bengal Paintings', *Rupam* (July–October 1926).

93 Bankim Chandra Chattopadhyay, *Bishabriksha* (1873).

94 Jogendra Chandra Ghosh, *Brahmanism and the Sudra* (Calcutta, c.1900), p. 128.

95 From the reminiscences of Dwijendranath Tagore, quoted in Gupta, *Puratan Prasanga*, p. 298.

96 Walter Hamilton, *Geographical, Statistical and Historical Description of Hindostan and Adjacent Countries*, VOL. I (London: J. Murray, 1820), p. 104.

97 Dutt, *Bengali Life and Society*, pp. 17–18.

98 William Jones and August Willard, *Music of India* (Calcutta: Sushil Gupta, 1962[1834]), pp. 3–5.

99 *Friend of India* (12 February 1876).

100 *Englishman* (26 February 1877).

101 *Indian Mirror* (19 February 1877).

102 Mitra, *Banglar Geetikar O Banglaganer Nanadik*, p. 3. This book also gives an exhaustive account of the different schools of classical music which were operating in nineteenth-century Bengal.

103 Sinha, *Nineteenth-Century Bengal*.

Conclusion

1 Richard Johnson, 'Three Problematics: Elements of a Theory of Working Class Culture' in John Clarke et al. (eds), *Working Class Culture* (London: Hutchinson, 1979), p. 237.

2 Excerpts from a song sung by Santal rebels:

Get up, arise,
Come forward for our birthland.

. . .

We alone will have to be alive,
No one will help us,
No one will give us shelter.
Let us rebel.

(Quoted in Samaddar, *Bangla Sahitya O Samskrititey Sthaniyo Bidroher Prabhab*, pp. 363, 365)

Excerpts from the rituals chanted by Munda rebels:

We shall assemble in large numbers with
Weapons in our hands.
The new sun of religion was born,
the hill and valley were lit up . . .
. . . Birsa Bhagwan is our leader . . .

(Quoted in Ranajit Guha, *Elementary Aspects of Peasant Insurgency in Colonial India* [New Delhi: Oxford Univeristy Press, 1983], p. 288.)

3 Asit Kumar Bandyopadhyay's introduction to Sinha, *Kabial Kabigan*, p. 1.

4 *Basantak* 2(10) (1874). Mahendranath Dutta tells us that women's panchali went out of fashion because the 'educated people began to denounce it'; the songs of 'mud and slime' sung on Navami (see Chapter III, NOTE 149) disappeared with the 'spread of English education and the emergence of Keshub Sen, the Brahmo reformer' (*Kolikatar Puratan Kahini O Pratha*, pp. 29–30). From another source, we learn that by the end of the nineteenth century, the 'akhdas' (rehearsal clubs) of jhumur and tarja artistes (see Chapter III, Section 4, for a description of these folk forms) had closed down because of 'police laws' (Lahiri, *Bangalir Gan*, p. 1041).

5 Freire, *Cultural Action for Freedom*, pp. 57–60. The 'silencing' of the lower orders by the Bengali elite of nineteenth-century Calcutta was carried out in many ways, ranging from suppression by laws to manipulation of their levels of consciousness. The latter technique found expression in the bhadralok society's attempts to remould the character of the lower orders through papers like *Sulabh Samachar* (see Chapter II, Section 15). The moralizing carried out in the columns of such papers was aimed at generating an inferiority complex in the minds of the lower orders about their folk culture. Just as a few generations earlier, the educated Bengali respectable classes were taught by the English to hate their own culture, so also the same process of 'silencing' was repeated by the 'reformed' gentry in relation to their subordinates—the lower orders. Promises of social and economic betterment if they imbibed the tastes and habits of the bhadraloks led many among the lower orders to give up their old cultural forms of expression. Illusions about an upward mobility often resulted in their discarding of the traditional forms of folk culture like jatra, panchali, jhumur and tarja.

6 Robert D. Storch (ed.), *Popular Culture and Custom in Nineteenth Century England* (London: Croom Helm, 1982).

7 Syamacharan Ganguli, 'Bengali Spoken and Written', *Calcutta Review* 65 (1877): 395–417

8 Rabindranath Tagore, 'Aikatan' (18 January 1941).

9 For an excellent study of Abanindranath Tagore and the Bengal School of Painting, see Jaya Appasamy, *Abanindranath Tagore and the Art of His Times* (New Delhi: Lalit Kala Akademi, 1968).

10 Bishnu Dey and John Irwin, *Jamini Ray* (Calcutta: Indian Society of Oriental Art, 1944), p. 30.

11 Hall and Whannel, *The Popular Arts*, pp. 68–70.

SELECT BIBLIOGRAPHY

Books

'Letter by a Traveller', *Calcutta Gazette* (22 April 1819) in Hugh David Sandeman (ed.), *Selections from Calcutta Gazette 1816–23*, VOL. 5. Calcutta: Government of India, 1869, pp. 302–04.

ACHARYA, Paromesh. 'Reforms of Language Textbooks at the Primary Level of Education in West Bengal' (Working Paper NO. 78). Calcutta: Indian Institute of Management, 1984.

AHMAD, Wakil. *Unish Shatokey Bangali Musalmaner Chinta Chetanar Dhara*, VOL. I. Dhaka: Bangla Academy, 1983.

AHMED, Rafiuddin. *The Bengal Muslims*. Delhi: Oxford University Press 1981.

ANISUZZAMAN, *Muslim Manas O Bangla Sahitya*. Dhaka: Muktodhara, 1983.

APPASAMY, Jaya. *Abanindranath Tagore and the Art of His Times*. New Delhi: Lalit Kala Akademi, 1968.

ARCHER, W. G. *Bazaar Paintings of Calcutta*. London: Victoria & Albert Museum, 1953.

———. *Kalighat Drawings from the Basant Kumar Birla Collection*. Bombay: Marg Publications, 1962.

———. *Kalighat Painting: A Catalogue and Introduction.* London: Her Majesty's Stationery Office, 1971; Santiniketan, 1986.

BAGAL, Jogesh Chandra. *Sahitya Sadhak Charitmala, 72.* Calcutta: Bangiya Sahitya Parishad, 1943–44.

BAKHTIN, Mikhail M. *Rabelais and His World.* Cambridge, MA: MIT Press, 1968.

BANDYOPADHYAY, Bhabanicharan. *Naba Bibi Bilas.* Calcutta; Subarnarekha, 1979[1830].

BANDYOPADHYAY, Bireshwar. 'Kolkatar Kumortuli'. *Purashree* (23 October 1978).

BANDYOPADHYAY, Brajendranath (ed.). *Sambadpatrey Sekaler Katha,* VOL. I. Calcutta: Bangiya Sahitya Parishat, 1949.

BANDYOPADHYAY, Chandrasekhar. *Jatadharir Rojnamcha: Orphe Gangadhar Sharma.* Calcutta: Pragyabharati, 1982[1883].

BASAK, Baishnabcharan. *Bharatiya Sahasra Sangeet.* Calcutta: Basak, n. d. (early twentieth century).

BASU, Amritalal. 'Calcutta As I Knew It Once'. *Calcutta Municipal Gazette* (Silver Jubilee Number, 1949).

BASU, Jogindranath. *Michael Madhusudan Dutter Jeebancharit.* Calcutta: Sanyal and Co., 1925.

BASU, Manomohan. *Manomohan Geetabali.* Calcutta: Gurudas Chattopadhyay, 1886.

BASU, Rajnarayan. *Rajnarayan Bosur Amarcharit.* Calcutta: P. C. Dass, 1912.

BASU, Swapan. *Gana Asantosh O Unish Shataker Bangali Samaj.* Calcutta: Pustak Bipani, 1984.

Bharatchandrer Granthabali. Calcutta: Basumati Sahitya Mandir, n.d.

BHATTACHARYA, Gaurishankar. *Bangla Lokanatya Sameeksha.* Calcutta: Rabindra Bharati University, 1972.

BIGSBY, C. W. E. *Approaches to Popular Culture.* London: Edward Arnold, 1976.

BISHOP HEBER. *Narrative of a Journey through the Upper Provinces,* VOL. 2. London: J. Murray, 1828.

———. *Heber's Indian Journal: A Selection, with an Introduction by P. R. Krishnaswami.* London: Oxford University Press, 1923.

BOSE, Babu Chunder Nath. 'Thoughts on the Present Social and Eco-
nomic Condition of Bengal and Its Probable Future' (1869) in Bela
Dutta Gupta (ed.), *Sociology in India: an Enquiry into Sociological
Thinking & Empirical Social Research in the Nineteenth Century, with
Special Reference to Bengal* Calcutta: Centre for Sociological
Research, 1972.

BOSE, Shib Chunder. *The Hindoos as They Are.* Calcutta: Edward Standford, 1883.

BRANDER, Michael. *The Victorian Gentlemen.* London: Gordon Cremonesi, 1975.

BURTON, Elizabeth. *The Early Victorians at Home: 1837–1861.* London:
Longman, 1972.

CAPTAIN STEEL. 'General Abstract of Census of Population and Houses
in Calcutta in 1831' [Appendix B] in F. W. Simms, *Report on the Survey of Calcutta.* Calcutta: J. C. Sherriff, Military Orphan Press, 1850.

CAREY, William. Introduction in *A Dictionary of the Bengalee Language.*
Serampore: Mission Press, 1818.

CARPENTER, Mary. *Six Months in India,* VOL. I. London: Longmans
Green, 1868.

Census of Calcutta, 1876.

CHAKRABORTY, Ramakanta (ed.). *Bismrita Darpan.* Calcutta: Sanskrit
Pustak Bhandar, 1971.

CHAKRABORTY, Usha. *Condition of Bengali Women around the Second
Half of the 19th Century.* Calcutta: Bardhan Press, 1963.

CHAKRAVARTY, Barun Kumar. *Loka-Samskriti: Nana Prasanga.* Calcutta:
Book Trust, 1981.

CHAKRAVARTY, Haripada. *Dasharathi O Tanhar Panchali.* Calcutta: A.
Mukherjee, 1960.

CHAKRAVARTY, Sudhir. 'Gabhir Nirjan Pathey'. *Ekshan* (Autumn) (1392
B. S. [1985]).

CHATTOPADHYAY, Gautam (ed.). *Bengal: Early Nineteenth Century
(Selected Documents).* Calcutta: Progressive Publishers, 1978[1965].

CHATTOPADHYAY, Kanailal (ed.). *Bharat Sramajibi.* Calcutta: National
Book Agency, 1975.

CHATTOPADHYAY, Nisikanta. *The Yatras or the Popular Dramas of Bengal.*
London: Trubner, 1882.

CHUNDER, Bholanath. 'The System of Banyanship' in Alok Ray (ed.), *Nineteenth Century Studies, 8*. Calcutta: Bibliographical Research Centre, 1974, pp. 462–3.

———. 'Calcutta: Its Origin and Growth' in Alok Ray (ed.), *Calcutta Keepsake*. Calcutta: Riddhi, 1978, pp. 8–35.

CLARK, G. Kitson. *Churchmen and the Condition of England, 1832–1885: A Study in the Development of Social Ideas and Practice from the Old Regime to the Modern State*. London: Methuen, 1973.

DANVERS, Frederick Charles et al. *Memorials of Old Haileybury College*. London: A. Constable, 1894.

DAS, Girindranath. *Bangla Pir Sahityer Katha*. Calcutta: Subarnarekha, 1998[1976].

DASGUPTA, Anil Chandra (ed.). *The Days of John Company: Selections from Calcutta Gazette 1824–32*. Calcutta: West Bengal Government Press, 1959.

DASGUPTA, Ranajit. 'Material Conditions and Behavioural Aspects of Calcutta Working Class, 1875–1899' (Occasional Paper NO. 2). Calcutta: Centre for Studies in Social Sciences, 1979.

DASGUPTA, Shantikumar and Haribandhu Mukhoti (eds), *Ishwar Gupta Rachanbali*, VOL. I (Calcutta: Sanskrita Pustak Bandar, 1954).

DEB ROY, Rama. *Glimpses on the History of Calcutta, 1600–1800*. Calcutta: Socio-Economic Research Institute, 1985.

DEB, Raja Binaya Krishna. *The Early History and Growth of Calcutta*. Calcutta: Riddhi, 1977.

DEY, Bishnu and John Irwin, *Jamini Ray*. Calcutta: Indian Society of Oriental Art, 1944.

DEY, Purnachandra Udhhatsagar. 'Kolikata Baghbajarer Pracheen Itihas'. *Desh* (20 January 1940).

DEY, Sushil Kumar. *Bangla Prabad*. Calcutta: A. Mukherjee, 1986.

DUFF, James Cunningham Grant. *A History of the Mahrattas* (S. M. Edwardes rev., annot. and introd.), 2 VOLS. London: Oxford University Press, 1921.

DUTT, Hur Chunder. *Bengali Life and Society: A Discourse*. Calcutta: Sanders, Cones and Co., 1853.

DUTT, Kylas Chunder. 'Scenes in Calcutta'. *The Hindu Pioneer* I(7) (March 1836).

DUTT, Romesh. *The Economic History of India under Early British Rule: From the Rise of the British power in 1757 to the Accession of Queen Victoria in 1837.* London: Kegan Paul, Trench, Trubner, 1908.

DUTTA, Mahendranath. *Kolikatar Puratan Kahini O Pratha.* Calcutta: Mahendra Publishing Committee, 1973.

DUTTA, Prankrishna. *Kolikatar Itibritta.* Calcutta: Pustak Bipani, 1981.

FANON, Frantz. 'On National Culture' in *The Wretched of the Earth.* Harmondsworth: Penguin, 1967, pp. 166–89.

FAYRER, Joseph. *The Thanatophidia of India: Being a Description of the Venomous Snakes of the Indian Peninsula.* London: J. and A. Churchill, 1872.

FREIRE, Paulo. *Cultural Action for Freedom.* London: Penguin, 1972.

GANGULI, Syamacharan. 'Bengali Spoken and Written'. *Calcutta Review* 65 (1877): 395–417.

GHOSE, Ajit. 'Old Bengal Paintings'. *Rupam* (July–October) (1926): 98–104.

GHOSH, Benoy. *Kolikata Shaharer Itibritta.* Calcutta: Prakash, 1975.

——— (ed.). *Samayik Patrey Banglar Samajchitra,* VOL. 4. Calcutta: Papyrus, 1980.

——— (ed.). *Selections from English Periodicals of 19th Century Bengal,* VOL. 2. Calcutta: Papyrus, 1980.

——— (ed.). *Selections from English Periodicals of 19th Century Bengal,* VOL. 3. Calcutta: Papyrus, 1980.

GHOSH, Jogendra Chandra. *Brahmanism and the Sudra, or the Indian Labour Problem.* Calcutta: City Book Society, c.1900.

GHOSH, Manmathanath. *Memoirs of Kali Prussunno Singh.* Calcutta: Barendranath Gupta 1920.

GHOSH, Prodyot. *Kalighat Pats: Annals and Appraisals.* Calcutta: Shilpayan Artists Society, 1973.

GHOSHAL, Jaynarayan. *Karunanidhan Bilas.* Calcutta, 1820.

GOGERLY, George. *The Pioneers.* London: John Snow, 1871.

GOSWAMI, Jayanta. *Samajchitrey Unobingsha Shatabdir Bangla Prahasan.* Calcutta: Sahityashree, 1974.

GRAHAM, Maria. *Journal of a Residence in India.* Edinburgh: Archibald Constable, 1812.

GUHA, Ranajit. *Elementary Aspects of Peasant Insurgency in Colonial India*. New Delhi: Oxford Univeristy Press, 1983.

GUPTA, Bipin Behari. *Puratan Prasanga*. Calcutta: Vidya-bharati, 1966.

HALL, Stuart and Paddy Whannel. *The Popular Arts*. London: Hutchinson, 1964.

HAMILTON, Walter. *Geographical, Statistical and Historical Description of Hindostan and Adjacent Countries*, VOL. 1. London: J. Murray, 1820.

HAVELL, E. B. *Ideals of Indian Art*. London: J. Murray, 1911.

JOHNSON, Richard. 'Three Problematics: Elements of a Theory of Working Class Culture' in John Clarke, Chas Critcher and Richard Johnson (eds), *Working Class Culture: Studies in History and Theory*. London: Hutchinson, 1979, pp. 201–37.

JONES, William and August Willard, *Music of India*. Calcutta: Sushil Gupta, 1962[1834].

KOPF, D. *British Orientalism and the Bengal Renaissance*. Calcutta: Firma KLM, 1969.

KOSAMBI, D. D. *The Culture and Civilization of Ancient India in Historical Outline*. New Delhi: Vikas Publications, 1977.

LAHIRI, Durgadas. *Bangalir Gan* (Asitkumar Bandyopadhyay ed.). Calcutta: Paschim Banga Bangla Academy, 2001[1905].

LESTER, W. *The Happy Era of One Hundred Millions of the Human Race, or the Merchant, Manufacturer and Englishman's Recognized Right to an Unlimited Trade with India*. London, 1813.

LONG, Reverend James. *A Descriptive Catalogue of Bengali Works*. Calcutta: Sanders, Cones and Co., 1855.

MANNAN, Qazi Abdul. *The Emergence and Development of Dobhasi Literature in Bengal up to 1855*. Dacca: University of Dacca, 1974.

MARSHALL, P. J. 'Indian Officials under the East India Company in Eighteenth Century Bengal'. *Bengal, Past and Present* 84 (July–December) (1965): 95–120.

MARSHMAN, John Clerk. *Life and Times of Carey, Marshman and Ward: Embracing the History of the Serampore Mission*, VOL. 1. London: Longman, Brown, Green, Longmans & Roberts, 1859.

MARTIN, James Ranald. *Notes on the Medical Topography of Calcutta*. Calcutta: G. H. Huttmann, Military Orphan Press, 1837.

MARTINEAU, William H. 'A Model of the Social Function of Humor' in Jeffrey H. Goldstein and Paul E. McGhee (eds), *The Psychology of Humor.* New York: Academic Press, 1972, pp. 101–25.

MCKENZIE, Mrs Colin. *Life in the Mission, the Camp, and the Zenana; or Six Years in India,* 3 VOLS. London, 1853.

MITRA, Arun Kumar. *Amritalal Basur Smriti O Atmasmriti.* Calcutta: Sahityalok, 1982.

MITRA, Asok. *Bharater Chitrakala.* Calcutta: Ananda, 1995[1966].

MITRA, Rajyeshwar. *Banglar Geetikar O Banglaganer Nanadik.* Calcutta: Punashcha, 1973.

MITTER, Partha. *Much Maligned Monsters.* Oxford: Clarendon, 1977.

MUKHERJEE, Hiren. 'The Crisis in Culture', speech delivered at the All-India Progressive Writers' Conference, Calcutta, 1938.

MUKHERJEE, S. N. *Calcutta: Myths and History.* Calcutta: Subarnarekha 1977.

MUKHERJI, Trailokyanath. 'Art Manufacturers of India'. Compiled for the Glasgow International Exhibition, 1888, Calcutta.

MUKHOPADHYAY, Harekrishna. *Gaudbanga Sathskriti.* Calcutta: Pustak Bipani, 1999.

MULLICK, Pramathanath. *Sachitra Kolikatar Itihas.* Calcutta: Sri Prabodh Krishna Bandyopadhyay, 1935.

NEOGY, Prithwish (ed.). *Rabindranath Tagore on Art and Aesthetics.* New Delhi: Orient Longman, 1961, pp. 60–4.

NYAYARATNA, Ramgati. *Bangla Bhasha O Sahitya Bishayak Prastab* (Asit Kumar Bandyopadhyay ed.). Calcutta: Bholanath Das, 1991[1873].

PAL, Prafulla Chandra. *Pracheen Kobiwalar Gan.* Calcutta: University of Calcutta, 1958.

PANDHE, Pramila (ed.). *Suppression of Drama in Nineteenth Century India.* Calcutta: India Book Exchange, 1978.

PAUL, Ashit (ed.). *Woodcut Prints of Nineteenth Century Calcutta.* Calcutta: Seagull Books, 1983.

RAHA, Kironmoy. *Bengali Theatre.* New Delhi: National Book Trust, 1978.

RAY CHOWDHURY, Subir and Swapan Majumdar (eds). *Bilati Jatra thekey Swadeshi Theatre.* Calcutta: Dey's Publishing, 1999[1972].

RAY, A. K. *A Short History of Calcutta: Town and Suburbs*. Calcutta: Riddhi, 1982.

RAY, Alok. Introduction in Bholanath Mukhopadhyay, *Aponar Mukh Apuni Dekho*. Calcutta: Pragya Bharati, 1982.

—— (ed.). *Nineteenth Century Studies*, VOLS 5, 6, 8, 9, 11. Calcutta: Bibliographical Research Centre, 1975.

RAY, Dinendra Kumar. *Palli Baichitrya*. Calcutta: Ananda, 1982.

RAY, Suprakash. *Bharater Krishak Bidroha O Ganatantrik Sangram*, 2nd EDN. Calcutta: DNBA Brothers, 1972.

REDFIELD, Robert and Milton B. Singer. 'The Cultural Role of Cities' in *Economic Development and Cultural Change* 3(1) (1954): 53–73.

RIJALUDDIN, Ahmad. *Hikayat Perintah Nageri Benggala* (C. Skinner trans. and ed.). The Hague: Martinus Nijhoff, 1982.

SAMADDAR, Ranajit Kumar. *Bangla Sahitya O Samskrititey Sthaniya Bidroher Prabhab: Sannyasi thekey Sipahi Bidroha Parjyanta*. Calcutta: 1982.

SANYAL, Hitesh Ranjan. 'Chaitanyadev ebong Bangali Samaj O Samskriti'. *Baromash* (April 1986).

SARBADHIKARY, Debaprasad. *Smritirekha*. Calcutta: Nikhilchandra Sarbadhikari, 1933.

SARKAR, K. *Shilpi-saptak*. Calcutta, 1977.

SARKAR, Sumit. 'The Complexities of Young Bengal' in *A Critique of Colonial India*. Calcutta: Papyrus, 1985, pp. 18–36.

SEN, Dineshchandra. *Bangabhasha O Sahitya*. Calcutta: Paschimbanga Rajya Pustak Parshad, 1986[1896].

SEN, Dineshchandra. *Brihat Banga*, VOL. 1. Calcutta: University of Calcutta, 1934–35.

SEN, Sukumar. *Battalar Chhapa O Chhobi*. Calcutta: Ananda, 1984.

SETH, Harihar. *Pracheen Kolikata*. Calcutta: Orient Book Co., 1952.

SHASTRI, Sivanath. *Ramtonu Lakiri Tatkalin Banga Samaj*. Calcutta: S. K. Lahiri, 1909.

SIDDIQUI, M. K. A. *Muslims of Calcutta: A Study in Aspects of Their Social Organisation*. Calcutta: Anthropological Survey of India, 1974.

SINHA, D. P. *The Educational Policy of the East India Company in Bengal to 1854*. Calcutta: Punthi Pustak, 1964.

SINHA, Kaliprasanna. *Hutom Penchar Naksha*. Available as: Arun Kumar (ed.), *Satik Hutom Pyanchar Naksha*. Calcutta: Sub-arnarekha, 1997.

SINHA, Pradip. *Calcutta in Urban History*. Calcutta: Firma KLM, 1978.

SINHA, Pradip. *Nineteenth Century Bengal: Aspects of Social History*. Calcutta: Firma KLM, 1965.

SOUDAMINI DEVI, 'Pitrismriti'. *Prabasi* (1912).

SRIMANI, Shyamacharan. *Sukshma Shilper Utpatti O Aryajatir Shilpachaturi*. Calcutta: Roy Press, 1874.

STEPHENSON, R. M. 'Conflict and Control Function of Humor'. *American Journal of Sociology* 56 (1951): 569–74.

STOKES, Eric. *The English Utilitarians and India*. New Delhi: Oxford University Press, 1982.

STORCH, Robert D. (ed.). *Popular Culture and Custom in Nineteenth Century England*. London: Croom Helm, 1982.

TAGORE, Rabindranath. 'Aikatan' (18 January 1941).

TENNANT, William. *Indian Recreations; Consisting of Thoughts on the Effects of the British Government on the State of India: Accompanied with Hints Concerning the Means of Improving the Condition of the Natives of That Country*, VOL. 3. Edinburgh: University Press, 1808.

TREVELYAN, C. E. *On the Education of the People of India*. London: Longman, Orme, Brown, Green & Longmans, 1838.

TROTSKY, Leon. *Literature and Revolution*. Ann Arbor, MI: University of Michigan Press, 1960.

TWAIN, Mark. *A Connecticut Yankee at King Arthur's Court*. New York: Scholastic Book Services 1979[1889].

WILKS, Mark. *Historical Sketches of the South of India, in an Attempt to Trace the History of Mysoor, from the Origin of the Hindoo Government of That State, to the Extinction of the Mohammedan Dynasty in 1799*. London: Longman, 1810–17.

WILLIAMS, Raymond. 'Communications of Cultural Science' in C. W. E. Bigsby (ed.), *Approaches to Popular Culture*. London: Edward Arnold, 1976, pp. 27–38.

WOLFF, Janet. 'The Interpretation of Literature in Society: The Hermeneutic Approach' in Jane Routh and Janet Wolff (eds),

SUMANTA BANERJEE

Sociology of Literature: Theoretical Approaches. Newcastle: University of Keele, 1977, pp. 18–31.

Periodicals

Anusandhan (17 Ashadh 1304 B. S. [1897])

Bangadarshan (Baishakh 1280[1873])

Bangadarshan (Kartik 1280 [1873])

Bangadarshan (Paush 1279 B. S. [1872])

Bangadarshan (Paush 1280 [1873])

Basantak 2 (10) (1874)

Bengal Past and Present 1 (July–December 1907)

Calcutta Gazette (6 September 1827)

Calcutta Municipal Gazette (Special Issue 1977)

Calcutta Review (October 1877).

Calcutta Review 13(25) (1850)

Calcutta Review 13(26) (1850)

Calcutta Review 57 (114) (1873)

Calcutta Review 21 (1853)

Dashi (July 1895)

Desh (10 Chaitra 1362 B. S. [1952])

Edinburgh Review (1809)

Englishman (26 February 1877)

Friend of India (11 September 1873)

Friend of India (12 February 1876)

Friend of India (18 October 1855)

Friend of India (25 September 1873)

Friend of India (7 June 1855)

Hindoo Patriot (10 September 1859)

Hindoo Patriot (13 April 1866)

Hindoo Patriot (13 August 1868)

Hindoo Patriot (15 April 1872)

Hindoo Patriot (21 June 1855)

Hindoo Patriot (3 December 1857)

Hindoo Patriot (3 May 1855)

Hindoo Patriot (4 May 1854)

Hindu Intelligencer (1 October 1855)

Indian Evangelical Review (January 1883)

Indian Mirror (19 February 1877)

Jnyananweshan (27 April 1833)

Kalikata Purashree (26 September 1980)

Madhyastha (Falgun 1280 B. S. [1873])

Morning Chronicle (January 1855)

Nabajeevan (Agrahayan 1291 B. S. [1884])

Samachar Chandrika (20 October 1827).

Samachar Darpan (16 October 1819).

Samachar Darpan (24 February 1821)

Samachar Darpan (27 November 1828)

Samachar Darpan (5 February 1825)

Samvad Bhaskar (11 December 1849)

Samvad Bhaskar (5 February 1856)

Samvad Prabhakar (15 October 1852)

Samvad Prabhakar (17 February 1851)

Samvad Prabhakar (18 Chaitra 1254 B. S. [1847])

Shilpapushpanjali, 1 (1292 B. S. [1885])

Somprakash (20 Chaitra 1270 B. S. [1863])

Somprakash (23 Chaitra 1270 [1863]).

Somprakash, (13 Jaisthya 1292 B. S. [1885])

Sulabh Samachar (1 Agrahayan 1277 B. S. [1870])

Sulabh Samachar (22 Agrahayan 1277 B. S. [1870])

Sulabh Samachar (24 Sraban 1278 B. S. [1871])

Sulabh Samachar (26 Magh 1277 B. S. [1870])

Sulabh Samachar (3 Falgun 1277 B. S. [1870])

Vishvakosh, VOL. 4 (Calcutta, 1893)

Reports

Indian Factory Commission, 1890 Report

Calcutta School Book Society, *Reports*, 1818–19

Calcutta School Book Society *Reports*, Third Report, 1819–20, Appendix 2

Report on Condition of the Lower Classes of the Population in Bengal. Calcutta: Bengal Secretariat Press, 1888.

Report on the Colleges and Schools for Native Education under the Superintendence of the General Committee of Public Instruction in Bengal, 1831. Calcutta: Military Orphan Press; G. H. Huttmann, 1832.

INDEX

Bandyopadhyay, Rangalal 186, 187, 189, 193, 199, 247–8n

Banerjee, Krishnamohan 53, 57, 64

Banerjee, Kali Charan 204

Banerjee, Nabin 146–7

Banerjee, Shashipada 81

Bangadarshan 180, 210

banians 25, 49, 71, 84, 94–5, 96, 111, 131, 138–9, 201; defined 1, 23–4; amassing fortunes 24, 25, 27, 31–2, 41–3, 250n14; as intermediaries 26–7, 31; as absentee zamindars 33–4, 37, 54; in trade and commerce 54–5; entertaining 26–7, 44; their wasteful expenditure 33–4; their role in the growth of the city 34; shaping elite culture 31–2; education 46; their mores 94; decline in their fortunes 45

Banshbedey 35

Baral, Raichand 218

Bardhaman 88, 164, 248n3

Barwell 30

Basaks 22, 23, 56, 62, 167

Basu, Amritalal 195, 206, 208, 209, 244n104, 246–7n135, 259nn153–4

Basu, Jogindranath 264

Basu, Kedarnath 119

Basu, Mohanchand 102, 119, 167

Basu, Nabin Chandra 180

Basu, Rajnarayan 78–9, 82

Basu, Ram 103, 106, 107, 110, 112, 165, 169

Battala: as centre of drinking 96, 97; its publications 14, 134–6, 154, 175–6, 204–205, 25n1026; its satirical sketches 197–9, 203; impact of its books 154, 172–3; its book illustrations 150–1; its

prints 14, 215; booksellers arrested and fined 175–6

Bauls 75–6, 110, 127–8, 229, 245n122

bazaars 22, 25, 32, 34, 37, 131

bazaar paintings, *see* Kalighat *pats*

Bedarelgafelin (Sekh Munsi Chamiruddin) 132

Belgachhia 44, 97, 181, 183, 202

Bengal Club 44

Bengal British India Society 54, 83

Bengal Gazette 28

Bengal Music School 218

Bengal School of Art 216, 230, 267n9

Bengal Theatre 208

Bengali language 13, 46, 150; Sanskritized 14, 87, 88–9, 90, 160, 165, 171–2, 173–4, 178–9, 202, 224–5, 255n96, 260n13; colloquial 14, 89, 90, 91, 194, 195, 198–9, 202, 204–205, 225, 229; the court language 88; the folk style 89, 90, 91; Muslim Bengali 128–130, 131–2; adoption of Arabic and Persian words 128–9; jargon 168–9; development of new literary language 14, 171–3, 229; linguistic disjunction 227–8

Benisamhar 181

Berger, John 3

Bethune, J. D. 176–7, 178

Beverley, H. 66, 67

Bhabani (Bhabarani), jhumur-wali 125–6

Bhabani Bene 111, 171

bhadraloks 15, 65, 102–103, 155; defined 60–1, 73, 242; attitude to rebellions 74–5, 207; their religious attitudes 63–4, 77, 85, 109

Pearson, *Teachers' Manual* 150

peasant revolts 74–5, 160–1, 205–6, 207–208, 224, 245n119

pirs 77–8, 79, 129, 133, 148

Pir Machandali 129

Permanent Settlement (1793) 1, 54, 56

Persian 4, 31, 47, 129–30, 131–2, 166, 224–5

Plassey, Battle of 22, 34, 166

The Police of Pig and Sheep 209

Positivism 216

Posta Raj family 57, 99, 235n8, 250n15

Poush-parban 194

poverty 35–7, 63

prabhati 101

Pramanik, Taraknath 139

Pratapaditya 81

Pratapchand of Bardhaman 164

Pratt, Hodgson 211

Prince of Wales 209, 218

prostitute, prostitution 107, 125, 147, 157, 199, 253n57

proverbs 14, 62, 93–4, 98–9, 100, 137, 147, 141, 156, 157, 159, 249–50

Radha 88, 89, 101, 103, 105, 106–7, 108, 115, 118, 125–6, 132, 150, 154, 156, 166, 168, 177, 180

Raghunath 76

Rajballav, Raja 55

Rajputs 14, 81–2, 100, 130, 186, 216, 247n136

Ramakrishna 77

Ramayana 72, 118, 150, 215; in Bengali 88, 173–4, 187, 189, 190

Rana Pratap 81, 82

Raphael 43, 213, 216

ratha, ratha-jatra 130, 136

Ravi Varma 215

Ray, Dasharathi (Dashu Ray) 119–122, 124, 154, 159, 175, 196, 222, 223–4; *Rukshmini-haran* 119–120, 121; *Sita-Anweshan* 120

Ray, Dinendra Kumar 130

Ray, Gurudas 29

Ray, Kali Kumar (Calee Coomar) 150

Ray, Narasimha 57, 250n15

Ray, Raja Sukhomoy 164

Ray Ramananda 253n55

Ray, Tinkari 119

religion, popular 75–8, 110, 245; bhadralok 78–9; colonial responses to 27, 39–40, 49–50; reconciliation of religions 103–4, 110; Hindu conservatism 57–6; Derozian reaction against conservatism 57; conversions to Christianity 57–8; reformists and rituals 59–60; reforms 57, 58–61, 63–4; religious hypocrisy 144, 146, 148, 155, 197, 210, 222, 257n125

Renaissance (Bengal) 5–6, 15

Rigaud, Monsieur 211

Roy, Baradaprasad 128

Roy, Jamini 215, 230

Roy, Rammohan 5, 6–7, 57, 58, 59, 63, 80, 98, 164, 179, 201

Roy Chowdhury, Santosh 145

Royal Academy of Arts 13, 165

Rukshmini-haran (Dashu Ray) 119–120, 121

Rupchand Pakshi, *see* Das, Rupchand